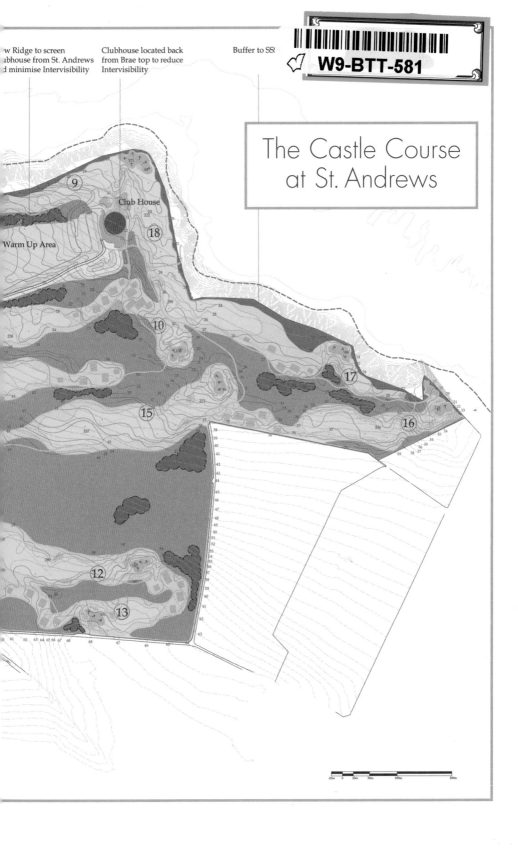

w Ridge to screen
ibhouse from St. Andrews
d minimise Intervisibility

Clubhouse located back
from Brae top to reduce
Intervisibility

Buffer to SS!

The Castle Course
at St. Andrews

Warm Up Area

Club House

The Seventh at St. Andrews

The Seventh
at St. Andrews

• • •

How Scotsman David McLay Kidd
and His Ragtag Band Built the First New Course
on Golf's Holy Soil in Nearly a Century

Scott Gummer

GOTHAM BOOKS

GOTHAM BOOKS
Published by Penguin Group (USA) Inc.
375 Hudson Street, New York, New York 10014, U.S.A.
Penguin Group (Canada), 90 Eglinton Avenue East, Suite 700, Toronto, Ontario M4P 2Y3,
Canada (a division of Pearson Penguin Canada Inc.); Penguin Books Ltd, 80 Strand,
London WC2R 0RL, England; Penguin Ireland, 25 St Stephen's Green, Dublin 2, Ireland
(a division of Penguin Books Ltd); Penguin Group (Australia), 250 Camberwell Road,
Camberwell, Victoria 3124, Australia (a division of Pearson Australia Group Pty Ltd);
Penguin Books India Pvt Ltd, 11 Community Centre, Panchsheel Park, New Delhi - 110 017,
India; Penguin Group (NZ), 67 Apollo Drive, Rosedale, North Shore 0745, Auckland, New Zealand
(a division of Pearson New Zealand Ltd); Penguin Books (South Africa) (Pty) Ltd,
24 Sturdee Avenue, Rosebank, Johannesburg 2196, South Africa

Penguin Books Ltd, Registered Offices: 80 Strand, London WC2R 0RL, England

Published by Gotham Books, a division of Penguin Group (USA) Inc.

First printing, October 2007
10 9 8 7 6 5 4 3 2 1

Copyright © 2007 by Scott Gummer
All rights reserved

"You Can't Always Get What You Want"
Written by Mick Jagger & Keith Richards
Published by ABKCO Music, Inc.
© Renewed ABKCO Music, Inc. Used with permission.
www.abkco.com

Gotham Books and the skyscraper logo are trademarks of Penguin Group (USA) Inc.

LIBRARY OF CONGRESS CATALOGING-IN-PUBLICATION DATA

Gummer, Scott.
    The seventh at St. Andrews : how Scotsman David McLay Kidd and his ragtag band built the
first new course on golf's holy soil in nearly a century / Scott Gummer.
    p. cm.
    ISBN 978-1-592-40322-6
    1. Royal and Ancient Golf Club of St. Andrews—History. 2. Kidd, David McLay, 1967– .
3. Golf course architects—Scotland—Biography. 4. Golf courses—Design and construction—
History—20th century. I. Title.
    GV969.R6G86 2007
    796.35209411—dc22   2007008203

Photo Insert Credits
Page one to page four: David McLay Kidd; page five: St. Andrews Link Trust; page six, top photo:
Hobbs Golf Collection; page six, middle and bottom photos: David McLay Kidd; page seven, The
New Inn: John Stewart; page seven, The Dunvegan: Prof. Sam Taylor; page seven, One Golf Place,
The Clubhouse, The Central: John Stewart; page eight: David McLay Kidd

Printed in the United States of America
Set in Janson Text • Designed by Elke Sigal

While the author has made every effort to provide accurate telephone numbers and Internet addresses at the time of publication, neither the publisher nor the author assumes any responsibility for errors, or for changes that occur after publication. Further, the publisher does not have any control over and does not assume any responsibility for author or third-party Web sites or their content.

For Lisa
For everything
Forever

Contents

• • •

Hole-by-Hole Commentary

• • •

David McLay Kidd

Foreword

• • •

David McLay Kidd

From the instant I first heard rumblings about a seventh course in St. Andrews, I knew I wanted to be involved. I felt the same way when, shortly after landing the commission for Course No. 7, I received an e-mail from Scott Gummer asking me if I wanted to take part in a book about the process.

I was extremely keen on the opportunity to present a fair and honest chronicling of how my team and I create a golf course. I may be listed as the course designer, but I wanted people to see that it is not a solo effort, that it is not just me coming up with ideas and inspiration that a bunch of robots implement.

Some incredibly creative people, from all walks of life and all corners of the globe, had a hand in the creation of the seventh course, and this book was a chance for me to help give them the recognition they rarely get but richly deserve. I merit no more credit for what I did than Paul Kimber does for what he did, or Mick McShane, or Conor Walsh, or Alan McGregor, or so many other talented and committed individuals.

I appreciated Scott's enthusiasm, and his participation from the get-go proved crucial in the telling of this story. I took part in a recent book about the story behind Bandon Dunes, but it was written five years after the fact and so many of the details were lost over time. This is the story as it happened, "warts and all."

There were bumps in the road, some sizeable but none insurmountable. The staff of the St. Andrews Links Trust has earned my admiration and respect for their commitment to the ultimate goal of creating the best golf course possible. The same can be said for their involvement with this book. They trusted us and left us to do what we do best, and in turn we felt the weight on our shoulders to exceed their expectations. I can honestly say, hand on heart, they were the best client I have ever had.

Scott and I agreed that this book would not be a dry technical examination of how to build a golf course. It is not a golf book; rather it is a book about people who happen to work in golf. Some people, like Mick McShane, can be tough nuts to crack, and I remember well introducing Scott to Mick in the pub at the Pilmour Hotel. Mick's first words to Scott were "You have no right to write about me!" Had Scott been insincere or even the slightest bit pretentious, this book would have never happened. Mick would have clammed up—or punched him.

For me, this book is a gift to my father, Jimmy, who taught me everything I ever needed to know about this business and about life. "I wasn't always there for you," my father said to me recently. "I worked early in the morning and late into the night, not to mention most weekends." Quite to the contrary, I told him, because even if I did not see him before I went to bed or after I woke up, I knew he was near. With my constant and far-flung travel, I am oftentimes neither near nor there for my family, and I realize that my wife and children pay a far higher price for my ambition.

The single most important reason why I wanted to be involved with this book was in the hope that one day my children will pick it up and read it, and they will understand not only what I did, but they will get some inkling as to why.

Preface

• • •

I had been watching Weather.com for weeks, hoping and praying for a sliver of sunshine along the Oregon coast. Despite having finagled travel writing assignments from Pebble Beach to St. Andrews and South Africa to South Korea, Bandon Dunes had eluded me. As a freelancer I'd pitched the idea everywhere, but all my editors, wisely, saved that assignment for themselves. So when I became an editor myself at *GOLF Magazine*, Bandon Dunes was all mine. As soon as the weather cleared in mid-December 2004 I made a beeline for the airport.

I can't say for certain why I had David McLay Kidd's mobile number saved in my cell phone. I'd spoken with him only once before, over the phone while working at *GOLF*, and he must have said, "If you ever make it to Bandon, give me a ring," a line I am quite certain the marketing-savvy Scotsman regularly proffers to writers. Still, as I drove to the Oakland airport, I felt compelled to give him a call. Kidd could easily have been anywhere in the world, but as fate would have it he was just across the bay at the San Francisco airport.

"Are you coming or going?" I asked.

"I am flying up to Portland then headed to Bandon," Kidd answered.

"I am flying up to Portland then headed to Bandon."

"I am on the 2:20 flight," he said.

"I am on the 2:20 flight."

"I'll be in the bar by the Horizon Air gates wearing a brown jacket and drinking a pint."

"I am wearing a brown jacket, and how about I buy you that pint?"

As it turned out, I was assigned seat 3B and Kidd 4B on the flight from Portland to North Bend. Had I not called him, we would have sat one row apart and never connected. Instead, we did connect, instantly. The pint at the airport bar led to many, many, many more pints and three straight days of exceptional golf (given the setting if not the scoring) during a memorable first visit to Bandon Dunes.

Shortly after Christmas in 2004 I received an unexpected gift from *GOLF:* a pink slip. The editor who had brought me on had been cut loose by his new boss, and the new editor wanted a travel editor based in midtown Manhattan, which I was not and would not be. The new guy's last words to me went something like "You certainly are taking this well; if I were you I might have come across the desk and taken a swing at me." Part of me still wishes I had, but a bigger part of me recognizes that the closing of that chapter opened this one.

——Original Message——
From: Scott Gummer
Sent: January 27, 2005
To: David McLay Kidd
Subject: now that I have more time on my hands . . .

David,

Hope this finds you well and staying warm.
Been thinking about you and the seventh course at
St. Andrews, and I wonder if you'd be interested in collaborating on a
book about the process.

Take care and keep in touch,
Scott

——Original Message——
From: David McLay Kidd
Sent: February 03, 2005
To: Scott Gummer
Subject: RE: now that I have more time on my hands . . .

Scott,

Sorry for the delay, I just got back from South Africa today, where I was opening my remodeled Montagu course at Fancourt this week.

As to the book, I'd be happy to oblige, let me know what I can do?

Cheers,
David

There is nothing David Kidd did not do. Freely and fully, he opened his files, his notes, his letters and e-mails, his office, his home, his fridge, his wallet, but mostly he opened his heart in an honest effort to share the singular adventure of creating this course at this time with this team in this place: his home, the home of golf.

Kidd was far from the only person to give so generously of himself and his time, from the folks at DMK Golf Design to the staff at the St. Andrews Links Trust to Fife councillors, staunch supporters, vocal opponents, local club members, university librarians, taxi drivers, and publicans—especially the publicans. This book endeavors to share various perspectives of one man's vision, ideally in a manner that reflects the most basic truth about the game of golf: it is just a game.

Golf is supposed to be fun, though so much writing on the subject waxes syrupy and ascribes preposterous meaning-of-life gravitas to the game. From the outset David Kidd and I shared a like mind and insistence that *The Seventh at St. Andrews* not be a tome for golf architecture wonks. If that is your bag, you'd best go buy a textbook.

For us, golf is about the people and the places. And this book is about some exceptional people in an extraordinary place.

The Seventh at St. Andrews

It is of vital importance to avoid anything that tends to make the game simple and stereotyped. On the contrary, every endeavor should be made to increase its strategy, variety, mystery, charm, and elusiveness so that we shall never get bored with it, but continue to pursue it with increasing zest, as many of the old stalwarts of St. Andrews do, for the remainder of our lives.

ALISTER MACKENZIE
The Spirit of St. Andrews

•   •   •

You can't always get what you want
You can't always get what you want
You can't always get what you want

But if you try sometimes
Well, you just might find
You get what you need

The Rolling Stones

1

Rumors

The two gents on the first tee had the Eden Course essentially to themselves. The weather was not unusual for late November in St. Andrews: clear blue but bitterly cold, the kind of cold that sets a nose spouting like a freshly tapped Vermont maple and can rub a nipple raw after eighteen holes spent scraping against the stitching of a golf shirt's embroidered logo. "They aren't Americans," thought the man standing behind a second-story window. He appeared to be frowning, but the jetty of blond hair on his forehead naturally furrowed his brow. In truth, save for the knot in his throat, he could not have been happier to be here. He now split his time between houses in London and Oregon, but Scotland was home.

Americans, he thought, would be swaddled from head to toe in Gore-Tex—if they had not bagged golf altogether in favor of a sauna and a massage at the Old Course Hotel's sparkling new Kohler Waters Spa. These blokes, with their wool sweaters and their beanies, were most certainly locals. They could be university professors or sheep farmers, or quite likely one of each, for in Scotland golf is not a game of kings but a game of the people, and in St. Andrews it is not a privilege but a right.

> Subject to the provisions of this Order
> the trustees shall hold and maintain the
> Links as a public park and place of public
> resort and recreation for the residents
> of the town of St. Andrews and others
> resorting thereto . . .
>
> St. Andrews Links
> Order Confirmation Act 1974

The history of golf in St. Andrews dates back over half a millennium, but it was the future, not the past, that preoccupied David McLay Kidd as he peered out the conference room window across the Eden, the Old, the New, and the Jubilee courses and out on to St. Andrews Bay. Watching the two men tee off was a momentary but welcome distraction from the painstaking wait for two other men, presently huddled in the hallway, to return with the verdict that would alter not only the path of Kidd's career but also the landscape of golf in St. Andrews forever.

St. Andrews is one of those special destinations where the reality eclipses the anticipation. It is, for golfers, like Disneyland is for children—a fact that many of the sixteen thousand locals lament, especially during the busy summer months when the narrow streets around town are clogged with cars piloted by tourists not used to driving on the left side of the road. Still, there is no discounting the giddiness a golfer feels driving in on the A91, when the trees clear and the "Auld Grey Toon" suddenly appears. The links are right there; the first turnoff leads straight to the practice center and the Eden Clubhouse. Past that turn, the A91 becomes Guardbridge Road, which parallels expansive playing fields that, rain or shine, always seem occupied by students engaged in spirited rugby matches. Beyond the pitch sits the stately Old Course Hotel, beyond which every self-respecting golfer knows sits the famed Road Hole.

Many visiting golfers never venture beyond the six golf courses that comprise the links and the three streets (North, South, and Market) that are the main arteries through the heart of town. In this way it is almost as if the northeast corner of St. Andrews—framed by the beaches of the West Sands, where the running scenes for *Chariots of Fire* were filmed, and the East Sands, just beyond the ruins of the St. Andrews Cathedral—has been zoned for golf, like The Strip in Las Vegas. St. Andreans who reside in outlying neighborhoods and opt not to go downtown can tend to their gardens, walk their dogs, shop for groceries, go to school, play in the parks, and live their lives in relative peace and quiet. Despite the ubiquitous tourists and the Starbucks, the old town retains an undeniable charm thanks to its cobblestone streets, ancient stone buildings, quaint shops, abundance of pubs, barbershop offering free whisky with every haircut, and generally lovely people, who speak with the most beautiful, if unintelligible, accent on Earth.

Try as he might to convince himself this was just another job, that if he did not get this there would be others, Kidd knew in his mind and in his heart and with every stitch of his soul that such thinking was complete and total shite. The commission to design the first new championship golf course for St. Andrews in nearly a century was simply beyond comparison. Pebble Beach and Augusta National are treasures to be sure, but neither comes close to the history, aura, and spirit that envelop St. Andrews. To Kidd, the only other place that maybe, just maybe, might present such a once-in-any-lifetime opportunity to create something special and lasting was the moon.

One problem with the moon is the lack of pubs. Kidd is keen on a right pub, and the longer he was left waiting in the conference room the more desperately he longed for a pint to help settle his nerves. Not that Kidd's bladder could handle it after all the coffee he'd drunk that morning and the soup he'd been served, as was custom at midday meetings inside Pilmour House, headquarters of the St. Andrews Links Trust, the body created by the aforementioned act of Parliament. In addition to managing and maintaining the Links as a public park and place of public resort and recreation, the act empowered the Links Trust to "lay out, open up and maintain new and additional golf courses." In 1993 the Links Trust added the 5,260-yard, par-69 Strathtyrum short course and the 1,520-yard, par-30 Balgove nine-holer, which, along with the Old, New, Jubilee, and Eden, gave the town ninety-nine holes, making it the largest public golf facility in Europe. However, not since the christening of the Eden on July 4, 1914, had the home of golf built a regulation-length course. The reasons for building a seventh course had been, and remained, a hotly debated topic around town, especially in light of the fact that a number of nearby courses not under the purview of the Links Trust were struggling mightily. But the train had left the station, the requisite signatories were all aboard, and the Links Trust was set to award the most coveted commission in the history of modern golf. Now, at the moment of truth, all David McLay Kidd could think about was how badly he had to use the loo.

Kidd was hesitant to leave the room and risk interrupting Alan McGregor and Gordon Moir, general manager and links superintendent of the Links Trust, respectively. Then again, perhaps they had ducked into McGregor's adjacent office and the muffled voices Kidd heard on the other side of the conference room door were a couple of coworkers chitchatting about last weekend's thrilling comeback by Rangers to tie Aberdeen on Barry Ferguson's penalty kick goal late in the match.

"You look worried," said Paul Kimber, Kidd's second-in-command. Kimber pushed his chair back from the table. Fidgety in the dress clothes he donned only when absolutely necessary, he stretched his long legs. Six-foot-six-inches tall with broad shoulders, his frame seemed more like a swimmer's than a golfer's. He did not fit easily at the conference table, plus he was still feeling the aftereffects of the brutally long plane ride to Scotland. Noting the pained expression on his boss's face only worsened Kimber's discomfort.

Kidd tried to blame his grimace on his bloated bladder, but just as Tonto knows when the Lone Ranger is not feeling his Kimosabe self, Kimber sensed that Kidd's confidence was teetering. Kidd's brain swelled like a popcorn bag going round and round in a microwave oven, kernels of thoughts exploding and cramming his mind with ifs, ands, or buts. Yes or no, the scenarios were infinite, and yet each ultimately weaved its way back to one inescapable conclusion: No was not an option. They had to "get to *Yes*" as Kidd likes to say. They had come too far.

• • •

Moving to Hawaii to build the exclusive Nanea Golf Club for billionaire golf nuts Charles Schwab and George Roberts was a dream come true for Kidd and his fiancée, Jill. The couple had been on the Big Island for all of five days and still had the giddy glow of young lovers on vacation when they greeted another impossibly glorious morning on September 11, 2001. By the time they poured their coffee and tuned in the morning news, the unfathomable had happened. Staring through tears at the aftermath of the 9/11 terrorist attacks— the broken New York City skyline, the burning Pentagon, the hole in the field in rural Pennsylvania where the heroes of Flight 93 gave their lives to save countless others—the thought of building a $30 million golf course could not have felt more indulgent.

Kidd acknowledged and accepted his responsibilities, not only to his clients but also to his crew. Job #1 was building Nanea, but Job #1a was building DMK Golf Design. The employee roll contained but three names (Kidd, Kimber, and UK office manager Elaine Alabaster), but Kidd took his role as provider of work and wages exceptionally seriously. As such, he was elated to receive an invitation to interview for the redesign of the Shore Course at Monterey Peninsula Country Club, whose surrounding eight square miles of prized California coast are second only to St. Andrews in the pantheon of golf's most holy lands. However, pitching that business meant hopping a plane, and Kidd was none too keen (and Jill even less so) about having to fly the suddenly unfriendly skies just weeks after 9/11.

Unique circumstances did not cost Kidd the Monterey Peninsula job; he just got schooled by an older and wiser adversary. The fact that Mike Strantz was frightfully talented certainly entered into the equation, but Kidd logged two entries in his "Learn From Your

Mistakes" file. The first was that there is strength in numbers. Kidd flew solo to the interview, while Strantz brought along an associate. Kidd was a wunderkind, but he was not Superman. One man does not a golf course make, and Strantz's decision to have a helper by his side projected, intentionally or not, the appearance of an organization versus a one-man band.

The other lesson learned was to be honest—to a point. Kidd laid out his busy workload in great detail for the Monterey Peninsula selection committee, but his plan to increase their interest by demonstrating his demand may have backfired, Kidd suspected, if the powers that be perceived him to be stretched too thin. Meanwhile, Strantz stepped up and offered his hand—even though he may well have already proposed to any number of other suitors, because in the golf design game clients don't give the green light, bankers do.

As it turned out, not only would Kidd have indeed been stretched beyond his limits (Lesson #3: Don't Let Your Mouth Write Checks That Your Butt Can't Cash), but also the committee made an inspired choice. The exquisite redesign at Monterey Peninsula proved to be a lasting legacy to the genius of Mike Strantz, who died of cancer at age fifty, one year after the reopening of the Shores course.

• • •

In the autumn of 2001, the trade winds delivered a rumor from half a world away. The morning started like any other: Kidd kissed Jill good-bye, poured a deep mug of piping-hot black Kona coffee, hopped into his Jeep, popped on his shades, cranked up the music, and hit the road. Cruising along the Kona Highway, Kidd kept an eye peeled for whale spouts. Marveling at the incredible November weather, he made a mental note to log onto metcheck.com and see what the weather was like back home in Scotland. On the seat beside him, Kidd's cell phone chimed. Probably Jill calling to say he forgot something, Kidd thought, or reminding him to slather sunscreen on his pasty white skin. Spying his caller ID, Kidd immediately recognized the UK number belonging to his parents.

"Is it sunny and eighty degrees in Scotland?" Kidd ribbed his father, Jimmy. Jimmy began talking at the speed of sound, but he was so wound up that Kidd couldn't make out more than a handful of words. So Kidd waited for his long-winded father to run out of breath.

"The only thing I understood was lunch, St. Andrews, and grass," said Kidd.

"I said," Jimmy started over, "that Alan McGregor sat next to me at lunch today at a conference in St. Andrews sponsored by Scottish Grass Machinery."

"I know Alan, from the Links Trust."

"Alan and I have known each other forever," said Jimmy, who is one of the world's most respected golf agronomists and for a quarter-century was estates and golf courses director at Scotland's exquisite Gleneagles Resort. "Today he drew me aside and very quietly mentioned that the Links Trust is going ahead with plans to build a seventh course in St. Andrews."

Kidd cranked the Jeep's steering wheel hard to the right and pulled over to the shoulder.

"He said that they are looking for a young, upwardly mobile, successful golf course designer with a worldwide reputation," Jimmy continued, "and he asked if I thought you might be interested."

"What did you say?" Kidd shot back.

"I did well not to spit my tea across the table," Jimmy admitted, "but as calmly as I could I said, 'Yes, I do believe David would be interested indeed.'"

Silence. Kidd's tongue could not catch up with his brain, which had shot into overdrive processing the profoundness of such a commission.

"Did you hear me, son?" Jimmy barked. "You got the job!"

Kidd knew better. He knew his father was the excitable sort and prone to hyperbole, especially if he'd had a wee nip to calm his nerves while waiting out the eleven-hour time difference between Hawaii and Scotland. Kidd also knew that the Links Trust was not about to award a commission of such magnitude without undertaking an exhaustive interview process. The names of likely candidates for the coveted post immediately began flashing in Kidd's head. Perhaps a revered Open champion, like Arnold Palmer, Peter Thomson, or Gary Player. Or possibly a respected player from a more recent era that had made a successful transition to course design, like Greg Norman, Ben Crenshaw, Tom Weiskopf, or Johnny Miller. Maybe a high-profile American, like Tom Fazio, Rees Jones, or Robert Trent Jones, Jr., whose name and reputation might help draw golfers across the pond from the States. Then again, Jimmy said that McGregor said that the Links Trust was looking for a young, upwardly mobile, successful golf course designer with a worldwide reputation, so maybe someone like Tom Doak, Kyle Phillips, Gil Hanse, or Doug Carrick. Scotland's best professional golfer, Colin Montgomerie, dabbled in course design. Even Tiger Woods had said he'd like to try his hand at designing. Imagine the media tsunami if Tiger fashioned his first course in St. Andrews!

Two names resonated above the din:

Nick Faldo. Great Britain's greatest golfer, winner of forty-three titles worldwide, including six major championships. His burgeoning course design business spanned the globe, with projects in England, Germany, Portugal, Cyprus, Northern Ireland, the Republic of Ireland, Denmark, Iceland, Russia, Turkey, Australia, China, Vietnam, Cambodia, South Korea, the Dominican Republic, Canada, Florida, California, and Kansas. Respected, if not loved, as a player and infinitely more likeable in semiretirement, Faldo's most compelling qualifications for the St. Andrews commission were three Open Championships, highlighted by a Claret Jug won in 1990 at the Old Course.

Jack Nicklaus. The most prodigious golfer in history had parlayed his name and fame into one of the most prolific golf course design operations in the business: 311 courses open for play in thirty-eight states and twenty-nine countries, with 254 of those bearing the Golden Bear's fingerprints, including 210 solo designs. Nicklaus was a natural for the commission, given his achievements on the Old Course (site of two of his three Open titles, in 1970 and 1978) and his stature in the community. In 1984, Nicklaus received an honorary doctorate from St. Andrews University, and in 1990 he joined a select group to receive honorary membership in the Royal and Ancient

Golf Club of St. Andrews. Nicklaus harbored deep affection and respect for the town and its citizens, so much so that when it came time to say good-bye to tournament golf, he chose the 2005 Open Championship at the Old Course as the stage. The result was a weeklong lovefest, golf's very own "Jackstock."

Had a whale jumped out of the ocean and landed in the passenger seat of his Jeep, Kidd would not have noticed, so far gone was his mind. He longed to share the news with someone—*anyone!* However, McGregor had told his father on the QT, and Kidd did not want to start off on the wrong foot by stepping on toes. Plus, the golf design business is a small fraternity, and Kidd suspected that telling Kimber and the rest of his crew might jump-start the rumor mill and drown him in an impossibly crowded pool of applicants.

Kidd grabbed his cell phone and started to dial Jill, then stopped. He tossed his phone onto the passenger seat, in part because golf was new to Jill and she would not grasp the enormity of the opportunity (and the reaction is, after all, what makes being the bearer of good news so much fun in the first place), but more so because Kidd feared an irreparable backlash if he woke Jill from a peaceful slumber to suggest a move from the Hawaiian tropics to frigid Scotland.

Going about business as usual, Kidd stopped at his favorite gas station, refilled his coffee mug, and loaded up on snacks, sodas, beer, and ice for the crew. The physical building of Nanea was excruciating and unlike anything Kidd had ever experienced or imagined. The mandate from Messrs. Schwab and Roberts was to create a challenging, walkable golf course akin to their favorite links layouts in England, Ireland, and Scotland. By definition a links course is built on sand—not lava. Save for molten lava, few surfaces on the earth are less hospitable than lava rock, yet that was Kidd's canvas at Nanea.

A man working outdoors feels more
like a man if he can have a bottle of suds.
That's only my opinion, sir.

—ANDY DUFRESNE
The Shawshank Redemption

Kidd agrees wholeheartedly, and his willingness not only to buy the beer but also to stick around and drink it with the crew after hours has earned him the respect and admiration of his men. "Be the loudest, so as to make sure your voice is the one that gets heard" was a lesson Kidd learned from his father, as was "Be the dumbest, to the extent that you empower your crew to believe that they are all experts." It's hard to picture an irrigation grunt draining longnecks in the shadow of a dozer with Jack Nicklaus, both because of his stature and his superhuman pace. (When your design firm opens as many as thirty new golf courses in a calendar year, who has time to lollygag?) But just as Nicklaus still approaches endeavors in his late sixties with the same drive and competitive fire as he did in his late teens, Kidd remains a greenkeeper's son at heart, more at home with the crew than the client and happiest when he has work boots on his feet and dirt under his fingernails.

Knocking back Budweisers with the boys at quitting time, Kidd kept quiet—no small feat for a guy who talks with his hands so expressively that he could pass for Italian if not for his milky complexion and blond hair. There could be no leak, Kidd told himself, if he just kept his big, fat floodgate shut. Standing on the slope of a dormant volcano, Kidd's secret gurgled like magma in his belly until, at three beers past six o'clock, he erupted. Kidd sang like a stool pigeon, babbling on about what a commission in the home of golf would mean to their careers, where in town the site might be, when the course could conceivably open, who the likely contenders were, why he wanted the job so badly, and how he aimed to get it against any and all odds.

• • •

As autumn turned to winter in Hawaii—a curiously invisible transition for someone who grew up in Scotland—Kidd heard nothing from the Links Trust and less still through the grapevine. It seemed certain that Kidd's irrepressibly exuberant father had spoken out prematurely. The ensuing silence was deafening. It was as if Jimmy's conversation with Alan McGregor was but a dream and there would be no seventh course at all.

Kidd had paying clients to worry about, namely Charles Schwab and George Roberts, whose first tour around Nanea was scheduled for December 27, 2001. Two days prior, Kidd and Jill had joined a group of friends on Hapuna Beach, a gorgeous half-mile stretch of golden sand rated the number one beach in America by *Condé Nast Traveler* magazine and a renowned hot spot for swimmers, snorkelers, divers, bodysurfers, and boogie boarders during the summer. In winter, however, the waters at Hapuna can churn ugly with thunderous waves, treacherous rip currents, and violent shore breaks. Wading in the warm Pacific on Christmas Day, Kidd caught a glimpse of Jill on the beach. Blond and tan with a bright, sexy smile, she was a vision. Then the lights went out.

A sneaky wave reared up like a horse on its hind legs behind Kidd, who stood knee-deep in the surf with his back to the ocean. He was smiling when it hit him. The wave blindsided Kidd, pounding him into the sand like a nail. It felt, he recollected in the hospital, like a piano had fallen on him from the sky. Kidd caught a glimpse of Jill in the emergency room. Her smile was no longer sexy. Sickened was more like it. His left arm was broken, his shoulder dislocated, he had two black eyes, too many cuts and scrapes and bruises to count, and the semblance of a nose shoved halfway to his ear. By the grace of God and modern medicine (Vicodin), Kidd survived and managed to endure the walkthrough at Nanea two days later.

It took the better part of that winter and the following spring for Kidd to push St. Andrews to the deep recesses of his mind and stop working himself up over what might have been. Construction at Nanea was coming along slowly but surely, and that provided a constant diversion, as did a docket of other projects DMK Golf Design was pitching. The adage about never knowing what tomorrow brings is especially true in the golf design business, as initial inquiries often arrive in the form of an unsolicited e-mail or telephone call from a guy with some land who wants a golf course. In early May 2002, Kidd received just such a message. He swore he heard his assistant, Elaine, right, but to be certain Kidd asked her to repeat the name of the caller who'd left a message. "Mr. Gordon Moir," she confirmed, "from the St. Andrews Links Trust."

Because of the time difference between the UK and the Big Island a day had passed since Kidd received Moir's message, and much to Kidd's chagrin, another sun would set in Scotland before he could return the call. Kidd got a taste of how excruciatingly fidgety his father must have been waiting by the phone for the morning to dawn on the other side of the globe before he could call his son with the news of the seventh course. When Kidd finally reached Moir, he played it low-key—a con job Kidd can pull off only by telephone because he possesses the world's worst poker face. He tells it like it is, often without ever having to say a word.

"We have a piece of land in mind for a seventh course," said Moir.

"I'd love to get over and see it," replied Kidd, not waiting on an invite.

Within a week Kidd was standing on terra firma in St. Andrews. As he settled into Moir's car for a ride out to the proposed site, Kidd had it in his mind that, logically and logistically, the only suitable site for a links layout would be to the west of the six existing courses along the Eden Estuary. However, Moir turned east instead of west, skirted the city center, and motored onto the Crail Road headed out of town. In ways he could not yet fathom, Kidd had no idea where this road might lead.

Hole 1

• • •

Par-4
374 yards / 363 yards / 341 yards / 309 yards / 289 yards

Part of the enjoyment of Scottish golf is walking a round of golf in three hours, so we want to get games out quickly. The Old Course is the perfect example of a course that is "self-loading." Golfers don't need a starter to tell them when to play away; as soon as the group ahead crosses the Swilcan Burn, the next group is clear to tee off.

Paul figured out that we could create a hollow in the first fairway, into which the group ahead would disappear then reappear. As soon as they reappear on the far side of the hollow, the next group can tee off.

We wanted to put in a practice putting green next to the first tees, but there was not sufficient room, so we ended up with the idea of wrapping the back tee and the practice green together on the same piece of turf.

Pace of play is critical, especially on a public course, so we built the biggest fairway we could get away with. There are two lines off the tee: a tight line off the right-hand side and a much wider line up the left. We faced two issues here: we wanted to ensure that the golfers could not see the water treatment works, and we needed to make sure the golf was not a danger to the clubhouse road, which runs to the right of the first hole. The route to the right is intentionally intimidating and tight so that only the best golfers attempt that.

Most players should hit out to the left, where a solid drive will set up a good look at the preferred angle into the green, which sits in a complete bowl. There are two very narrow entryways, left and right, with the left being slightly wider.

The green is receptive the whole way around, and it should be a reasonably easy hole to get away on. The bunkering on the right side of the green is the most severe, and again that is intended to keep golfers on the left. This green will prove fairer in many people's heads than some others. Golfers are liable to get a more favorable bounce here than at many of the other greens they will encounter.

—David McLay Kidd

2

The White Elephant

The eastern boundary of St. Andrews is marked by a 30 mph sign. Beyond the last roundabout the row houses and brick buildings give way to open fields. On the left, between the tight two-lane byway and the sea, sits a caravan park. Up a piece on the right an auto shop occupies the intersection where the B9131 road veers south toward Anstruther and the A917 continues onto Crail. Kidd knew the latter road well, for seven miles on sits Kingsbarns, a drop-dead-gorgeous links course that opened in 2000 to instant international acclaim. Kingsbarns appears completely natural in its seaside setting, though nothing could be further from the truth. Conceived by developer Mark Parsinen and golf course architect Kyle Phillips, a couple of Californians, Kingsbarns is a marvel of earthmoving crafted by lead shaper Mick McShane, a da Vinci with a dozer who transformed lackluster hayfields into rollicking dunes that deservedly earned a spot on every reputable list of the world's best new courses.

The Links Trust wouldn't stray that far out of town, Kidd told himself. Nor could he imagine their building beyond the two ho-hum golf courses at the St. Andrews Bay resort. Located three miles out along the Crail Road, the 520-acre, 209-room, £50 million hotel and conference center opened in 2001 under a cloud of controversy for running roughshod over construction restrictions and erecting a clubhouse on the cliff's edge that, along with the caravan park, defaces what once was a picturesque vista from town.

Between those ugly bookends sat a patch of equally ugly, flat, brown farmland that represented the only other chunk of land on the seaward side of the road that could accommodate a golf course. The Links Trust had looked everywhere for a suitable plot. They dismissed a parcel across the Eden Estuary for being too low-lying, difficult to access, and a bit close for comfort to the RAF Leuchars air force base. Woodlands out near the Old Course Hotel's Duke's Course were uninspiring and too far removed from the water, a key feature in the trustees' minds. Portions of the Strathtyrum Estate and adjacent Easter Kincaple Farm might have worked, as could a different site on the Strathtyrum Estate on the south side of the A91 road into town, but the folks at Strathtyrum sought a partner, not a buyer, and the Trust was verboten from entering into a joint venture to build and operate a golf course.

The Links Trust's interest in, but struggle to find, land for a seventh course was no secret, and such was the way that a local farmer named Sandy Fyfe came to suggest the Trust ride out and have a gander at 250 acres composed two-thirds by Fyfe's Kinkell Farm and one-third by Brownhills Farm, owned by John and Sheena Raeside. The property boasted 1.1 miles of rugged braes (bluffs) overlooking the bay and across the North Sea, plus fantastic views looking back into town. Described as such it sounded ideal for eighteen holes, but as Moir turned left onto a paved driveway, it quickly became clear to Kidd why no enterprising golf course developer had snatched up the land. Kidd was struck by its nothingness. There was nary a contour to be seen and but one tree. The only existing feature of note was an inextricable tenant.

At the end of the driveway, occupying 161,459 square feet of primo cliff-top real estate just west of center on the site, sat the sparkling new St. Andrews Waste Water Treatment Works. The cutting-edge facility could treat waste from more than double the town's population of sixteen thousand and featured a two-step process that purified the effluent before an ultraviolet light treatment expunged leftover bacteria in the sewage, after which it was flushed at sea. Cleverly hidden from town sight lines, the plant was also concealed from Kidd's passenger-seat view by the grade of the site, which sloped gently from the Crail Road down to the sea. As they climbed out of the car, Moir prattled on about soil conditions, weather, prevailing winds, annual rainfall, yada, yada, yada, but there was no ignoring the three-and-a-half acre white elephant lying before Kidd's eyes, and the red flag flying in his brain screamed, "They want to build a golf course around the town shitter!"

21 May 2002

Gordon Moir
St. Andrews Links Trust
Pilmour House
St. Andrews
Fife
KY16 9SF

Dear Gordon,

It was a pleasure to meet you last week and have the opportunity to discuss the new course being proposed at St. Andrews.

After we talked, I went back and took some more pictures, even going down to the waterfront at St. Andrews and looking back at the site. The views from and to the site are exceptional. I have learnt that golf is a pastime enjoyed as much by the eyes as the body, especially for the golfers with lesser ability. This site will provide them with a great deal of pleasure, of that I have no doubt.

Once on the site it is apparent that generations of farming have removed every subtlety from the terrain. Imaginative golf design must restore these subtleties. You mentioned that you have had the STRI [Sports Turf Research Institute] *do some site investigation work; this will be very useful in directing the design and construction effort to make the best use of the ground in the most cost-effective manner with long term sustainability in mind.*

It barely needs saying but to make sure you are in no doubt, I would love to be selected as the Golf Architect for this golf course. My approach is completely hands-on; for this reason I only work on one course at a time and try to select each one carefully. If selected I would intend to move to St. Andrews for the duration of the construction process, ensuring that I can coordinate the design at every stage day by day.

When the time is right I look forward to discussing the project further with you.

Best regards,
David McLay Kidd
Golf Course Architect

Kidd's visit to St. Andrews resulted in more questions than answers, chief among them: "How do I get to *Yes?*" Throughout his life that mantra had helped Kidd focus on achieving objectives fraught with obstacles. Getting to *Yes* with the Links Trust, Kidd suspected, might well prove as lofty a goal as getting to *I Do* with Jill.

Kidd knew beyond a doubt that he could do the job—but not by telling the whole truth. His biggest fear at this stage was being put in a position where he had to be honest. Buzzwords like "minimalist" and "natural" and "traditional" are favored not only by provincial locals but also by politicians, who exist to make a golf course designer's job either incredibly difficult or downright unbearable. Upon parting ways with Moir, Kidd rang Kimber back on the Big Island.

"So what do you think?" Kimber asked anxiously.

"I think we're gonna have to move a shitload of dirt."

Two-and-a-half million pounds sterling was plenty of money to build a golf course, but it was not half enough to create *the* golf course Kidd envisioned. Opportunity was knocking, and yet Kidd felt the Links Trust was turning a deaf ear. They struck him as resigned to the limited potential of the chosen golfing grounds, content with any old eighteen holes just as long as they relieved the increasing overcapacity issues on the existing links. For £2.5 million the trustees might as well present the designer with the same wheelbarrow, spade, and shovel that the Royal and Ancient Golf Club gave Old Tom Morris when he was made the first keeper of the green back in 1864. Kidd had no interest in building a snoozer, much less losing money in the process. Compared to the bottomless pockets of his über-rich clients at Nanea, signing on with a charitable trust would, on the best of days, be like working in a straightjacket and shackles. But Kidd was determined to turn the process upside down, to flip the Links Trust's resignation into enthusiasm, and flop the perception of limited potential into the promise of infinite possibilities.

• • •

Kidd's pre-takeoff routine on long-haul flights rarely changes: remove his shoes and slip on the socks that come in the overnight kit; order a gin and tonic; pull his laptop from his carry-on case, stow the case in the overhead compartment, and stash the laptop in the seat pocket in front of him; greet the person sitting next to him with standoffish cordiality lest he or she be a golfer who wants to talk shop for twelve hours; check the in-flight magazine to see if anyone has already done the Sudoku puzzle; sip the first gin and tonic and order a second before the flight attendant gets away; resolve to actually learn how the hell to do a Sudoku puzzle someday.

Properly settled in, Kidd pulled out a pen and, in true visionary form, set to work on the back of a cocktail napkin. On one side he drew the plot of land as best as he remembered it, complete with the immovable Wastewater Treatment Works lodged front and center and the clubhouse site favored by the Links Trust set between the sewage plant and the Crail Road. Even on the most rudimentary of sketches there was no getting around the fact that the only way to get around the buildings required diminishing the key asset, the view, and forcing golfers to trudge up the grade with their backs turned away from the water.

Determined to look for the bright side, Kidd flipped over the napkin and charted the pros and cons of the St. Andrews gig.

+

in St. Andrews
on the water

–

no landforms
no character
no vegetation
bloody walking path below the braes
routing challenges
the town shitter

By the time Kidd arrived back on the Big Island, the only thing he'd determined for certain was that there was absolutely no way in hell he would give this gig a second thought were it not in St. Andrews.

Days then weeks then a full month passed without a word. Kidd's growing sense that it was only a matter of time before the bad news came was confirmed the last week of June when a letter arrived from the Links Trust. "A letter," Kidd thought. "Brilliant." Gordon Moir had picked up the telephone and placed a personal call to make the initial inquiry, so the letter caught Kidd off guard. Therein lies the simplistic beauty of the letter, the most ordinary yet devastating of severing tools, a weapon capable of cutting out the heart without breaking the skin, wickedly impersonal yet impossible to mistake because everything is right there spelled out in black and white.

24 June 2002

Mr. D. McLay Kidd
DMK Golf Design Ltd
The Heybridge Center
Colchester Road
Heybridge
Essex CM9 4NN

Dear Sirs

Dear Sirs?!? As if a letter were not cold enough, the Links Trust could not even bother to tell him to bugger off by name? Kidd's eyes jumped to the bottom of the page.

Yours faithfully,
Alan J. R. McGregor
General Manager

Not good. It was signed by the big boss, just like the dreaded rejection letter from the president of the university that says, in essence, nice try but you are not invited to our party. Out of morbid curiosity Kidd read the guts of the letter.

The St. Andrews Links Trust is applying for planning permission to build a 7th course to add to their portfolio of golf courses at St. Andrews.

. . . We are writing to 10 golf architectural firms and intend inviting up to 5 for interview. Should you wish to be included in this short list please reply explaining why you would be right and what you would intend charging for this prestigious project probably valued at around £2.5 million.

[In fact, the Links Trust wrote to sixteen firms and invited six to interview.]

Two words jumped off the page: *Why you?* Kidd set out to craft his response not knowing which other firms had received the same missive from McGregor. In fact, of the possible candidates Kidd initially envisioned, Arnold Palmer, Peter Thomson, Greg Norman, Ben Crenshaw, Tom Weiskopf, Johnny Miller, Tom Fazio, Rees Jones, Robert Trent Jones, Jr., Tom Doak, Doug Carrick, Colin Montgomerie, and Tiger Woods all failed to make the cut.

The most surprising omission was Jack Nicklaus, who the Links Trust suspected would command too steep a fee for their modest budget. Typically the design fee runs somewhere in the neighborhood of

6 to 12 percent of the construction budget, which worked out to £150,000 to £300,000 for Course No. 7 based on the £2.5 million suggested price tag. With the going rate for a Jack Nicklaus Signature reported to be upward of $2 million, the Links Trust opted to end the conversation before it began—though they may have acted prematurely.

Kidd could not afford to lose money on the deal, but he knew others could, namely, Nicklaus. Do the math: according to his Web site, "Nicklaus Design has opened 110 courses over the last seven years—an average of almost 16 courses a year—including a record 27 in 1999." The company outdid itself with thirty new courses scheduled to open in 2006, fourteen of which were Jack Nicklaus Signature Courses. Designing No. 7 gratis would be the ultimate gift to the town and the people of St. Andrews, not to mention a shrewd PR move. Nor would it be without precedent, as Nicklaus had donated his services to his alma mater, Ohio State University, for the renovation of the school's Scarlet Course, as well as to the redesign of the North Palm Beach Country Club near his longtime Florida home. Luckily for Kidd the Links Trust never broached the subject with Nicklaus, nor did Nicklaus ring Pilmour House offering a freebie.

The Links Trust's list of targets featured far fewer recognizable names than anyone might have expected. Save for the most hardcore of golf architecture fanatics (a surprisingly thriving subculture), most people outside the industry would not recognize the names of many of the sixteen candidates:

Nick Faldo, London, England
Martin Hawtree, Oxford, England
Gary Player, Palm Beach Gardens, Florida
Rich Hurley, East Stroudsburg, Pennsylvania
Dennis Griffiths, Braselton, Georgia
Jonathon Tucker, West Yorkshire, England
Howard Swan, Essex, England
David Williams, North Wales
David McLay Kidd, Essex, England

Jonathon Gaunt and Steve Marnoch, Derbyshire, England
Robin Hiseman, Aberdeenshire, Scotland
Jeremy Slessor, Berkshire, England
Donald Steel, West Sussex, England
Dave Thomas, Cheshire, England
Kyle Phillips, Granite Bay, California
Calum A. Todd, Dundee, Scotland

There was no rhyme or reason to the lineup or ranking of the candidates; however, had Kidd been privy to the list, he would have been more unsettled by Faldo's top billing than by his own name appearing ninth. Kidd had buckets of talent, but Faldo had boatloads of trophies. Three Claret Jugs and three green jackets aside, Faldo's place in history as Europe's greatest golfer was cemented by his Ryder Cup heroics. His marks stand to this day for the most appearances (eleven), most matches played (forty-six), most points won (twenty-five), and most matches won (twenty-three). Golf is the most individual of endeavors, and yet Faldo flourished in the team atmosphere in spite of burnishing an image during his playing days as a loner who cared more about winning than anything or anyone. (Upon collecting his third Open prize at Muirfield in 1992, Faldo took center stage at the awards ceremony, stepped to the mic, waited for the crowd to hush, and before a worldwide audience, proceeded to thank his friends in the media, "from the heart of my bottom.")

The polar opposite of the pro game, golf design requires a team effort, and Faldo is once again flourishing, in large measure because he has had the good sense to ally himself with talented, respected designers such as Americans Brian Curley and Steve Smyers and Aussie Tony Cashmore. Kidd routinely gets approached by representatives of tour players who think it would be neat to play course designer; however, he politely declines such overtures. Professional golfers make Kidd nervous because he views them, by and large, as the epitome of the amateur architect, seeing things innately from a player's view and focusing mostly, if not solely, on the design without an understanding of or appreciation for three equally important, if less sexy, considerations: construction, maintenance, and operation, which along with design compose an essential, interdependent matrix.

Each of the four elements directly and proportionately affects the others. Just because a hole can be envisioned does not mean that it can be effectively or efficiently built, kept up, or managed. Adding a seemingly innocent bunker, for instance, may be aesthetically pleasing from a design standpoint, but it could prove problematic in terms of construction. The area might sit where water naturally collects, meaning that one good rain would wash that bunker out. Maintenance-wise, a bunker designed for visual intimidation may require unnecessarily time-consuming upkeep. The son of a greenkeeper, Kidd worries about such consequences. Operationally, the placement of that bunker could affect pace of play or force golfers along a shaded path where the grass will become worn and unsightly and struggle to recover due to too much traffic and not enough sun.

Courses codesigned by professional golfers, more often than not, are a nice way for the golfers to line their pockets and stroke their egos, not unlike the proliferation of PGA Tour gentleman winemakers. Greg Norman, Ernie Els, and Mike Weir are among those who have their names on labels, but they aren't the ones picking and crushing the grapes. They probably got in the game because they like wine, it's a fun hobby, and they were presented with a business opportunity. (Make no mistake: on or off the course those guys don't play to lose.)

Developers drive the tour-pro codesign business because Marketing 101 teaches that you can sell more real estate faster on a course bearing the seal of Phil Mickelson than Phil Wogan. Wielding a rubber stamp and popping by the site a few times when the press is tagging along does not make you a golf course architect, yet that is essentially the extent of the involvement of some big-name player-architects. It irks Kidd that they get the same "Designed By" credit for a cameo that Kidd gets for a leading role, as does the specter of missing out on a truly special piece of land simply because some incredibly wealthy golf geek/developer (of which there is no shortage) wants to have his mug snapped with a famous golfer for a photo that goes in the clubhouse to prove what a swell guy the owner is.

Kidd contends that if developers don't know enough to want him, then he knows better than to want them. He is too busy to stop and stew about the injustices of due credit, and in fact Kidd was more amused than bemused when Kimber dropped in Kidd's lap a *LINKS* magazine cover from early 2006 that trumpeted:

Davis Love III leads a new breed
of throwback player-architects known
for their hands-on work styles
and timeless designs

" 'Hands-on work styles'?" Kidd bellowed as he chucked the issue back to Kimber without even opening it. "Look at his bloody getup!" Striking a pose like the Ralph Lauren model he is, Love sported spotless boots, clean blue jeans, a pristine Polo shirt, and perfectly coifed hair. "Hands-on," Kidd chuckled. "My arse."

Hole 2

• • •

Par-4
441 yards / 414 yards / 397 yards / 375 yards / 341 yards

The tees at the second hole are set down low, and as golfers prepare to hit slightly up-hill and across some grown-up grass, it appears as if there is just no good place to drive the ball.

During the build, we had a busy construction road that ran across the fairway just short of the landing area, and when we were shaping the hole, I really worried and fretted for weeks with Paul over whether golfers could see anything at all off that tee. My main concern was more about safety than playability. Once golfers come over that hill, they will see there is plenty of room; however, we don't want people on the tee driving into people they cannot see in the fairway.

When the haul road was removed and that area shaped, sure enough, it opened up the line of vision, though just enough. It worked out just the way we wanted, and I believe it will be a very exciting tee shot, a lot like some of the great Irish courses, including Ballybunion and Lahinch, where you stand on the tee and you just have no clue. It requires taking a giant leap of faith, stepping off into nothing, and believing you are not going to fall.

The fifth hole at Lahinch and the eighth hole at Pebble Beach are two great holes where golfers use a rock as their aiming point off the tee, and it could be that we end up doing something like that to show the best line on some of these holes where the tee shot is partially blind.

Mick shaped all the greens on the course except at the second hole. Conor did that; though they did not tell me which green he had shaped. When I saw it for the first time, I thought the second green looked very McShaneish, with all the characteristics of what Mick had done elsewhere. It matched everything else.

For better or for worse, Conor is a McShane in the making!

—David McLay Kidd

3

Why You?

Had Kidd seen the Links Trust's list, he'd have been disappointed he was not facing more heavyweight contenders. Regardless of his feelings about Nicklaus and Faldo, the one name Kidd would have most wanted on the list was Tom Doak.

Kidd and Doak are like a couple of actors who keep getting sent up for the same roles. Their mutual trademark has been a bespoke method of design and construction; though devoting such a focused level of time and attention to any one project grows more difficult as the demands for their services grow. Both are known for making the most of a site's organic ingredients rather than concocting the kinds of synthetic features, such as artificial waterfalls, fancied by burgeoning golf baron Donald Trump. (Trump's handlers invited Kidd to consider collaborating on the proposed Donald J. Trump Signature Design at Trump International Golf Links near Aberdeen in northeast Scotland; however, Kidd was not keen to play second banana.)

Like Arnie and Jack back in the early days, Kidd and Doak are respectful rivals, more friendly than friends, Kidd the gregarious one and Doak the diffident sort. A Pete Dye protégé and Alister MacKenzie aficionado, Doak, who is nearly seven years Kidd's senior, has worn multiple hats, including published author, accomplished photographer, learned golf historian, and freakish trivia sponge. His Traverse City, Michigan–based operation is named, appropriately, Renaissance Golf. The two men are inextricably linked by their most celebrated works, which sit side-by-side along the Oregon coast at the Bandon Dunes golf resort. Kidd's wild and woolly Bandon Dunes course put the resort on the golfing map in 1999, and Doak's rough-hewn Pacific Dunes, opened in 2001, cemented Bandon as a pilgrimage all golfers must make before they die.

From Bandon, Kidd and Doak followed wildly divergent paths. Kidd took on two ultra-expensive, ultra-private projects: Nanea, on the Big Island, which cost in the neighborhood of $30 million, and Queenwood, in the suburbs southwest of London. Reportedly built for a mere $7 million, Queenwood owns the distinction of being the most expensive private golf club in the United Kingdom and the favored hangout of tour pros Ernie Els, Retief Goosen, Adam Scott, Thomas Bjorn, Paul McGinley, David Howell, Justin Rose, and Darren Clarke, who is the two-time defending club champion. Each course draws raves from the fortunate few people who play them; however, neither Nanea nor Queenwood garners much praise from the media because at both establishments golf writers and course raters rank on par with telemarketers: thanks, but no thanks. Kidd took two utterly divergent canvases and created truly exceptional works that showcase his artistry—but mum's the word. It would be like a painter receiving private commissions to create a portrait with oils and a landscape with watercolors, and succeeding spectacularly, yet the only people who ever see the works are the owners' friends and family.

While Kidd took the high-ticket road, Doak took the low road Down Under. Cape Kidnappers in New Zealand and Barnbougle Dunes in Tasmania were built for less than $7 million—combined. On the heels of Pacific Dunes, Doak could have easily ridden the wave of acclaim and plucked a cushy gig close to home, but both plots of exotic land were so raw, so visually spectacular, so otherworldly. Both were ideal not only for golf courses (sand by the sea), but also for photography, and the eye-popping images that subsequently graced the pages of every notable golf magazine on the planet wound up buying Doak incalculable PR. It was a ballsy play, but it paid off handsomely.

Doak was not in the St. Andrews stakes, but Kidd did not know that. (Some time later, Kidd asked Doak why he did not throw his hat in the ring for No. 7, and Doak replied, curiously, that he did not know how to get in touch with the Links Trust—this despite having caddied on the links the summer after his college graduation.) Still, Kidd's competitors were capable and formidable. As he set about answering Alan McGregor's "Why You?" letter, all he knew was that the Links Trust had invited him to the table, and regardless of who the other players were, Kidd was all in.

29 July 2002
Mr. Alan McGregor
St. Andrews Links Trust
Pilmour House
St. Andrews Fife
KY16 9SF

Re: St. Andrews Links No. 7

Dear Mr. McGregor,

Thank you for your letter of 25th July 2002. I am flattered to be considered for this prestigious commission. I am extremely keen to be selected for this project and hope that I can sufficiently articulate all of the reasons I believe my team and I to be the most suitable choice.

Nine single-spaced typewritten pages were more than sufficient. McGregor counted the pages and had a good chuckle. Even in print, the kid was a natural talker, just like his father.

The possibility of being involved in the creation of a new course for the St. Andrews Links Trust was exciting in itself and after seeing the site and the views from it, I am brimming with enthusiasm.

Your letter asked why I believe that I would be the right choice for this project. In my opinion the reasons are numerous and diverse. I feel I have the background, experience, team and talent to create an exceptional golf course with professionalism and efficiency. I offer the following personal and company biography to support our bid for the opportunity to interview for this commission.

I was born and raised in the Scottish lowlands, son of a respected greenkeeper.

Kidd's thesis encompassed his experience growing up at Gleneagles, studying at Writtle College, the largest land sciences college in the UK, interning for Southern Golf, the largest golf construction company in the UK, joining a small architectural firm called Swan Golf Designs as a designer/project manager, returning home, where he spent the 1990s as director of design for Gleneagles Golf Developments, then hanging out his DMK Golf Design shingle in 1999. After explaining DMK's five-stage design process (routing, scheme design, detailed design, construction, grow-in), Kidd did his best to skirt the issue of money.

I would deeply regret losing the opportunity of working on this project because of cost so I am reluctant to define fees at this early stage. . . .

Our method of work varies from many of our competitors as it sees us concentrate all of our efforts on the construction of one project at a time, ensuring it to be the very best it can be. As there is a constant presence on site from our team there is the opportunity to offer more than a design service. Project management, construction management or even a complete design and build package can be provided. Consequently, comparing golf design fees is often not an "apples for apples" comparison, especially when comparing the time the principal and his staff might spend on-site against the fee charged.

Kidd intentionally tucked the money card up his sleeve even though McGregor's letter clearly stated, "please reply explaining . . .

what you would intend charging for this prestigious project." By citing DMK's reluctance "to define fees at this early stage" because "our method of work varies from many of our competitors," Kidd not only ensured a return engagement—if the Links Trust liked what they saw, they would have to ask him back to find out how much it would cost— Kidd also shifted the paradigm of how the Links Trust would select the architect. The question "What am I going to pay you?" became "What are you going to provide me?" Kidd's only hope to "get to *Yes*" was to turn the process upside down, and by presenting the opportunity for the Links Trust to get more for their money than strictly design service, he had succeeded in conceiving that new reality, one in which the Links Trust was now on offense instead of defense. Any player who now came to the table offering anything less than the design, project management, construction management, and/or the complete design-and-build package that DMK was prepared to deliver would put the Links Trust in the position of comparing apples to applesauce.

Kidd summarized his dissertation with a list of "Key Points That Make DMK Golf Design the Right Choice":

- *Born & raised in Scotland*

- *Greenkeeper's Son*

- *Academically Qualified*

- *Familiar with Daily Fee Golf Design, Maintenance & Operations*

- *Familiar with local weather and people*

- *Familiar with expectations of international visitors esp. USA*

- *All plans created in 3-D CAD* [Computer-Aided Design], *allowing accurate quantification and control*

- *Team includes Shapers with outstanding reputations*

- *Track record of success*

- *Experience gained in every facet of golf business from maintenance, through construction, operations and design*

- *Knowledge, experience and talent of team combined with hands-on method of work guarantees exceptional results*

- *Proven ability to work within a budget to allocate resources, control schedules and deliver on time*

- *Able to integrate quickly into a team, communicate effectively, consult and collaborate with others to establish the most effective and creative solutions*

- *Fundamentally, a practical common sense Scotsman who has built a team of like-minded professional people who wish to create fun, challenging, classically beautiful golf courses for all.*

Please forgive this lengthy response; it further illustrates my enthusiasm for the project and deep desire to be selected for an interview in the coming months.

Yours sincerely,
David McLay Kidd

Armed with the responses, the Links Trust brain trust gathered to whittle the field. McGregor felt compelled to present a balanced mix representing various nationalities and levels of experience. The deliberations proved drawn out and difficult, though not nearly as tedious as the wait Kidd endured back in Hawaii. As August passed without a peep, Kidd braced himself for another extended, excruciating silence; however, when a letter arrived from Pilmour House in early September, Kidd wondered whether the response had come too soon, like a jury returning a verdict after curiously brief deliberations.

4 September 2002

Mr. D. McLay Kidd
DMK Golf Design Ltd
The Heybridge Center
Colchester Road
Heybridge
Essex CM9 4NN

Dear Mr. McLay

An inauspicious opening, but an improvement over "Dear Sirs."

I am now writing formally to invite you to come to St. Andrews to present your case to be the course architect for St. Andrews Links No. 7. You are one of 6 that have been short-listed.

The signature was that of Links Superintendent Gordon Moir; however, that letter might as well have been a golden ticket signed by Mr. Willy Wonka himself. The five other lucky recipients were notable primarily for their lack of notability:

Martin Hawtree, Oxford, England
Robin Hiseman, Aberdeenshire, Scotland
Jonathon Tucker, West Yorkshire, England
Rich Hurley, East Stroudsburg, Pennsylvania
David Williams, North Wales

• • •

Where's Faldo?
One would have thought that, having made the long list, Faldo might merit a bye to the short list simply for being Faldo. As for the others, die-hard golf architecture wonks might have heard of Hawtree—though not necessarily Martin. His grandfather, Frederick William Hawtree, collaborated with five-time Open winner

J. H. Taylor on a number of designs, including the overhaul of Royal Birkdale to Open Championship standards in 1932, and among the notable works of Martin's father, Frederick George Hawtree, was the enhancing of Royal Liverpool for the 1967 Open. Continuing the family tradition, Martin has established himself as Britain's Open surgeon with a docket that includes toughening up multiple Open venues, including Royal Birkdale, Carnoustie, and Muirfield.

The most recognizable name on Robin Hiseman's CV is Royal Dornoch—the wee Struie course, not the world-renowned Old Tom Morris course people immediately associate with Royal Dornoch. Jonathon Tucker's official title is head of golf course development service for Great Britain's Sports Turf Research Institute, and Richard Hurley's is adjunct professor in turfgrass management and turfgrass breeding at Rutgers, the state university of New Jersey. David Williams looks like a jovial bloke judging from the snapshot on his rudimentary Web site, but ask the average American golfer if he's ever heard of the Williams-designed Caversham Heath, Clandon Regis, or Gwynus, and you are likely to get the same blank, befuddled look you'd get asking the average Scot if he's ever heard of Bandon Dunes. The fact of the matter was that for the all of the accolades Kidd rightfully earned for Bandon Dunes in the USA, in UK golf circles he remained firmly, if not exclusively, known as Jimmy Kidd's kid.

As for Faldo, his firm was indeed keen for a crack at No. 7 and responded to Alan McGregor's cordial "Why you?" missive with a thoughtful, reasoned case for delivering a world-class golf course and perhaps a branded golf academy, as well as the added value Nick Faldo's name generated from a promotional standpoint. Money was not an object; they offered to deeply discount their usual commercial terms and made clear that the design fee would not be an obstacle. To their minds, nothing that Faldo Design put in their letter could have put off the Links Trust.

However, the absence of any "name" finalists suggests that the Links Trust was focused on the product regardless of any marketing potential. After all, why pay for ancillary marketing when your tagline is "The Home of Golf?" From the outset the Links Trust stated unequivocally that the primary objective for pursuing a seventh course was to ease capacity, not draw tourists. In the end availability trumped visibility. The Links Trust wanted the principal present and accountable, and the iconic status that begets diverse business empires all but ensured that any of the big-name player-architects would pop in for photo ops then delegate day-to-day duties to an underling. (Many big-name player-architects are contractually obligated to make four to six site visits, including the grand opening. In Kidd's letter he offered to move to St. Andrews.) Cachet goes a long way with golf community developers and the home buyers they target, but Course No. 7 was never about sales. It was just about golf.

Kidd still did not know whom he was up against, nor could he have cared less. Suffused with confidence, he welcomed all comers. With Nanea nearing completion, Kidd kicked his rear into gear and shifted his focus toward making absolutely certain that the Links Trust could not conjure one good reason not to hire DMK Golf Design.

Having made the cut and received the formal invitation to present, Kidd focused on the fine print of Moir's letter, which posed six questions that each finalist would be expected to address:

1. *Who would be the principle* [sic] *architect?*

2. *Would he be permanently on-site and if not how often would he visit?*

3. *Would you sub-contract any specialist work i.e. irrigation, soil testing, drainage etc? If so, who would you use and would the cost be included in your quotation?*

4. *Do you use the same construction company on all your projects? If so, which one and if not, how would you go about selecting a suitable construction company?*

5. *What is your likely timescale for the project?*

6. *What is your fee proposal?*

The first five were fairly easily answered: (1) Kidd would be the principal architect, assisted by an associate who would work exclusively on this project; (2) between Kidd and his associate they would provide a full-time on-site presence; (3) yes, DMK would sub-contract specialist expertise; (4) no, they do not use the same construction company on every project; and (5) the time frame would be broken out into five phases: routing (five weeks), scheme (six weeks), detail (eight weeks), construction (twenty-five weeks) for Year 1/April to October, and grow-in (twenty-one months) for Year 1/August to Year 3/May.

"What is your fee proposal?" Number six was a direct question that begged a direct answer, although Kidd had hoped to skirt the money issue until he was sitting across the table from the Links Trust. Measuring himself against the specter of big hitters like Nicklaus and Faldo, Kidd tried to make the argument about time versus money, for those guys had plenty of the latter but not enough of the former. If Kidd could tip the discussion toward time spent instead of money saved, he could expose a glaring weakness in his opponents. Unfortunately, there was no wiggling out of the undesirable position of having to throw out the first number, and the quote Kidd provided for designing the most anticipated golf course in the world fairly insured that DMK Golf Design's profit margin would be almost exactly nil.

•   •   •

In late October 2002, Kidd and Kimber arrived to find Scotland positively arctic. Eighteen months spent living on a tropical island had warmed their blood. Kidd got the OK to give Kimber a look about the site the day before their presentation. Clambering out of the rental car, they were pounded by an icy wind that sliced through their every stitch of clothing and layer of skin and made their bones ache with every shuffle of their feet.

Both were shocked to find they were not alone. A solitary figure wandered down toward the braes. Kidd and Kimber agreed that the only loon half-cocked enough to be out kicking dirt clods on a day like this had to be another candidate for the job. Heavily bundled, the bloke was unrecognizable, so Kidd and Kimber started after him.

They figured to say a quick hello, commiserate about the weather, lament the inadequacies of the site—nothing too probing. Really they just wanted to see whom they were up against; have a quick peek then beeline it back to a pub. It quickly became apparent that the gent did not share their curiosity. As Kidd and Kimber moved toward him, he moved away. They zigged, and he zagged. That mouse wanted no part of these cats, and with their surreptitious veil of a chance encounter lifted, they joked that their best hope of getting a good look at him was for Kimber to chase after and try to tackle the bastard while Kidd peeled off to one side and blocked his path back to his rental car. Sensing that this course of action might not endear them to the Links Trust, the lads let the mouse scurry on his way.

The site was as advertised by Kidd: flat and boring, with a three-acre poop plant plopped front and center. Kimber's first impression was direr than Kidd's, though Kidd knew that his own experience afforded him greater vision. Whereas Kimber saw a glass half-empty, Kidd saw a glass in need of Scotch. The night before their presentation the two hunkered down in the living room at Kidd's parents' house in Auchterarder, a quaint village an hour's drive west of St. Andrews. Fueled by a few wee drams of whisky, Kidd and Kimber burned the midnight oil and polished their pitch.

Hole 3

· · ·

Par-3
222 yards / 207 yards / 187 yards / 154 yards / 147 yards

The third hole offers the first set of par-3 tees on the golf course. On a par-3 the tees are set much tighter and closer together, and these have been completely sculpted to nestle into one another. I sincerely hope golfers will begin to get the sense that the tees we have created at this course are miniature works of art all by themselves.

Tees at so many golf courses are an afterthought—if they receive any thought at all. The typical flat, round, tiny helicopter pads set one after another have no artistic value whatsoever.

Here, we did something completely different and tried to put as much effort into the tee sets as we put into everything else. The tees on this course have taken as much, and arguably more, effort than some of the greens complexes, which runs completely and utterly contrary to conventional golf course design.

The sophisticated golfer who investigates these kinds of things will realize that we built this from whole cloth, and will hopefully appreciate the exacting attention to detail. This was a potato field, not an ancient landscape into which we softened a golf course. The whole thing has been created, and I think these tees look especially amazing, like something that could be five hundred years old.

At the third hole we employed a trick we commonly use on par-3s: we excavated out truckload after truckload of earth between the tees and green so as to give golfers the illusion that they are hitting over something. It raises the stakes—and the heartbeat—and as a result a golfer will often take an extra club, but we counter that by penalizing shots that go long. Big and right here is bad. Golfers who see that might try to take something off of their tee ball, but we counter that with a rather large slope in front of the green. The green is huge here, and the best play is a decisive play.

—David McLay Kidd

4

Thank You for Coming

Jimmy Kidd was a boy of modest means who grew to acquire a taste for the finer things in life. His penchant for fine wine, fancy restaurants, and snazzy cars is outdone only by his predilection for dapper duds. The clothes make the man, Jimmy has long believed, and so it was that on the eve of Kidd's big day his father bestowed his favorite tweed jacket upon his son. Slipping it on, Kidd felt like a Masters champion donning golf's fabled green jacket, only this was more sentimental than ceremonial. Jimmy is old school with his emotions, whereas Kidd is distinctly New Age. Tears bubble just below the surface, and the dam is perpetually on the brink of collapse, especially when the subject turns to family. Ask Kidd, for instance, how he copes with spending so much time away from his beautiful baby daughter, and the instantaneous, inaudible answer is "Not well." Kidd knew how much his landing this commission meant to his father because the accomplishments of a child validate the dedication of a parent. Like Tiger Woods, David Kidd benefited from a father who worked tirelessly to create both the environment and the opportunities for his son not just to succeed but also to flourish. Kidd's working in St. Andrews would be no different than Tiger's winning at St. Andrews in that both represent shared triumphs for the father *and* the son rather than mere vicarious victories for the father *by* the son.

Like a knight receiving a suit of armor to wear into battle, Kidd accepted the tweed jacket humbly and appreciatively. No words were spoken. None were necessary. Not that Kidd could have eked out so much as a syllable without bawling anyways.

•   •   •

DMK Golf Design was the third of the six finalists to present to the Links Trust. Given a choice, Kidd preferred to lead off in hopes of wowing the client and setting the bar so high that anyone who came after simply could not measure up. He dreaded going last for fear that his audience would be as bored and burned out as a school-teacher subjected to sitting through a parade of oral reports. At least back then each student got to see the others perform. Not knowing who he was up against here further fed Kidd's anxiety. Was this a true, open competition or was he just the token Scot brought in to appease locals before the Links Trust went ahead and crowned the safe and popular pick they'd wanted all along?

Neither Kidd nor Kimber talked much on the drive from Auchter-arder to St. Andrews. There was nothing left to say or do. Their props were all good to go—laptop charged, PowerPoint presentation loaded, leave-behind kits assembled. Each of them knew his own part as well as the other's, lest one of them forget a line. They left nothing to chance, not even the traffic, pulling into St. Andrews with time enough to re-fuel on coffee before their 11:00 A.M. appointment at Pilmour House. The band of inquisitors included Dr. Duncan Lawrie, chairman of the trustees; Jim White, chairman of the links management committee; John Devlin, chairman of the greens subcommittee; Moir; and Mc-Gregor. Introductions were made and pleasantries exchanged; then Kidd got right down to business.

Each finalist was allotted two hours to present, which, going in, felt padded to Kimber but pressed to Kidd. Engaging and instantly likeable, Kimber mixes easily in any company, though he does so less enthusiastically than Kidd. Schmoozing is an art Kidd employs as a weapon to his extroverted advantage over a great many competitors who are content to let their work speak for themselves.

As with most job searches, the finalists were all fairly equal on paper. Each of the contenders was perfectly capable of laying out eighteen playable golf holes. Everyone delivered informative lectures and polite answers. All trotted out tidy support materials chock-full of buzzwords and superlatives that ultimately blended together like one humongous run-on sentence after six different people said essentially the exact same thing about tees with varying angles and elevations that appeal to golfers of all skill levels, and fairways that are generous, rolling, and tight on the attack line, marked by strategic bunkers and penal rough, guarding undulating putting greens, offering multiple pin placements blah blah blah. The fundamental objective of any interview process is not to find the most qualified candidate, but rather to find the most compatible. That's where intangibles come in: a sense of humor, a firm handshake, eye contact, the gift of gab.

Kidd blew past the two-hour time limit like a runaway train. Kimber knew better than to jump in front of this locomotive; better to just sit back and enjoy the ride. Luckily the panel seemed more interested in Kidd's pitch than their own rumbling stomachs. What piqued their interest, what managed to set DMK apart, was Kidd's bid to serve as general contractor. Golf courses are no different than houses in that the architect designs and the contractor builds. The two functions are typically mutually exclusive, but taking on the entire process offered a significant upside. DMK was going to break even on the design fee but could earn at least a reasonable profit on the construction. By managing all the subcontractors, DMK could control the entire construction budget, spending strategically and making sure resources were dedicated based on their wants rather than the needs of a contractor more interested in making a buck than a killer golf course. Contractors build what they bid, but Kidd designs in the dirt. The fancy drawings are to sell the client, land the commission, justify the budget, and secure the permits. After that, the two-dimensional plan on paper never bears too close a resemblance to the three-dimensional reality in dirt. Plus, given Kidd's contention that they were going to have to move a shitload of dirt, he wanted his own handpicked shaping crew, muckshifters who possessed the vision, the talent, and the balls to lead and not just follow. The downside of taking on the kit as well as the kaboodle was that DMK Golf Design bore significant added responsibilities, like processing the ordering, delivering all of the necessary equipment and materials, and insuring the total liability for health and safety on the project.

Three-and-a-half hours later the only words Kimber had managed to shoehorn in were "hello," "thank you," and "good-bye." Kidd walked out of the meeting feeling like they had just aced a final exam.

"Did I talk too much?" asked Kidd.

"It didn't feel like it," Kimber answered honestly. "Even though the allotted time was two hours and you talked for nearly four." He could not resist a friendly needling.

"Did anyone look pissed bored to you?"

"No," said Kimber, retracing the faces of the assembled audience. "I wouldn't say so."

"You hesitated."

"No one looked bored," said Kimber. "Hungry, yes, but not bored."

4 November 2002

Mr. Gordon Moir
St. Andrews Links Trust
Pilmour House
St. Andrews Fife
KY16 9SF

Re: St. Andrews Links No. 7

Dear Gordon,

Thank you very much for giving me the opportunity to present my company and myself to you and your colleagues last week. I hope I didn't talk too much! I had no idea how long I had been talking until the very end. I can assure you that was unusual and my father is by far the champion in that regard.

I wished to reiterate the point that, possibly unlike many if not all of our competitors, we have not offered you merely a design service but a design and construction management combination that will guarantee that the construction proceeds as smoothly and efficiently as possible. We are happy to manage any structure of construction you wish. I will be on site virtually full-time with a design associate from my company assigned entirely to the project.

I look forward to hearing the conclusion of your group's deliberations, if there are any unanswered questions or anything we have not been clear about please do not hesitate to contact me.

Yours sincerely,
David McLay Kidd

cc: Alan McGregor

Good news traveled fast, as Kidd and Kimber had barely been back in Hawaii long enough to readjust to the heinous time change when McGregor reached Kidd on his mobile phone.

"Dammit!" Kidd cursed, startling Jill as he hung up from McGregor.

"What's the matter?" she asked gingerly.

"They want us back in St. Andrews for a follow-up interview."

"But that is good news."

"In two weeks!"

Kidd was ecstatic about getting the callback, though he was none too thrilled about having to make the agonizing journey again so soon, and less elated still about the pounding his credit card was taking. Business class air fares from Honolulu to Edinburgh topped $10,000, and flying coach for such a long haul was not a reasonable option for him. Unlike Nicklaus and Norman and a growing number of rich tour pros–cum–course designers, Kidd does not own a private jet, and unfortunately there are no nonstops from the Big Island to St. Andrews.

After back-to-back red-eye flights from Hawaii to Los Angeles, then Los Angeles to Heathrow, Kidd and Kimber bunked overnight at Kidd's home in Essex, southwest of London. The plan was to catch a reasonable night's rest in an actual bed before hopping a shuttle from nearby Stansted Airport up to Edinburgh on the morning of their follow-up interview. Leaving nothing to chance, they booked a flight that arrived in Edinburgh hours in advance of their afternoon appointment and anticipated potential delays caused by weather or traffic—but not amnesia. Passing through security, Kimber felt Kidd's peculiar glare.

"Have you forgotten something?" asked Kidd.

"I don't believe so," Kimber replied as he collected and checked his belongings. Plane ticket, rental car reservation, laptop, mobile phone, pens and paper, business cards, breath mints. Everything looked to be accounted for.

"Where is your sports coat?"

Kimber's heart sank. "In my suit bag."

"Where's your suit bag?"

"Hanging."

"Hanging where?"

"In the closet at your house."

Kidd cursed loudly enough to draw the ire of more than a few passersby. Seething, he shook his head; then suddenly his eyes widened.

"Where are you going?" asked Kimber, hot on Kidd's heels as he marched through the terminal.

"*You* are going *there!*" Kidd said, pointing to Austin Reed, a popular British clothing chain with a mercifully convenient outpost at Stansted. As if paying inflated airport prices was not hard enough, Kimber had to scour the store for a size 44 long to fit his six-foot-six-inch frame. Amazingly he found a presentable tweed that fit—so long as he did not cross his arms or reach above his head. Kimber was forced to fork over £150 for a jacket that anywhere outside the airport probably cost half as much.

The follow-up interview took place in the same meeting room at Pilmour House, only this time it was just McGregor and Moir, and instead of sitting at the massive conference table, they gathered at a smaller, more intimate table in one corner of the room. Kidd hoped the cozier setting might help him pick up hints in their interviewers' eyes or body language, but for different reasons both men were tough reads. Moir, forty-eight, has deep, droopy eyes and a stoic visage that fairly belies emotion. Reared in Fraserburgh, the most northeasterly point of Scotland, he started in the trade at age seventeen, as an apprentice, and worked his way up to head greenkeeper at Fraserburgh Golf Club before moving to the Links.

What Moir lacks in expression McGregor makes up for tenfold. So animated is he that the creators of the 2004 movie *Bobby Jones: Stroke of Genius* cast McGregor as the starter who announces the contestants at the 1930 British Amateur. His booming baritone, crisp enunciation, and lilting accent make the sixty-year-old grandfather of five the ideal bedtime storyteller. His own story of the road to Pilmour House is a winding tale. An army officer with the Royal Highland Fusiliers for nine years, McGregor left the military and got serious about the killing game, accepting a post with Scotland's largest pest control business. Management positions in the pharmaceutical and business machine industries led to the CEO seat at United Auctions PLC, the UK's largest livestock auctioneer. One random Sunday McGregor's younger brother, Calum, rang to ask if McGregor had seen the advert in the newspaper seeking applicants for general manager of the St. Andrews Links Trust.

McGregor was not looking for a job; however, there was declining job satisfaction in steering Britain's largest livestock auction at the height of the mad cow crisis. Also, he had a soft spot for St. Andrews after spending six years there in a prep school run by a headmaster who was a three handicap, a member of the R&A (The Royal and Ancient Golf Club of St. Andrews), and given to concocting feeble reasons to cut the school days short any time a big tournament came to town. As a preteen McGregor witnessed Peter Thomson and Bobby Locke's triumphant turns around the Old Course in the 1955 and 1957 Open Championships, respectively. Figuring nothing ventured, nothing gained, McGregor submitted his CV and was called for an interview, which he likened to a parole board grilling. Fortunately, the diplomatic skills he'd honed working with the farming community closing auction marts came in handy, and in September 1998 McGregor ascended to the hot seat.

Kidd began to feel the heat as the two sides got down to the nitty-gritty. The Links Trust approved of Kimber as the associate; however, they required confirmation of Kidd's commitment as the principal architect. In his "Why me?" response Kidd had said he would move to St. Andrews and essentially work full-time on-site. Push had come to shove: was that a bona fide offer or a campaign promise? Kidd would commit in writing to no less than sixty working days on-site during construction. Also, the Links Trust made clear their intention to install a head greenkeeper at the outset of construction. *Fine.* And use Links greenkeeping staff. *Dandy.* Plus, Kidd would be expected to work closely with the buildings architect, Fraser Smart. *Naturally.* The trustees wanted to nominate certain subcontractors for consideration. *Agreed.* They wanted sign off on DMK's routing plan. *Fair enough.* They planned to call past clients for references. *Please do.* They reiterated that if DMK were to serve as general contractors they would be responsible for a litany of administrative tasks, from maintaining health and safety documentation to liaising with local bureaucracies and on and on and on. *Whatever it takes.* The project budget, and the line item for earthmoving in particular, needed to be discussed and mutually agreed upon. *Brilliant, so long as everyone is clear that we are going to move Heaven and earth.* Now, about your fee . . .

And everything had been going so smoothly.

Kidd fully expected McGregor to take a stab at cutting DMK's proposed fee, and in fact he'd have been disappointed if McGregor hadn't. Part of what made DMK Golf Design a successful firm was the business acumen of its leader, and Kidd wanted a savvy client, someone who was not a pushover, who scratched and clawed for the best deal but refused to sacrifice quality to get it. Kidd needed to see how his potential partner dealt with conflict.

"We need to sharpen the pencil on your fee," said McGregor, so disarmingly charming he could likely get the whole of Scotland back from the queen if he set his mind to it.

"There's nothing left to shave," Kidd replied earnestly. "That's what we have to work with."

McGregor sat back in his armchair. Resting his chin in his hands, he squinted his eyes as if that might help him see things more clearly. Kidd sat tall in his seat, never once fidgeting, never once breaking eye contact. The cards were on the table, and the only thing left up anyone's sleeve was the price tag in Kimber's new tweed jacket, which he planned to return for a refund on the way back through the airport.

"Excuse us a moment, will you?" McGregor said, standing. "Gordon?"

Moir followed McGregor out of the conference room.

"Do you think they are debating whether to move us on to the next round of interviews or whether to give us the job?" asked Kidd.

"What more is there to say?" replied Kimber.

"Yea," said Kidd. He walked to the window and gazed toward St. Andrews Bay. Like the ebb and flow of the tide, Kidd's confidence came and went, came and went. "Or nay."

Just outside the window two gents on the first tee had the Eden Course essentially to themselves. "They aren't Americans," Kidd thought. In addition to an anxious knot in his throat, Kidd had to pee like a racehorse, but he was hesitant to leave the room and risk interrupting McGregor and Moir's powwow.

"You look worried," said Kimber, his own expression suddenly turned concerned.

"I'm not worried," replied Kidd. "I just have to pee so bad it's gonna start seeping out my tear ducts."

The door handle jiggled, and Kidd slithered nonchalantly back to the table. McGregor, displaying a military formality, marched into the room, spine straight, shoulders back, chin up. "Gentlemen," he said, presenting his hand to shake. "Thank you for coming."

Hole 4

• • •

Par-5
565 yards / 552 yards / 546 yards / 496 yards / 443 yards

The team debated the fourth hole probably more than any other. We had a real challenge in rerouting a burn that ran down through the site. Originally we brought it in front of the fourth green, but in addition to that making the hole too similar to the fifteenth hole, we also found that the grade was too steep and water would run too fast.

We needed to slow the water down, and I suggested that we bend the burn so it crossed the fairway at a softer angle farther out from the green. Once that was done we realized that the average player likely faced a second to a gap that was incredibly tight—maybe fifteen yards wide for about a sixty-yard stretch—with water on the left.

After hitting driver off the tee, the choices were to either lay up short of the water or try to bust one all the way to the green. Had it been left the way it was, I argued that a mid-handicapper would have to hit driver, wedge, 4-iron, and that seemed really screwed up. So we moved the burn for a third time, this time even farther out so that now the average player can hit driver, 4-iron, wedge, a more conventional play that also makes it much easier to get the second shot over the burn.

The fourth green was the last to be built. By then the creativity was really cooking, as Mick would say, and the result is that the fourth green is one of the boldest on the entire golf course—maybe even on par with the wild fourteenth green.

The fourth green is kind of like a heart shape looking from the top down, with a crease in the middle that must appear like a ten-foot slope, though it is not even half that much. It swings from the high front right down to the back left, and there are all sorts of friendly contours to feed a ball into that green.

There are a bunch of different ways to play this hole and plenty of places where you might get an extremely favorable bounce—but that will all balance out because there are plenty of other places on the course where you won't.

—David McLay Kidd

5

The Links (Mis)Trust

The St. Andrews Links Trust enjoys/endures a love/hate relationship with the constituency it is charged with serving. There is no arguing that the condition of the golf courses and the quality of the facilities are today immeasurably superior to when the Links Trust was established in 1974. Back then golfers on holiday, more often than not, would pull up to the Old Course to have a look and snap a pic then climb back in their car and motor on to a course that did not resemble the raggedy carpet in a St. Andrews University dormitory. Golfers who did stay to play changed their shoes in the car park. It was quaint, but the experience did not meet the reasonable expectations of tourists who shelled out to tee it up at the home of golf. Food or drink? In town. Souvenirs? Pluck a sprig of gorse. Service? Sod off.

The golf courses formerly fell under the purview of the St. Andrews Town Council, but in the mid-1970s that body was abolished under a redistricting that proposed shifting the government seat across the Firth of Tay to Dundee, the negative side effect of which would bring a flood of Dundonians to the links. So as to keep control of the hallowed grounds in St. Andrews, an order "enacted by the Queen's most Excellent Majesty, by and with the advice and consent of the Lords Spiritual and Temporal, and Commons, in this present Parliament assembled, and by the authority of the same" constituted the

Links Trust, "to vest in the said Trust the control and management of the Links of St. Andrews; and for purposes connected herewith."

This was not the first act that affected the links. Kings James II, James III, and James IV issued acts in the years 1457, 1471, and 1492, respectively, that banned the playing of golf. "It is stature and ordained that in na place of the Realme," decreed James IV, "there be used fute-ball, golfe, or uther sik unprofitable sportes." But cooler heads prevailed, and in due time the citizenry were no longer being "taken be the Kingis officiares," per James II, for the atrocious transgression of "tuitching . . . the golfe." Golfers returned to the links, though they had to share with neighbors who helped themselves to peat to fuel their fires and carved-out chunks of turf for roofing.

Then there were the rabbits. In a text titled *Historical Notes & Extracts concerning the Links of St. Andrews, 1552–1893*, author D. Hay Fleming wrote:

> *The earliest documentation concerning the Links . . . is dated, at St. Andrews, the 25th of January 1552, and bears the signature of Archbishop Hamilton* [who] *acknowledges that he had obtained "licience and tolerance," by the free consent of the provost, bailies, council, and community of St. Andrews, to plant and plenish rabbits within the . . . "commond Linkis nixt adjacent to the Wattir of Eddin"; but reserving always . . . "all manner of rycht and possessioun proprietie and communitie of the saidis Links . . . to thair uis and profit, playing at golf . . . with all uther maner of pastime, as ever thai pleis."*

Perhaps the provost, bailies, council, and community of St. Andrews did not know then what we know now about the horny habits of rabbits and their proclivity to reproduce; otherwise they might have rethought the whole free consent deal, for it seems to have ignited a tug-of-war that raged for centuries. In 1797 the cash-strapped town council sold "the lands of Pilmor and Pilmor Links," and when the new owner flipped the land in 1799 to a father and son named

Charles and Cathcart Dempster, the town council tacked a caveat onto the disposition it granted:

> *All and whole the Lands belonging to the patrimony of the said city of St. Andrews called Pilmor, with the remanent Links . . . lying in the parish of St. Andrews and the sheriff-dom of Fife, bounded by the Sea and the Swilking Burn on the east, the Water of Eden on the north, and parts of the Lands of Strathtyrum on the west and south parts respective; Reserving . . . that no hurt or damage shall be done thereby to the Golf Links; nor shall it lie in the power of any propri-etor of said Pilmor Links to plough up any part of said Golf Links in all time coming, but at the same time shall be re-served entirely, as it has been in times past, for the comfort and amusement of the inhabitants and others who shall re-sort thither for that amusement.*

Untold acrimony may well have been avoided had the Dempsters not been rabbit farmers. It did not take long for the rabbits to trash the place, or for the locals to turn up the heat on the town council. They never said anything about allowing the links to be converted to a rabbit warren. Had they advertised that option, the land would surely have attracted more buyers and commanded a much better price for the town. However, the deal was done, and the pressing is-sue was the clause about the links being "reserved entirely, as it has been in times past, for the comfort and amusement of the inhabi-tants." The golfers, clearly, were not amused. Siding with their con-stituents, the council in 1806 backed the plaintiffs in a court case seeking "that the inhabitants of St. Andrews and others shall be at liberty to take, kill or destroy the rabbits, in the same way they were in use to do." The court ruled against the Dempsters. Obstinate bug-gers, the Dempsters appealed to the House of Lords. While awaiting that ruling, the plaintiffs, along with their friends, families, and any-body else who was game to take a whack, abided the lower court or-der and mashied every rabbit they could get a niblick on.

By this time the Old Course boasted an established eighteen-hole layout, having been reconfigured in 1764 from a twenty-two-hole loop that saw golfers play eleven holes out, turn around, then play the same eleven holes back in. Given that each putting green had only one hole (double greens were not introduced until 1832, and golfers could not mark their ball with a Sharpie, as the indelible marker favored by golfers was not invented until 1964) confusion surely reigned when incoming and outgoing matches collided head-on. In addition to a few bloody noses, this conflict may have incited the advent of golf etiquette, the unwritten code that complements the official rules of golf, which are administered by the USGA in America and the R&A everywhere else in the world. The original "Articles & Laws in Playing the Golf" were set forth by the Honorable Company of Edinburgh Golfers in 1744:

1. *You must tee your ball within a club length of the hole.*

2. *Your tee must be on the ground.*

3. *You are not to change the ball which you strike off the tee.*

4. *You are not to remove stones, bones or any break club for the sake of playing your ball, except upon the fair green, and that only within a club length of your ball.*

5. *If your ball come among water, or any watery filth, you are at liberty to take out your ball, and throwing it behind the hazard 6 yards at least, you may play it with any club, and allow your adversary a stroke, for so getting out your ball.*

6. *If your balls be found anywhere touching one another, you are to lift the first ball, till you play the last.*

7. *At holeing, you are to play your ball honestly for the hole, and not to play upon your adversary's ball, not lying in your way to the hole.*

8. *If you should lose your ball, by its being taken up, or any other way, you are to go back to the spot where you struck last, and drop another ball, and allow your adversary a stroke for the misfortune.*

9. *No man at holeing his ball is to be allowed to mark his way to the hole with his club or any thing else.*

10. *If a ball be stop'd by any person, horse or dog, or any thing else, the ball so stop'd must be played where it lyes.*

11. *If you draw your club in order to strike and proceed so far in thee stroke as to be bringing down your club; if then your club shall break, in any way, it is to be accounted a stroke.*

12. *He whose ball lyes farthest from the hole is obliged to play first.*

13. *Neither trench, ditch, or dyke made for the preservation of the links, nor the scholar's holes or the soldier's lines, shall be accounted a hazard, but the ball is to be taken out, teed and played with any iron club.*

The Old Course may have been laid out, but it was not designed in any traditional sense. Naturally firm sand glazed with short grass is inherent to the linksland and ideally suited to a game where one swings a stick at a projectile, attempts to retrieve it, then hits it again. The earliest bunkers were not built but rather formed, most likely by whipping winds and burrowing animals seeking shelter from said winds. Tees were dollops of sand, and holes were just that: pocks in the turf. And so it was until Old Tom returned home.

Born in St. Andrews in 1821, Tom Morris grew up just up the street from the Old Course and started in the business as an apprentice club and feather ball maker. His mentor was Allan Robertson, widely regarded as the father of professional golf. Robertson's gift for making golf equipment was outdone only by his ability to make use of it. A hustler who was not above a wee sandbagging to better his odds on a match, Robertson talked a good game and had the featheries to back it up: in 1858 he carded a 79 on the Old Course, acknowledged to be the first round under 80. Robertson also dabbled in course design, fashioning the original layout at Carnoustie in 1850, later upgraded by Morris. Like his boss, Old Tom wielded a mighty brassie. He placed second in the inaugural Open Championship in 1860 and won top honors in 1861, 1862, 1864, and 1867. (His son, Young Tom, matched the old man by reeling off the next four Open titles.)

Morris Sr. was living on the west coast of Scotland and working at Prestwick, a course of his own design, when, in 1864, the Royal & Ancient hoped to lure him back to St. Andrews to serve as the keeper of the green at the links. The offer: an annual salary of £50, a wheelbarrow, a shovel, a spade, and a helper two days a week. Old Tom took the job and kept it for nearly forty years before retiring at the tender age of eighty-two. Among his contributions to the links were the addition of the putting greens now played at the first and last holes, the clearing of forests of gorse (no small feat with a shovel and a spade), the removal of cattle in favor of sheep (much more efficient grazers and fertilizers), the placing of metal cups in the golf holes, the use of heavy rollers to smooth the greens, and the introduction of the invention that above all others revolutionized the game forever: the lawn mower.

Golfers everywhere have Edwin Beard Budding to thank for this brainchild. The Gloucestershire, England, native drew inspiration from the spiral-bladed nap-cutting machines at the textile mill where he worked, which gave freshly woven cloth a smooth finish. Budding envisioned a like contraption that would trap blades of grass between blades of metal, and in 1830 he patented his idea. In partnership with the Phoenix Iron Works, Budding engineered a nineteen-inch cast-iron mower that operated much the same way scissors do, with spinning blades that lopped off grass as they passed alongside a stationary blade. Within a decade, more than a thousand Budding lawn mowers had been sold, forcing flocks of sheep to look for a new line of work.

The development of the railways toward the end of the nineteenth century also stoked the wildfire popularity of golf. According to the British Golf Museum, 1,500 miles of train tracks crisscrossed Britain in 1837. By 1870 that figure jumped to 15,620 miles, and by 1890 it was up over 20,000. The splendor of St. Andrews, its golf and its beaches, became increasingly accessible from hither and yon. However, with but one golf course that all comers could play for free, congestion fermented into frustration on the links until the town council and the R&A swung a deal to acquire additional linksland adjacent to the Old Course from the laird of Strathtyrum (who, no dummy, wrangled free golf for his family and any visiting friends on all existing and future St. Andrews courses, as well as the prerogative to dig seashells by the seashore where the estuary met the bay). The logically named New Course, with a routing by Edinburgh engineer W. Hall Blyth, opened in April of 1895. Tougher and tighter than its neighbor, the New would surely garner greater accolades were it set anywhere other than right beside the most famous golf course in the world.

Two years hence the Jubilee Course opened, so dubbed because it debuted on the sixtieth anniversary of Her Majesty Queen Victoria's coronation. Set between the New and the West Sands, the original 2,669-yard, twelve-hole course (expanded to eighteen holes in 1905) was built in less than three months for £178 and change and was intended for women and beginners, whose arses the real golfers wanted off of the Old and the New. It's not as if the lads and lassies were a complete afterthought, as the chieftains did bother to strike a compromise with the honchos of the abutting Rifle and Artillery Volunteer Corps to see that golfers were not in play when the corpsmen's guns were blazing. Still feeling squeezed, in 1914 the Town Council extended the reach of the links inland with the H. S. Colt–designed Eden Course, which borders the Old Course along the east and hugs the estuary to the north. In 1972, the wee Balgove nine-hole course opened on twenty-six acres purchased from the Strathtyrum estate.

Those were the assets the Links Trust inherited when it was established in 1974. There was no cash reserve, no sustainable income, no growth potential, and no resources. So grim was it that if the head greenkeeper needed turf for the Old Course, he carved out chunks from the other courses, like the paupers who filched sod to patch their roofs five hundred years before. The one thing the first trustees did have, however, was vision. Recognizing the unique station the links and the town enjoyed as the home of golf, the trustees embarked on an effort to raise money and awareness so that they might upgrade their assets, which in turn would enhance their image, which in turn would attract tourists, who in turn would spend pounds, dollars, yen, and so on, so that the Links Trust could generate a surplus, which could then be plowed back into the links.

A clear strategy supported by fiscal prudence put the Links Trust in a position, in 1981, to take a mortgage on the venerable Rusacks Hotel, which overlooks the eighteenth hole of the Old Course. A proper locker room was added to accommodate golfers in need of a loo or a place to change, and four years later the Links Trust sold the hotel at a profit. The proceeds helped fund the upgrade of the Eden Course, a new and improved Balgove, and the addition of the 5,620-yard, par-69 Strathtyrum Course, as well as the practice center, Eden greenkeeping facility, and the Links Clubhouse, which opened to much hullabaloo in 1995.

At the time it was the only clubhouse in town that did not require membership, a place where tourists and non-affiliated locals could eat, drink, shop, shower, and change clothes. Located at the south end of the West Sands, it served the Old, New, and Jubilee courses, as well as the "Himalayas," the popular humpy-lumpy layout beside the second tee of the Old, where the Ladies' Putting Club of St. Andrews staged their competitions and gaggles of people just out for giggles gathered to play. Local merchants did not welcome the competition from the sparkling new clubhouse or the supposed charity that ran it. In a scathing letter to the local newspaper, the *St. Andrews Citizen*, the captains of five local golf clubs charged that the foray of the Links Trust into commercial enterprise was a disgrace and an abuse of the power with which the charitable trust was vested.

Three entities comprise the Links Trust. The executive team, headed by McGregor, is responsible for day-to-day business and answers to two higher authorities: the Links Management Committee, which oversees the operation of the golf facilities, and the Trustees, who set policy and ensure that the links are kept within the spirit and the letter of the 1974 act of Parliament. The latter two are both eight-person bodies. The Management Committee has four members nominated by Fife Council and four by the R&A, while the Trustees see three nominated by the landowner (formerly the Town Council and now the Fife Council), three nominated by the R&A, one nominated by Scottish Parliament, and one local member of UK Parliament. Volunteers all, they bring to the party an eclectic mix of backgrounds and perspectives. Among those serving at the time Course No. 7 came together were the provost of Fife, a University of St. Andrews professor, a former Olympic runner, a hotelier, a farmer, the owner of a local launderette, the proprietor of an old folks home, a landscape gardener, a housewife, and a minister.

At every turn, mistrust trails the Links Trust like a shadow at sundown. Rancor continues to reign over another Links Trust initiative more than a decade after its undertaking: tired of watching the cash registers ring for a proliferation of tour operators who bought tee times on the links at face value and then sold them at a premium as part of a package, the Links Trust decided to get in the game and made a deal with Keith Prowse Ltd. of London. Since 1995, Keith Prowse has enjoyed an exclusive agreement with the Links Trust to deliver *The Old Course Experience*, a luxury travel package that guarantees golf's most precious commodity: fail-safe tee times on the Old Course. There are various methods for getting on the Old, but the vast majority of the golfing public must roll the dice in a daily ballot. Considering that the trek to St. Andrews is a once-in-a-lifetime proposition for most golfers, an extra thousand or three is an ersatz insurance premium against missing out on St. Andrews's main attraction. Detractors of the arrangement claim that the 800 or so prime tee times that Keith Prowse buys annually come at the expense of "the residents of the town of St. Andrews and others resorting thereto" per the Links Act, whether Keith Prowse sells them or not. On the other hand *The Old Course Experience* is a plump bird in the hand, a golden goose that delivers guaranteed income that the trustees can reinvest in projects like the state-of-the-art Jubilee greenkeeping center, the Eden Clubhouse, and, now, Course No. 7.

The briar patch in which the Links Trust occasionally finds itself is due partly to an institutionalized aversion to controversy that inevitably invites more. In rebuffing a *Golf Digest* request for details of the Keith Prowse deal under Britain's Freedom of Information Act, the Links Trust's official no comment was an affronted "The Trust is not a public authority and is not covered by this legislation, so it has no relevance." However, the sticky situations are more often the result of having to serve multiple, usually mutually exclusive, constituencies.

Firstly, there are the aforementioned "residents of the town of St. Andrews," for whom the Links Act provides that the trustees shall maintain the links as a place of recreation. No stipulation is made for how that is to be maintained, but since its inception the Links Trust (and the Town Council before it) has offered annual tickets to permanent, voting-eligible residents of the town. The ticket entitles residents to unlimited golf on the links. Times are variously restricted for tournaments, scheduled upkeep, and advanced bookings, but St. Andreans rarely have no place to play. Some 1,900 residents, 550 students, and 4,000 others in various and more restrictive categories (members of the R&A, members of an approved local golf club living in North East Fife, members of an approved local golf club living outside North East Fife, etc.) purchase the annual tickets, which are, without question, the biggest bargain in all of golf: £125 in 2007, or about $220, for unlimited golf across the links. That's the same price as one round on the Old for visitors, or half the cost of one round at Pebble Beach.

Secondly, the Links Trust serves the local golf clubs (though it has no legal obligation to do so). There are five men's clubs: the Royal & Ancient, the St. Andrews Golf Club, the New Golf Club, the XIXth Hole, and the Thistle Golf Club, as well as three ladies' clubs: the St. Rule Club, the St. Regulus Golf Club, and the Ladies' Putting Club. The links courses are all munis and do not belong to any of the golf clubs, however members do enjoy special privileges on the links.

Then there are the "others resorting thereto." Despite the fact that golfers who pay to play the links support over five hundred full-time jobs in town and pump more than £20 million into the St. Andrews economy, 90 percent of which comes from outsiders, there is a sizeable faction of St. Andreans who are less welcoming of change than the Amish and would love nothing more than for the tourists to take their business anywhere so long as it was elsewhere.

Serious golf nuts will find the means to make their way to St. Andrews. Fewer Japanese are gearing up along Golf Place since their economy tanked, and Americans are reeling from the hammering the dollar has taken from the British pound, which has increased in value nearly 30 percent against the dollar since 9/11. But a more pressing reason why locals feel squeezed on the links is a spike in the number of recognized residents, which includes an influx of links ticket-eligible university students. When the Links Trust took over in 1974, the university's twenty-five hundred students made up 25 percent of the town's ten thousand residents, roughly speaking. Today, the student populace has nearly tripled, to seven thousand, which accounts for 43 percent of the sixteen-thousand-plus who now call St. Andrews home.

The upsurge of interest in the university, Scotland's first (est. 1413) and one of the UK's finest (St. Andrews is to Oxford and Cambridge as Princeton is to Harvard and Yale) can be traced to the announcement of Prince William's intent to enroll in 2001. A 44 percent increase in applications flooded the university from kids who were eager to befriend or betroth the heir to the throne.

There is no way to say what effect the prince, a keen golfer while at St. Andrews U, had on the uptick in rounds played, but in 2001, the year William arrived, the links saw a record 215,000 rounds played, besting the previous mark of 208,000 in 1997. On his desk when McGregor signed on in September of that year was a strategic plan that showed the Old, New, and Jubilee courses running at capacity, the others nearly full, and the links as a whole flirting with the estimated breaking point of 220,000 rounds per annum across all six courses. Desperately seeking solutions, McGregor organized an off-site meeting at Cameron House, a bucolic retreat on the banks of Loch Lomond, in the spring of 1998. Out of this confab came the very first mention of a seventh course.

• • •

The Links Trust assembled a Working Party charged with studying individual and collective golf course loads and limits, trends in golf tourism and both town and university population, as well as yield management for the yearly tickets offered to residents. Traffic on the Old Course reached forty-nine thousand rounds in 1990, topping the target threshold by four thousand. (Exceeding the limit was possible because any golfer who arrived before the first or after the last tee time was free to play away.) Factor in that there is no Sunday play on the Old, the course is closed one month each year for rest and repair, and weather makes golf practically unplayable for maybe another month or two, and that leaves roughly 230 potential golfing days per year. If each of the forty-nine thousand rounds were played as part of a foursome, which never happens, sent off at intervals of eight minutes, as was the custom back then, the result would be a tee sheet that is booked solid for seven hours every golfing day. To ease the load, the Links Trust in 1990 extended the interval between tee times from eight to ten minutes and posted opening and closing times from 7:00 A.M. to 6:00 P.M. However, that was merely a Band-Aid, applied only to the Old Course. The other courses, which allowed play on Sundays, were all suffering from chronic inundation, a condition for which there are only two cures: limit demand or increase capacity.

Jacking up green fees would limit demand by pricing out a portion of the less affluent golfing public, but golf is an everyman's game in Scotland, and the Working Party never considered such cutthroat tactics. They did ponder tightening the screws on yearly tickets, a program beset by a Byzantine hierarchy of categories, waiting lists, and guest policies run on point systems. Instituting additional constraints on residents' access to their links might well have exposed the trustees to torturous repercussions straight out of *Braveheart*.

Increasing capacity could be achieved by extending playing hours and/or allowing play on the Old Course on Sundays; however, the former would exacerbate wear and tear on the links, and the latter not only promised to further exceed the threshold of 42,000 rounds on the Old, but it also flew in the face of Old Tom Morris's time-honored ipse dixit: "If the gowfer disna need a rest, the course does." Another option was to look forward by looking back: a century before, similar struggles with overcrowding on the links led the town to pony up for the New, the Jubilee, and the Eden, all opened in a span of less than twenty years. The home of golf had outgrown the existing links, and the most logical course of action, the Working Party concluded, was to seek more spacious digs.

In the autumn of 1998 the Links Trust hosted a public gathering in the Links Clubhouse, where the executive team presented the findings of the Working Party to an audience of some sixty people, most of whom were affiliated with the local golf clubs and interest groups, including the Community Council, an organized, articulate, and particularly hard-nosed lobby that takes exceptionally seriously its stated purpose, "to ascertain, coordinate and express to the local authorities for its area, and to public authorities, the views of the community which it represents, in relation to matters for which those authorities are responsible, and to take such action in the interests of that community as appears to it to be expedient and practicable." The Community Council is the group that notoriously snubbed Jack Nicklaus during his swan song at the 2005 Open Championship. Nicklaus's nomination to receive the award of the title Honorary Citizen of the Royal Burgh of St. Andrews was killed by the council, whose dissenters, according to the meeting minutes, submitted that the award "should be for people who had done something directly for St. Andrews over a substantial period of time." Perhaps the councillors would have been perfectly content without the windfall of publicity and tourist dollars Nicklaus helped generate around the world over five decades. In truth, this title of Honorary Citizen seems a tougher title to achieve than knighthood; in the five years since the council established the award, the number of recipients so honored tallies exactly zero.

The Links Trust expected resistance to their plan, most likely from the proprietors of area golf courses that were not battling overcrowding. The Old Course Hotel had a tough sell getting guests to shuttle up to its Duke's Course on the outskirts of town, in part because it was a snoozer Peter Thomson design (when Herb Kohler bought the hotel in 2004, he promptly ordered a major upgrade), but more so because guests who stay on the links want to play on the links. Up the road at St. Andrews Bay, the largely uninspiring Torrance and Devlin courses made the least of some prime waterfront. Even the universally acclaimed Kingsbarns struggled to draw St. Andreans off their links, despite practically giving golf away by offering £15 green fees to resident ticket holders, a whopping 90 percent discount off the regular £150 rate.

What caught the Links Trust off guard was the unexpected opposition from camps they assumed would be in their corner, most notably the Scottish Incoming Golf Tour Operators Association, the Kingdom of Fife Tourist Board, and the St. Andrews Hotel and Guest House Association. A seventh course certainly seemed in their collective best interests given that the parties were in the business of attracting and housing predominantly golf tourists. However, they wondered whether the new attraction might just deepen the advantage already enjoyed by *The Old Course Experience*, which operated unrivaled in guaranteed access to the Old Course and placed guests in the fancy hotels, not mom-and-pop B&Bs. Notwithstanding the fact that the Links Trust was providing residents with a world-class course and the promise to not jack the annual ticket fee excessively, locals remained skeptical. Rumors were rife that the Links Trust aimed to drive residents, as well as the local clubs' monthly tournaments, up onto No. 7 so as to free up the Old for rich tourists paying big-ticket green fees. Of all the arrows flung his way, McGregor found that to be the most ludicrous. The barb McGregor felt the deepest questioned whether the Links Trust manipulated their facts and massaged their figures (by basing their claims on growth relative to 1995, an Open year, when the Old Course was closed for an additional four weeks for tournament preparations) as a means of justifying their empire building. The exact percentage of growth was irrelevant. No matter how you sliced the pie chart, there was simply not enough golf to go around. Resolved that they could not please all of the people at any time, the Working Party pressed on.

Hole 5

• • •

Par-5
558 yards / 537 yards / 515 yards / 472 yards / 419 yards

The wind across Scotland blows predominantly west-southwest, a fact I learned growing up on the west coast and then later in central Scotland. I had never lived on the east coast, but when we reviewed the weather statistics as we considered different routings, that same wind pattern looked to hold true.

What we didn't understand until we started work here was the effect of St. Andrews Bay. The big body of water between Carnoustie and St. Andrews creates sea breezes and causes the winds to shift about. Wind gets stronger as you rise in elevation, and we are up on the braes, so the wind is at least as strong at No. 7 as it is down on the links. A prevailing wind at St. Andrews is a golf oxymoron, like the metalwood.

At Bandon Dunes the wind shifts 180 degrees between the summer and the winter; here at No. 7 it shifts 180 degrees between the drive and the approach. The fifth hole plays into the alleged prevailing west-southwest wind toward the southwest corner of the site. We were able to keep the golfing grounds well away from the Crail Road thanks to the fact that we had lots of room—220 acres to fit eighteen holes is quite generous.

The soft side-slope allowed us to do some shaping that creates an exciting drive. I think the third shot into the green really typifies the collaborative dynamic between Paul, Mick, and me. Much of what I did at No. 7 was tempering Paul and Mick's enthusiasm, and in many cases overenthusiasm.

Paul plays to about a six handicap, I hover around eight, and Mick is somewhere in the neighborhood of a sixteen. Paul may be capable of hitting the shots he perceives in his head, but I am not, and Mick certainly is not. However, Mick does not shape to suit his game; rather, he is hell-bent on defending against offensive-minded golfers like Paul.

The way they originally had the fifth green, it fell sharply away from incoming approach shots, and there was no way to hold that green—I didn't think. After much discussion, Mick altered that green a bit to make it slightly fairer than it was.

That said, we are agreed that we have no intention of making the whole golf course "fair."

—David McLay Kidd

6

Gobsmacked

"We didn't get it."

The words hit Jimmy Kidd like a bullet to his belly. His eyes fixed on nothing, his mouth unable to form words, Jimmy slumped into his favorite armchair like a gunslinger who never saw it coming. Racing home from Gleneagles, he'd felt a jolt of adrenaline when he spotted his son's rental car in the driveway.

"We didn't get the job," Kidd sighed. Kimber stood expressionless behind him.

What of the prophecy?

Jimmy is a devotee of *The Celestine Prophecy*, the New Age best seller by James Redfield, which postulates that there are no coincidences in life. It was not mere happenstance, Jimmy believed, that Alan McGregor popped in only for the luncheon portion of that Scottish Grass Machinery conference in St. Andrews, wound up seated right next to Jimmy, providing McGregor entree to share the Links Trust's desire to hire for the planned seventh course "a young, upwardly mobile, successful golf course designer with a worldwide reputation." Who could fit that bill better than Jimmy's boy?! Surely Kidd's being a Scot could not have worked *against* him, although it had not helped when he lost out at Southern Gailes to American Kyle Phillips and at Loch Lomond to Canadian Doug Carrick. Even the most cynical of skeptics had to acknowledge the curious connection to Tom Kidd, winner of the 1873 Open Championship, the first time it was contested in St. Andrews. Granted, David Kidd was not a known descendant of Tom Kidd, but it was still suspect! (Years later Jimmy's belief that there is no such thing as coincidence was irrevocably validated when he learned that he and McGregor, less than one year apart in age, both grew up in the same small village of Bridge of Weir but did not know each other.)

"Their loss," Jimmy offered, forcing a fake smile.

Looking up, he wondered why Kidd and Kimber were both grinning, and not just wee crescents but big banana grins. In addition to *The Celestine Prophecy*, Jimmy is a devotee of practical gags. This time, the student had duped the master.

"Hell yes, we got the job!" Kidd shouted, pulling his gobsmacked father out of his armchair and into a bear hug. Kimber popped the cork on a bottle of champagne and wrapped his arms around Kidd's mum. "I knew you would get it, I just knew it," Jimmy repeated as he embraced his son, whose eyes were wet and glistening. The news meant everything to Jimmy, and being able to share it face-to-face with his father meant everything to Kidd. He'd thought twice about tricking the old man like that, but it was a testament to how close they are. A few hours and bottles of wine later, Kidd spied his father across the house sitting back in his favorite armchair, sipping his whisky and shaking his head. Jimmy beamed with an inner glee as he repeated a refrain over and over in his head. *A golf course in St. Andrews, designed by David McLay Kidd.*

Kidd was an early Christmas gift in 1967, the year Jimmy received a job offer at the ripe young age of twenty-one to be head greenkeeper of the Killermont Course at Glasgow Golf Club, one of the oldest golf clubs in the world. The job came with a cottage; however, to get the cottage the head greenkeeper had to be married, which forced Jimmy's hand with his girlfriend, June McLay. His admittedly shoddy proposal the previous winter went something like "I've got this great opportunity in Glasgow, and it even comes with a cottage, but I have to be married to get the cottage, so whaddaya say?" To Jimmy's great good fortune she accepted, and this year they'd celebrated their fortieth wedding anniversary.

Jimmy and June grew up together in Bridge of Weir, a small village west of Glasgow famous for its leatherworks. Five tanneries in town produced exceptional leather for the likes of Rolls-Royce, Cunard cruise lines, and Kinghorn Tacky Grip, the golf club grip of champions, including "The Great Triumvirate" of the early 1900s, J. H. Taylor, Harry Vardon, and James Braid. June was an only child, while Jimmy was the eldest of seven. Both of Jimmy's parents labored in the leather trade, as did June's father. Circumstances being what they were, Jimmy left school and went to work as a teen in the lab at one of the tanneries. The tedium constrained his artistic sensibilities, and Jimmy longed to be outside. The only other industry in the village was golf, as at the time Bridge of Weir boasted two eighteen-hole courses and a nine-holer. Jimmy had never so much as picked up a club when, at the age of fifteen, he switched careers and took a job as an apprentice greenkeeper at Ranfurly Castle Golf Club.

Kidd was Jimmy's right-hand lad from the get-go. To supplement his modest income, Jimmy picked up side gigs after hours and on off days, tending to other golf courses and building lawn bowling greens. Wee Davey would sit with a bottle of Coke and a bag of chips and watch his father for hours. When the boy grew old enough and strong enough to manage a wheelbarrow, the old man put him to work running loads of sand and gravel. Kidd was an indefatigable worker, never asking for or taking a break. He was also a diligent saver. As a schoolboy he convinced his sister, Tracy, four years his junior, to join his campaign to eat less and pocket half their lunch money, which Kidd socked away along with the token wages his father paid him, so that come Christmas they would have booty to buy wonderful presents.

Kidd and Tracy were close as kids. As tots they loved to visit relatives in Bridge of Weir and play in St. Machars Church, where Jimmy and June had been married and generations of McLays and Kidds had been christened. Jimmy's father was a deacon at St.

Machars and his mother the caretaker. While their grandparents prepared for and then tidied up after church services, Tracy would dance to the "music" Davey made tickling the ivories on the house organ. The Kidds also frequented Macrahanish, where they camped by the beach in a cozy caravan. Despite easy access to the exceptional Old Tom Morris–designed course, Kidd whiled away endless hours with a fishing rod instead of golf clubs. Even as a boy he possessed impressive powers of concentration, spending extended stretches tying intricate flies.

Kidd began making the pilgrimage to St. Andrews as a teen—but not for golf. He and his mates drove the hour from Auchterarder most weekends, and bypassed the golf courses on a beeline for the beach, where the odds of meeting girls were exponentially better than on the links. Their modus operandi was to buy a case of beer and bury it in the sand, so it wouldn't get nicked while they spent the day windsurfing.

When the head greenkeeper job at Gleneagles Resort came open in 1982, it was the most prestigious such post in all of Scotland. It was no walk in the park, as the resort was clocking 117,000 rounds per year on their four courses, the Kings, Queens, Princes, and Glendevon. Jimmy was one of ninety applicants. The pool was winnowed to twenty-eight, then ten, then six, then three. Gleneagles wanted someone who not only knew agronomics but could also represent and help promote the resort. Jimmy accepted the post—then quit six weeks later. The courses were overburdened and the crew underequipped. He reconsidered only when management met his demands to decrease play by 25 percent and raise fees by 25 percent, changes that bought Jimmy time and money to restore and prepare the courses properly and were validated by famed British golfer and commentator Peter Allis, who was quoted as saying, "Thank God somebody cares about Gleneagles at last."

Jimmy's earliest recollection of his son's interest in the family business dates to an otherwise ordinary night when Kidd showed his dad a proposed class schedule for high school.

"Why biology?" asked Jimmy curiously, as his boy had never shown a keen interest in science.

"I figure I am going to need it," replied the boy, "if I am going to design golf courses."

Kidd would go on to Writtle College in England, the largest land sciences college in the UK, for a program that called for eighteen months in the classroom and one year working out in the field, followed by a final year back on campus. Kidd lined up a practicum gig landscaping cemeteries in Oxfordshire, but that plan changed after Jimmy stopped by Collingtree Park Golf Course north of London to see course designer Ron Kirby. Kirby was working with Johnny Miller there, as well as collaborating with Jack Nicklaus on the Monarch's course at Gleneagles, which Jimmy was overseeing. (Gleneagles's Princes and Glendevon courses were scrapped in 1993 to make way for Nicklaus's Monarchs Course, later renamed the PGA Centenary course.)

"Interested in a young, up-and-coming designer?" Jimmy asked Kirby as they walked the site.

"Always," answered Kirby. "Who?"

"My son, David."

Kirby put in a good word with the higher-ups at Southern Golf, the contractor building Collingtree Park. Kidd bagged the grave-mowing gig when Southern Golf gave him a job, his first in the industry out from under Jimmy's wing. Kidd appreciated the opportunity but became frustrated working for absentee designers who would turn up on-site with random infrequence. He learned to shape first and answer questions later. Kidd also learned to manage not only the people above him but also those working under him. One petulant shaper driving a dozer at Colne Valley Golf Club in Essex saw fresh meat and hounded the baby-faced Kidd mercilessly about his bonus. Fed up, Kidd went to the store and bought a case of dog food called Bonus, which he presented to the ornery muckshifter in front of the crew.

"There's your Bonus," said Kidd with authority. "That's the end of it till the job is finished."

In 1991, Kidd returned to the Gleneagles nest and accepted the position of director of design for Gleneagles Golf Development. He was twenty-four years old. Over the next five years he padded his portfolio with designs including Gokarna Park Golf Resort in Kathmandu, Nepal, and Golf de Andratx in Majorca, Spain. Then Kidd landed another far-flung commission: Bandon Dunes in Oregon.

Kidd's strongest inspirations did not come from other course designers, though the influence of James Braid is readily apparent. The five-time Open champion went on to fashion or fiddle with 250-plus courses across the British Isles, including Carnoustie, Brora, Nairn, Blairgowrie, and both the Kings and Queens courses at Gleneagles. Far from home and at times wondering what in the hell he'd gotten himself into, Kidd borrowed from Braid, incorporating into Bandon elements that work wondrously at the Kings: see the steep slope fronting the green at the Kings' first hole and Bandon's seventh, as well as the tabletop green at the Kings' fifth hole and Bandon's sixth. More so, Kidd's inspiration came from artists. He cites Van Gogh and the way he changed his technique and method over time, which resulted in varied interpretations and evolving styles. Kidd was also indelibly impressed with the technique Monet used with his water lilies, which appears so intricate up close but so effortless at a distance.

Kidd discovered Monet at the Louvre courtesy of his first wife, Lyn. Classmates at Writtle, they were best mates and dated for a half dozen years, not unlike Kidd's own parents. Kidd was back in Bandon when they discovered she was pregnant with their son, Campbell, born in 1998. Alas, they were better friends than spouses, and distance and circumstance conspired against them. The marriage was over and Kidd was separated from Lyn when he met Jill Schultz, a local girl who had recently moved back home to the Oregon coast from Florida, after her own marriage fizzled. Presented with opportunities to work as an office assistant for an eye doctor in Coos Bay or as a bartender at this new golf resort in Bandon, Jill chose the latter. The couple married on the Big Island during the building of Nanea in February 2003 and the following year welcomed a daughter, Ailsa. Kidd suggested the name, though he failed to mention that Ailsa is the name of the Open Championship venue at Turnberry on the west coast of Scotland. Many months passed before Jill learned the truth while overhearing her husband set up a golf game for a friend.

"You named our daughter after a golf course?!" she barked the moment Kidd hung up the phone.

"Ailsa is a cute name," reasoned Kidd. "At least I didn't name her Troon."

The sense of humor comes from his father, as does Kidd's work ethic, artistic dexterity, and antagonistic streak. From his mum Kidd inherited studied patience and quiet strength. When a storm is brewing in Kidd's life, he turns inward and silent. On the other hand, happy tears are forever only a hug away.

•   •   •

Kidd replayed McGregor's theatrics in his mind. "Gentlemen," said the former military man as he marched back into the conference room. "Thank you for coming." Neither Kidd nor Kimber knew quite what to think, and Moir's expression, or lack thereof, offered no clues. McGregor never actually said the job was theirs; his smile and slap on Kidd's back said it all.

Kidd and Kimber left Pilmour House on a beeline for a pub, though not in town. Too many prying ears. Buzzing through Cupar, ten miles clear of St. Andrews, Kimber spotted a sign for the unassuming Imperial Bar on Saint Catherine Street and ducked into the first open parking spot. Inside, they quietly ordered two pints of Guinness and retired to a booth in the back corner. Had they been aware of the world around them, Kidd and Kimber might have noticed that they appeared to be either terrorists or lovers.

"Cheers," offered Kidd, raising his glass.

"Cheers," said Kimber. "Now what?"

Back in St. Andrews a palpable air of elation and relief filled Pilmour House. Their to-do list was intimidating, but the Links Trust felt confident that they had found a cornerstone piece of the puzzle. From the outset they were impressed that DMK Golf Design offered an unconventional approach and were unabashed about it.

Whereas other candidates provided answers, DMK posed questions. They rebuffed preconceptions by refusing to be prescriptive. They dodged the money issue until pressed. They never presented a routing, evading any hint of commitment by decrying the notion of imposing oneself on the land, instead insisting on inspiration to see how the land might reveal itself. Others had plans all laid out, which ultimately worked to their disadvantage when DMK hammered home the point that the way to get a truly great golf course is to unearth it. DMK did not assume, as all the other candidates had, that the Links Trust would naturally hire a contractor to build the course. The traditional model secs the architect compile the design, which is then put out to bid, which is awarded to a contractor, who builds to the plan on the paper with little input from the designer and even less from the client. DMK proposed taking on design and construction in part because it worked to their ultimate advantage, but also because Kidd and Kimber realized and respected that this client fully intended to be an active partner. One-stop shopping appealed to the Links Trust because it meant fewer cooks in the kitchen; plus centralized control allowed the brass, not a one of which had ever undertaken an endeavor of this size or scope, to keep a close eye on the project at every turn.

Other candidates offered more experience, more detail, and more of a safety net. The trustees, a dependably pragmatic lot, were inclined to lay up but instead decided to go for it with Kidd. The other candidates were more practical, but DMK was more inspired. Kidd's loquacious three-and-a-half-hour presentation did not bore; rather it demonstrated the level of enthusiasm and determination the trustees sought. They knew this was a critical time for DMK, both as a company and as an individual. Kidd made sure that they knew. DMK was hungry, and come cards-on-the-table time the Links Trust simply believed that No. 7 meant more to David McLay Kidd than it did to the others.

Kimber returned his tweed jacket for a full refund at the Austin Reed shop in the Edinburgh airport, then returned with Kidd to Essex; however, Kimber did not make the trip back to Hawaii. Surprised and a tad disappointed, he understood Kidd's decision to keep him posted at the home office and begin work on No. 7 immediately. Still, Kimber had poured his heart and soul into Nanea and to this day has never been back to see the finished product. Letting go is the hardest part of the golf design business, perhaps most of all for the principal's deputy, who spends more time on-site making the day-to-day decisions that impact the outcome. Kidd draws an analogy to being a surrogate mother: you've been with this baby for months and months, nurtured it from conception through delivery, and then one day the quitclaim comes due and you hand it over and walk away. With any luck at all you may be invited to visit, although that courtesy rarely extends to the circle of friends who invested their time and energies to provide essential support along the way. Kimber has never been invited to the grand opening of any course on which he's worked. Not that he expects it, but not that he would mind getting the nod, either.

• • •

One could fell an entire forest for all the paper that is required to get a golf course approved. While DMK began tinkering with potential routing plans, the Links Trust set about the task of producing the myriad reports required for the planning application to Fife Council. The Links Trust could not afford a misstep, as they started out with one strike against them thanks to the fiasco that marred the development and construction of neighboring St. Andrews Bay Golf Resort and Spa.

Americans Don and Nancy Panoz, founders of Georgia-based Château Élan Hotels and Resorts, opened St. Andrews Bay in 2001. (In 2006 the resort was sold and reflagged by Fairmont Hotels and Resorts.) Even before ground was broken, controversy engulfed the project, with charges that Fife Council played fast and loose with the rules to railroad through the massive £50 million resort complex. Despite vociferous opposition, the application was approved, although Fife Council did subsequently address locals' concerns by setting stringent rules regarding access to the site, the roads that were to be used, and the number of trucks allowed to come and go daily. Not a week before the official start date, the developers were already in hot water for utilizing an unauthorized access road. Once construction began, the crew paid no heed to the stated limit of ten truck deliveries a day. Even when Fife Council relented (by a vote of eight-to-seven) and doubled the daily number of trucks allowed, the order was flat-out ignored. One councillor reported witnessing eight trucks barrel onto the site within one half-hour period. Roads were damaged, some so extensively they had to be closed; litter despoiled the site; workers disrupted drainage and caused significant excess water to run off the cliffs, which resulted in advanced erosion; and developers ran afoul of not only Fife Council but also Scottish Natural Heritage, when workers building the eighth hole on the Devlin course plowed through a designated Site of Special Scientific Interest (SSSI).

"The Resort," waxed St. Andrews Bay's Web site, "was designed in keeping with the historic nature of the area as Don and Nancy were dedicated to preserving the landscape's natural beauty, stunning vistas and the spirit and traditions of the game of golf." History is written by the victors, but the complaints did not end when the resort finally opened, as a good many St. Andreans viewed the £2 million clubhouse, plopped on a promontory in plain view from town, as a blight on the skyline. Forget the Links Trust's capacity debate, when word got out that another golf course was planned right next door, there was an initial groundswell to deny planning consent to the proposed Course No. 7 based solely on the shenanigans at St. Andrews Bay.

The Links Trust hired the independent firm of SQW Consultants of Edinburgh to prepare the *Economic Impact Statement*, which made the case supporting the Links Trust's resident-driven capacity concerns. In a section titled "Risk of Failure to Provide Additional Capacity," SQW determined:

> *If pressure on the other courses continues to increase there*
> *will inevitably be greater pressure on starting times on the*

Old Course and the chances of success for visitors and locals will diminish. If that continued to happen, it could discourage visitors to the extent that they would cease to come to St. Andrews.

If the Trust were to try and replace lost visitor income through increased charges to local golfers, very substantial increases would need to be imposed to replace the lost income. This would be difficult to achieve and would have little benefit to the local economy.

If there was a substantial, and sustained, fall in revenues, the Trust would have to reduce costs, whether by closing facilities or reducing the quality of the courses. Both of these would have a detrimental effect on the desirability of St. Andrews as a tourist venue, leading to a further reduction in income.

There is a parallel to this scenario when Carnoustie lost its place on the Open Championship rota. Over a period of years the course effectively became a backwater and it took major investment from both the public and private sectors to raise the quality of the venue so that it could once again be considered a worthy venue. The difference is that, whereas Carnoustie Links had relatively little impact on the local economy, St. Andrews' dependence on the golf courses is substantially greater.

Not quite a doomsday scenario; however, the conclusion that something needed to be done was incontestable:

There is proven demand. There is overwhelming data to show the importance of St. Andrews Links to the St. Andrews, Fife, and Scottish economies. . . . There is clear evidence that without a new course the quality of experience enjoyed at St. Andrews by local and visiting golfers will suffer.

An *Environmental Statement* produced by the William Cowie Partnership of Aberdeen reported precisely what everyone who'd set foot on the proposed site already knew:

> *Currently the site has very little ecological value as it has been intensively farmed for many years.*

The only species discovered on the entire site possessing any ecological value was a tiny patch of flowers called maiden pinks (*Dianthus deltoides*), which the Links Trust promised to protect. Other than that, the site supported the maxim that land ideally suited for golf is usually ill suited for almost any other productive use. To wit: Scottish links, Florida swamps, Carolina lowlands, Arizona desert. The report outlined the significant ecological enhancements a golf course would provide, including new habitats with the transformation of over half the site into indigenous grasslands, increased biodiversity in and around a pond and wetland, fewer fertilizers and chemicals than would be used on a farm, and management and protection of the braes, part of which were designated SSSI. In sum, it was a different way of saying the same thing Kidd deduced on that frigid autumn day when he first showed Kimber around the site. "Once you step back from the braes, we haven't got crap." Kidd paused and rethought that. "Actually, that's all we've got."

One man's crap is another man's treasure; however, no treasures were discovered during the *Archaeological Assessment* by local archaeologist Neil Cunningham Dobson:

> *The area of Kinkell has long associations with St. Andrews. . . . Standing on the brae above Kinkell Harbour there was a castle, chapel, and dovecot of the middle ages. Records show that by the 18th century it was in a ruinous state and in 1883 the remains were still there. . . . Today no remains can be seen, however earthworks and the building of the clubhouse and car park may reveal remains of foundations and associated structures.*

A castle! Kidd would've killed to work around a castle, maybe lead golfers from one hole to the next under a portcullis, or set a tee box in a bailey, or employ a turret as a target like the Victorian cupola atop the former Grand Hotel behind the eighteenth green on the Old, which golfers use as an aiming point on the inward nine. Instead, Kidd got to work around the town shitter.

Hole 6

• • •

Par-4
470 yards / 447 yards / 426 yards / 402 yards / 359 yards

The water is the be-all and end-all of golf at St. Andrews. We knew that the culmination of delivering golfers down to the water for the first time coupled with surprising them with how close we actually are to the town was going to be a fantastically dramatic effect.

So as to build up the drama, we created the sixth hole with a tee shot where very little can be seen, maybe a long distance horizon view of the water—nothing new that golfers have not already seen as they have played the course.

The fairway is big and wide with massive contours in it. A drive played to the right leaves the best line into a green that is laid in diagonally from right-to-left. A really good tee shot here can make it up onto an elevated bench on the middle right of the fairway, whereas a tee shot to the left can roll down into a hollow and requires the golfer to approach the green from the wrong angle, so everything left conspires to make stopping a shot on that green much more difficult.

For the most part, any balls flown into greens on this golf course are going to have a hard time stopping because the greens and the surrounds are all rock-hard sand, just like down on the links. Nothing else is sand but the greens and surrounds, so golfers need to try to check the ball first, and then it might stand a chance of stopping, maybe. However balls are not going to stop on the second bounce within four feet of the flagstick like they do on the US PGA Tour. It's just not going to happen here.

The big thrill comes after golfers walk through a swale at the end of the fairway and emerge up on the green. There it is, the old town. It truly is breathtaking, seeing the beach at the East Sands for the first time and looking right at the cathedral. It is so close that it appears you could tee up a driver and start lacing balls at the spires.

Pace of play might slow here while people take pictures. On a clear morning, of which there are many, this is one of my favorite spots on the whole golf course.

—David McLay Kidd

7

Moo

Routing a golf course requires the delicate balancing of the ultimate golf experience with pivotal considerations ranging from environmental ramifications to construction costs to the impact on operation and maintenance. There is a domino effect, not unlike plotting the seating chart at a wedding. Setting Aunt Edna at table 1 with her back to Uncle Emil at table 2 could cause a ripple that makes waves all the way to table 18. Variables in routing a golf course include the ease or difficulty of securing planning approval and permits, as well as the relationship of the individual holes and the course as a whole to the setting and related facilities like the practice area, clubhouse, and in the case of No. 7, the sewage plant. Emphasis on one factor often comes at the cost of another. Weaknesses that aren't so glaring on paper can become so in dirt, and making changes can get scary expensive fast, all of which puts the architect on the spot to get it right the first time. Kidd and Kimber drafted two dozen different renderings before they presented a routing to the Links Trust.

In late January 2003 the two spent three days plodding over hill and dale to chart their course. Kimber took digital photographs from the property looking back into town and from town looking up to the property to ascertain optimum sight lines so that the course would be less obtrusive while still affording golfers picturesque views of the spires of St. Andrews. In his mind's eye Kidd pictured strategic shaping of landforms that would act as meurtrieres, the slits in castle walls through which archers could see out but outsiders could not see in. The criteria also called for two nine-hole loops that began and ended at the clubhouse. The Links Trust was insistent on this, and it was not unreasonable considering the wide rectangular plot and sizeable acreage (180 acres is Kidd's minimum for 18 holes; here he had 220). The path of the sun, prevailing wind directions, and slope of the site from the Crail Road down to the braes suggested that the first hole best play west, away from the water, and uphill on a gentle grade, while the finishing hole play in the exact opposite direction.

Greens on the water are sexier than tees on the water, Kidd contends, and while both are ideal, if forced to choose, Kidd wants people putting on the water so that they can spend more time soaking up the scenery. This 1.1 miles of coastland (almost identical to the amount Kidd had at Bandon Dunes) looked to be able to accommodate two holes on the town side of the sewage plant and another three on the east. Try as they might, Kidd and Kimber were vexed by how to get around the wastewater treatment works without forcing golfers to turn their backs on the view, play away from the braes, and climb uphill to the clubhouse, which the Links Trust envisioned halfway between the braes and the Crail Road.

Kidd and Kimber submitted their *Routing Design Study* in February 2003. They dutifully delivered a plan, dubbed "Route A," which was designed around the client's vision. Here, golfers first encountered the braes at the fifth hole, a par-4 with a green tucked in the northwesternmost corner of the site. A par-4 and a par-3 playing along the coast followed, and then golfers returned to the braes at the tee at the twelfth, a par-3 that hugged a rugged cove. The thirteenth hole was a long par-5 down to Kinkell Point; then the fourteenth was a short par-4 that doglegged left, skirted the sewage plant, and started back up the hill toward the clubhouse. The plan was convoluted; a par-3 at the second hole would likely slow play, there would be no holes on the water after the fourteenth, and there were five holes close to the sewage plant, which dominated the view from the Links Trust's proposed clubhouse site. In their explanation DMK wrote:

> *The Clubhouse location . . . lays on a steep slope which makes opening and closing holes difficult to route and requires significant earthworks to "bench in" greens and tees.*
>
> *The Practice range, on this example, plays into the rising sun and the teeing area is set on a severe slope . . . [and] playing the range west forces the 18th to become an uphill hole, which may be considered a weakness.*
>
> *The wastewater treatment plant is in front of the clubhouse and no amount of screening will prevent it from feeling dominant on the site.*

In other words: this sucks.

Luckily, Kidd and Kimber had a Plan B. They radically rearranged the pieces based on assumptions they had no right to make. They rerouted the access road and moved the clubhouse down to Kinkell Point, where it would be separated from the sewage plant by the practice area. Golfers' first encounter with the braes remained in the northwest corner, though at the sixth hole. The seventh and eighth still played along the coast, only instead of routing golfers around the back of the sewage plant DMK proposed ushering them in front of it on a small strip of land they wanted the Links Trust to buy, thereby allowing the ninth hole to play along the water. On the back nine, the par-3 that hugged the cove and the subsequent par-5 to Kinkell Point became the climactic seventeenth and eighteenth holes, with the ninth and eighteenth sharing a massive double green.

> *Routing B has been designed with minimal consideration to the potential planning objections and maximum consideration to create the very best routing the land can yield.*
>
> *A round of golf is more than sport, it is an experience and an adventure. Finishing holes in this manner will add immeasurably to the golfing theatre. Pebble Beach is an exam-*

ple of how a stunning closing hole can elevate a great golf course to legendary status. No. 7 could have two closing sequences [on both nines] *that would be hard to better anywhere in the world.*

DMK implored the Links Trust to give "Route B" serious consideration, "because of the weight of history and anticipation hanging on the decisions we make," wrote Kidd. The Links Trust bit. They discovered that the one-plus acre in front of the wastewater treatment works belonged to the utility that operated the plant, Scottish Water. The company had a policy of offering any land for sale to the general public; however, given that the brambly strip served no useful purpose to anyone besides the Links Trust, Scottish Water obtained approval to sell it for the pathway between the eighth green and the ninth tees.

While they were at it, Kidd and Kimber entreated the Trust to look into a plot in the far northeast corner of the site. Adding the five-or-so acres would allow the sixteenth hole to finish atop the braes, upping the number of greens on the water to seven. The proposed par-3 seventeenth looked over a woolly cove, but Kidd and Kimber wanted it to *play* over the cove. An outcrop behind the existing property line would provide a set of tees that would transform the shot into a play at once as thrilling and terrifying as the infamous approach over space and time at Pebble Beach's otherworldly eighth hole.

"This hole will be the best." Kimber assured McGregor.

"The best in St. Andrews?" queried McGregor.

"Think big, Alan!"

"In Fife?

"No!"

"The best in Scotland?" asked McGregor. "The UK?"

"This hole will be the best," insisted Kimber, "in the world."

McGregor was convinced. Not that the seventeenth would be the best hole in the world necessarily, but that Kimber believed it would be. Unfortunately, acquiring the annex would be a stickier wicket. A 4×4 motorbike track occupied a goodly portion of the land, which belonged to Sandy Fyfe, the farmer who first suggested that the Links Trust come have a gander at the site, two-thirds of which comprised part of Fyfe's Kinkell Farm.

Raised on the farm, Fyfe returned in 1992 after posts as an accountant in London and Glasgow. In addition to raising cattle (ten suckler cows and one very lucky bull), he operates Kinkell House, a bed and breakfast; Kinkell Byre, a venue for corporate events, charity functions, weddings, and the like; as well as Fyfe Off Road, featuring a Land Rover driving course and the 4×4 track. For the right price and a promise that DMK's crew would reroute the 4×4 track, the Links Trust secured the coveted annex.

They also considered buying the braes, the strip of land between the golfing grounds and the water on which Fyfe grazes his cattle as part of an agreement with Scottish Natural Heritage. The organization encourages the grazing to help spur wildflower growth and effectively mow the grasses, so every autumn Fyfe marches his herd down, and every spring he marches them back up—straight across the fifteenth and eighteenth fairways in Kidd's preferred routing plan. The Links Trust made a cursory offer, which the occasionally prickly farmer declined because it was, he claimed, not substantial enough compensation for the cattle's relocation. Fyfe did not want to leave his cattle exposed (the brae tops offer shelter to the animals from the harsh winter weather), nor did he have a barn in which to house the animals. He also resisted trucking them elsewhere and back, claiming that the bovines were wild, not used to handling, and had never even seen a vehicle much less been packed into the back of one. Despite DMK's prodding, the Links Trust could not see spending money on land not used for golf. In hindsight they have wondered whether it would have been money well spent to avoid ongoing schisms with Fyfe over issues like property boundaries, fence lines, and cattle routes across the golf course.

The cattle route required a single entry and exit point, so said Scottish National Heritage, to lessen the impact on the braes. The road on which DMK, the Links Trust, and Fyfe all eventually—painstakingly— agreed would drive the cattle to the left of the sixteenth tees, around the back of the fifteenth green, along the length of the left side of the tenth hole, then across a road that bisects the fairway at the eighteenth between a golfer's drive and second shot. Underhoof would be a road of crushed rock made to look like a country path, which is the style of all the maintenance tracks and cart paths. Kidd and Kimber were infinitely less aggrieved over the road across the eighteenth—it's better than the aesthetically displeasing paved Granny Clarks Wynd that cuts across the home hole at the Old Course—than they were about the presence of cart paths. Concerned about the slope of the site (and bowing to market pressure), the Links Trust planned a small fleet of golf carts, an act that Kidd and Kimber deem tantamount to sacrilege.

The Links Trust was adamant that No. 7 be accessible and enjoyable to all. "If we produce a golf course that the locals will not go and play," McGregor insisted, "then we have failed." The trustees were especially emphatic that the course not be a brute to the ladies. Ladies golf is an integral part of the St. Andrews scene, but equally, if not more, important is the life lesson McGregor shared with his new partners at DMK. "Keep the woman happy," McGregor advised Kidd and Kimber, "and the world will take care of itself."

Another key element of this routing was eliminating the need to reroute the access road, which posed serious logistical, financial, and approval problems. Now the front nine would be played largely on the west side of the driveway, the back nine on the east, and golfers had to cross only once, going from the first green to the second tees. The only back nine configuration that made clear sense called for a par-35, which meant that in order to keep the front nine at par-36 there would have to be back-to-back par-5s at holes four and five, which did not concern Kidd and Kimber as much as the fact that the fourth and fifteenth were essentially mirror images of each other: long, downhill doglegs left with a burn fronting the green.

There were infinite ways to differentiate the fourth hole from the fifth and the fifteenth—favor opposite sides of the fairways, maximum versus minimum bunkering, run one of the burns through a culvert then fill in on top of it so players would not face identical forced carries. The fourth hole would prove hard to fiddle with, as moving the tees forward would make for an unreasonably long walk from the third green, and moving the green violated one of Kidd's cardinal rules: never compromise the green. DMK's final solution was, not surprisingly, very similar to "Route B," Kidd and Kimber's first choice. Just as a real estate agent might show a buyer the perfect house the first time out but still show that buyer other homes as a way of setting the hook for the first house, the exercise of drafting two dozen routings for No. 7 allowed DMK to demonstrate what did not work and lead the Links Trust to the same conclusion Kidd and Kimber had known all along.

This routing achieved each of Kidd and Kimber's objectives: a relocated clubhouse that overlooks the water rather then the wastewater works; a reasonably shielded sewage factory; good pacing utilizing the whole of the site; five tees and seven greens on the braes; both nines building anticipation to and finishing dramatically on the water; a stunning par-3 at the seventeenth hole that plays over the cove; a fantastic finish for both loops on a double green perched on Kinkell Point. The only perceived negatives were a par-3 to open the back nine, which could slow the pace of play, and the issues with holes four, five, and fifteen. Kidd did not fret over these questions. The answers would reveal themselves in due course. They always did.

Hole 7

· · ·

Par-4
465 yards / 450 yards / 422 yards / 392 yards / 340 yards

When we were routing the golf course, we had the seventh hole on the plans as a par-5 for a long time. The nagging problem we encountered, however, was that in order to get the sixth green on the water we would have to move the seventh tees forward and make it a par-4. That, in turn, would mean having back-to-back par-5s—facing opposite directions so one would play into and the other with the wind—at the fourth and fifth holes.

Paul and I went round and round, but we kept coming back to the fact that we had to have the sixth green on the water in that far corner of the site, so the seventh became a par-4. At 465 yards from the back tees, it looks like a par-5 on the scorecard, but it is allegedly downwind and certainly downhill, and unless a breeze is blowing in the player's face an average golfer will probably only hit a mid-iron into that green, not much more.

It is a big sweeping dogleg that dives to the left. Trying to cut the corner brings the braes into play for the first time. Overinflated egos will result in many lost golf balls here. The smart play, especially when playing a match, is the middle of the fairway, where there sits a slot that will shoot well-struck drives to a flat landing area.

The green is huge, one of the biggest on the golf course. It falls away back left, and when it was first shaped I worried about its potential to hold approach shots. Mick and Paul were adamant about the design, but I needed to address my worries. The solution we came up with was to extend the green some fifteen feet at the front, which not only added all sorts of front pin placements but also provided sufficient room for golfers to land a ball and run it all the way to the back.

There are some pretty aggressive shapes left and right of that green. There are also some spill-offs, as we call them, which in time will be covered with shaggy grass. Anyone trying to fly a ball in will be flirting with those spill-offs. A run-up shot is the play, which could put lob wedge–loving Americans at a disadvantage here.

—David McLay Kidd

8

Red Tape

The Links Trust submitted the planning application for Course No. 7 to Fife Council in September 2003. The typical wait for a response was two months, but the Links Trust's planning consultant, Harry McNab, suggested that his clients brace themselves for double that, given that Fife Council would be triple-checking every dotted *i* and crossed *t* in the application and putting a microscope to the *Economic Impact Statement* and *Environmental Assessment*.

There was no denying that the Links Trust had done their due diligence. The application included consultations with the Architectural Heritage Society of Scotland, the Association for Protection of Rural Scotland, Boarhills and Dunino Community Council, the Health and Safety Executive, Historic Scotland, the Kingdom of Fife Tourist Board, Royal Burgh of St. Andrews Community Council, the Royal Fine Art Commission for Scotland, the Scottish Environment Protection Agency, Scottish Executive Development, Scottish Executive Rural Affairs, Scottish Natural Heritage, the Scottish Rights of Way and Access Society, Scottish Water, SportScotland, the St. Andrews Merchants Association, and Transportation Services. Only the Architectural Heritage Society, the Community Council, and Scottish Natural Heritage lodged objections; however, protocol dictated that a departure hearing could be called if an application appeared to diverge from set development guidelines or if the Office of Planning and Building Control received ten formal letters of objection. They received twenty-two:

The Links Trust give the impression that St. Andrews would be left a ghost town if the seventh course is not built. That is simply absurd! On the other hand, I can imagine people wanting to move away from a place that is already starting to look like some of the tackiest areas of the USA.

Deborah Moffat

This growth surely has to be stopped before St. Andrews bursts. Traffic is seizing up, cars are parked everywhere and the great danger of the town losing its country setting and charm is just around the corner. I could go on and on.

James Docherty

We want to be assured that we will not be in the line of any stray golf balls.

Alastair Macqueen,
Brownhills Cottages

Some people are concerned that this area of Fife could be enveloped by a de facto golfers' theme park. Au contraire, overprovision and overhasty approval of new schemes could presage serial commercial failures creating a coastal safari park of white elephants, replacing farm land that contributed to feeding a hungry world.

J. Michael Buchanan

The farmland is a staging post for migrant birds from Scandinavia and Russia that . . . depend on foraging in winter cereal crops and stubbles.

J. Staples

*The applicants' case for a new course is an amalgam of
statistical and legal arguments, but neither of these stands is
pursued with sufficient precision to be persuasive.*

DR. IAN GOUDIE,
St. Andrews Community Council

*It is clear that the new course is not being built for locals—it
is a device to get locals off their own courses so that even
more visitors can be accommodated. One has to ask who
really stands to gain from all this? The answer is obvious—
the Links officials in terms of higher salaries and the various
commercial interests like Keith Prowse, who are making
money out of something they do not own, and at the expense
of locals who are being forced off their own courses.*

COLIN MCALLISTER

Colin McAllister was a gadfly in the ointment for the Links
Trust. A retired community college economics lecturer and former
captain of the New Club, as well as a member of the St. Andrews and
the Thistle clubs, McAllister is an affably quirky bloke who lives
alone in an apartment overlooking South Street. With no spouse, no
children, no mobile phone, and no computer, he has, and seems to
devote, ample time to ferment his mistrust of the Links Trust. His
bone to pick is with the "aggressively commercial policies," sneers
McAllister, "that protect the salaries of McGregor, Mason and their
crew." Listening to McAllister, sixty-five, spin yarns about their having "perverted the purpose of the Links Act," with motives to "divide
and rule," there emerges a similitude, in both visage and manner, between McAllister and Russell Crowe's portrayal of conspiracy theo-
rist John Nash in *A Beautiful Mind*. McAllister's beef was never really
with the seventh course per se; the debate simply afforded him an
audience.

Squeezed together cheek by jowl, an overflow crowd of nearly
one hundred concerned citizens braved a nasty night in February

2004 to bear witness and testimony at the departure hearing. One might reasonably expect a weighty matter like the future of the first championship golf course to be built by the town of St. Andrews in nearly a century to be decided in chambers by gentry vestured in black robes and powdered wigs. However, because the project site is actually physically closer to the hamlet of Boarhills than it is to St. Andrews, the venue for the hearing would be Boarhills Village Hall.

The blink-and-you'll-miss-it turnoff to Boarhills (pop. 100) sits four miles up the Crail Road. By daylight the 140-year-old church just west of the farming community appears all by its lonesome in a vast field. The village hall is even easier to miss than the turnoff. Down a one-lane gravel road there is an oversized corrugated metal shed with green siding and a red roof. And there you have it. Inside the 1,250-square-foot corrugated metal shed with the green siding and the red roof are wood slat floors and planks built into the wall for benches. At the north end there is a stage of sorts.

Gatherings include regular Beer & Quiz Nights and the annual Burns Supper. A commemoration of the life and works of Robert Burns (1759–1796), Scotland's beloved bard, Burns Suppers are celebrated all across the country, in some instances quite formally and in others quite drunkenly. Any which way, the evenings tend to adhere to a time-honored ritual that begins with a few words from the host before the guests are seated and join in the saying of the "Selkirk Grace." Soup is served; then everyone stands as the sound of bagpipes heralds the entrance of the haggis. Someone recites the "Address to a Haggis," during which the orator sharpens his knife and plunges it into the sheep's stomach in which the haggis has been boiled, drawing raucous cheers. A whisky toast is then made to the haggis. Post-meal, a parade of toasts continue: to the health of the monarch, to Robert Burns, to the lassies (guys drink to the girls), to the lads (girls drink to the guys). Poetry gets read, people dance, the guests all sing Burns' "Auld Lang Syne," then everyone goes home blotto.

Revelry did not exactly describe the mood inside Boarhills Village Hall the night of the departure hearing, as already contentious spirits were further dampened by a cold, driving rain. Kidd rode out to Boarhills with Links Trust external relations manager Peter Mason, and the two shared a disbelieving chuckle at the sight of a woman pedaling out the treacherous stretch of dark road on a Brompton folding bike. The hearing began at 7:00 P.M., once Councillor Jane Ann Liston had arrived and dried out after pedaling her Brompton folding bike from St. Andrews to Boarhills.

The purpose of the hearing before the East Fife Area Development Committee, so entered into the record, was to allow those both for and against to speak their piece. First up was Stewart Raeside, chairman of the Boarhills and Dunino Community Council, who stated that the majority of the area residents harbored no objections to the plan whatsoever. Next to speak was Colin McAllister. Peter Mason breathed a heavy sigh. Fiercely loyal to the cause and protective of the message, Mason cringed at the mere mention of McAllister's name, especially when preceded by "Have you seen the Letter to the Editor . . ." McAllister's frequent missives to the *Citizen* were earnest yet convoluted by theories on bureaucracies and monopolies, philosophical positing such as appeals to the maxim of Occam's Razor, wherein entities should not be multiplied needlessly, and impractical propositions including "a total ban on visitors before 8:00 A.M. and after 4:00 P.M. on all courses." Such was McAllister's departure hearing diatribe, which cited, in order, Policy C4, Policy SS8, and Policy N6 of the Fife Structure Plan.

Representatives of the Community Council, the Hotel and Guest House Association, and Fife tour operators spoke, as did a few residents, all of whom reiterated the issues raised in the nearly two dozen letters of objections: was a seventh course necessary, was it premature, and was there benefit to commissioning an independent economic study? The prosecution having rested, planning consultant Harry McNab addressed the assemblage and offered the Links Trust's take on the laundry list of issues raised in the letters of objection:

- *Contrary to development plan*

- *Not sufficient demand for development*

- *Unacceptable visual impact*

- *Detrimental impact on area of great landscape value*

- *Development of a prominent site*

- *Inappropriate site for proposals*

- *Surface water concerns*

- *Traffic generation*

- *Access unsuitable for additional traffic*

- *Footway required*

- *Inadequate visibility*

- *Problem will be caused by construction traffic*

- *Economic impact on St. Andrews and other golf courses*

- *Danger to walkers from golf balls*

- *Cumulative impact on coast*

- *Premature to Green Belt*

- *Development in Green Belt*

- *Doubts over visibility of proposals*

- *Light pollution*

- *Impact on SSSI*

- *Consider increasing capacity of existing courses*

- *Proximity of waste water treatment works*

With no more witnesses to be called, the team leader advised the audience that the committee would take the matter under advisement before voting on the planning application. No timetable was set. The hearing adjourned at 9:40 P.M. Councillor Jane Ann Liston hopped on her bike and rode home.

Seven weeks later, at 2:00 P.M. on March 30, 2004, the East Fife

Area Development Committee convened in Cupar. On the docket were forty-four planning applications seeking approval. Mr. and Mrs. Dando of Rose Cottage in Elie received thumbs-up for dormer extensions to their dwelling, as did the owners of Denview Cottage in Ceres to convert a field into a garden. The committee decided to ask Mrs. Hamilton a few more questions about her request to form a taxi office in her home at 10 Crawley Crescent in Cupar. Denied were Auchterlonies golf shop in St. Andrews, which sought to add on a tearoom, and Mr. Robertson of Tayport, who hoped to erect a garden shed. Both applications were refused "in the interests of visual amenity."

In the matter of application 03/03141/EEIA, "Site at Brownhills Farm/Kinkell Farm, St Andrews—Formation of 18 Hole Golf Course and Practice Area, Erect Clubhouse, Maintenance Facilities, Form Access Driveways and Cycleway/Footpath Associated Parking/Servicing Areas," Councillor Liston (who diligently pedaled the ten miles from St. Andrews) moved that the application be refused in the interest of the aforementioned visual amenity, as well as the impact on traffic and pending green belt proposals. When no one piped up to second the motion, Councillor Liston requested that her dissent be noted for the record.

Just as the committee prepared to vote, Councillor Andrew Arbuckle threw a wrench in the works by moving that clauses be added requiring the Links Trust to (1) offer Boarhills residents golf rates consistent with St. Andrews residents, (2) kick in £100,000 toward the implementation of a traffic plan, (3) pony up another £50,000 for children's play facilities in town, (4) fork over an additional £200,000 *annually* for cultural and leisure activities in St. Andrews, and (5) maintain the Fife Coastal Path for the length of the development. Arbuckle's sweeping motion failed; however, the committee agreed to include a provision requiring the Links Trust to maintain the coastal path along the site.

• • •

The watched phone finally rang in Alan McGregor's office. He pressed his planning consultant. "Tell me then, Harry, how did it go?"

"We're there," McNab confirmed.

"Thank God!"

"But only just."

Indeed. The vote went five to four. The ayes had it, but by the slimmest of margins. Fife Council granted permission for Course No. 7—subject to twenty-seven conditions. None were terribly onerous, as most dealt with fine-print items such as allowable working hours, maximum vehicle movements, signage, lighting, fencing, and the council's right to approve details from the colors on the buildings to the chemicals on the course.

The gig was booked. Now all Kidd needed was a band.

Hole 8

• • •

Par-3
146 yards / 141 yards / 130 yards / 112 yards / 108 yards

The eighth hole has my favorite set of tees on the entire project. They are just amazing, a bunch of small, old-fashioned teeing grounds all nested together. Once that is all textured up with gorse and heather and whins and tall grasses it's going to be an adventure just figuring out where your tee is on any given day.

The hole plays downhill all the way, which makes the tee shot look and feel more like a chip shot to an elevated green. Originally we had some bunkers in front of the green, but I worried that those would just be penalizing someone who has already hit a bad shot. Also, the hole looked overly bunkered, like something in Florida somewhere, so we took that out. We did, however, leave some really nasty bunkers that are front right of the green. If you go in those, well, you are not going to be happy.

The right side of the green features a very tight pin placement—one that would have been even tighter if Mick had had his way. When it was first shaped, I paced it, and I doubt it was eight paces across. Playing downhill and potentially downwind, that pin placement is tough if not impossible to hold. After much discussion, Mick widened it a bit and, more importantly, created a little more area right and back of the green so that shots that run through will result in a chip back onto the green, not a lost ball.

Another challenge for us design-wise was to conceal the water treatment works, which sits between the eighth green and ninth tees. A massive amount of shaping has essentially hidden the facility, and when that all gets grown up with a wall of gorse, I don't think players will even be aware there is anything behind there.

The tees at the eighth hole offer golfers the first opportunity to get a good look down the eastern coast, with a long vista of the beach all the way down toward Kinkell Point. In its own way the eighth tee delivers a view that is every bit as impressive as the sixth green's, only looking in the opposite direction. Here, too, cameras will be clicking.

—David McLay Kidd

9

Kimber

A wedding is a lot like a round of golf. Both are time-consuming affairs that can be hard on the feet. The fun ones are always over too soon, while the dreary ones drag on forever. A wee nip is a good thing; a cell phone is a bad thing. Both are best enjoyed with good friends, yet both are a great way to meet people. The object of both, in the end, is to score.

Kimber hoped he might meet a pleasant, pretty young bird at the wedding of his friends Kevin and Catriona Hampton in the summer of 2000. What he found instead was a job. Also on the guest list that day was a friend named Emma Appleton, who worked as a landscape architect. Knowing she was going to see Kimber at the nuptials, Appleton brought along an advert she'd clipped for him from a trade magazine. The ad sought a golf course design associate who "must have good AutoCAD skills and be prepared to travel."

Kimber applied to DMK Golf Design—as did four dozen other aspiring golf course architects. Kidd combed the stack of CVs and narrowed the field down to six seemingly qualified candidates. On the invitation he extended to each of the finalists to join him for a look around Queenwood, Kidd noted, "Please dress appropriately." The wording was intentionally ambiguous so that Kidd could judge the job seekers on their interpretation of appropriate. Knowing that

Queenwood was the most expensive and exclusive club in the UK, two blokes turned up sporting a suit and tie. Kidd immediately lopped them off the list. Kimber came round for his walkabout wearing golf attire and work boots. Brilliant.

Physically and metaphorically Kimber was clearly head and shoulders above the rest. However, the one topic that concerned Kidd the most was taboo, as laws governing fair-hiring practices prevented him from asking Kimber about his personal life, regardless of the fact that the information was crucial to Kidd's decision-making process.

"Have you any potential conflicts or attachments?" asked Kidd.

"Not that I know of," answered Kimber quizzically.

"Are you," Kidd said, struggling to find the right word, "encumbered?"

"Do you mean am I married?"

Kidd sort of half-shrugged and half-nodded at the same time.

"I am not married," said Kimber, "but I do have a girlfriend."

"How is that going to work?" asked Kidd.

Kimber stopped and thought about it for a brief moment. "I can get rid of her" were Kimber's exact words.

Following a short stint at headquarters in Essex, the newly single Kimber jumped right into the fire at Powerscourt Golf Club in Ireland, immediately after which he was posted a world away at Nanea on Hawaii. Must be prepared to travel indeed.

Kimber has never set roots very deep for very long. Born in England in 1971, Kimber was but four months old when his accountant dad and teacher mum moved the family to Jamaica. They stayed two years before returning to the UK, where they never stayed in one place for too terribly long. By Kimber's count St. Andrews is his thirty-fifth temporarily permanent address. He took up golf at age thirteen and had visions of life as a tour pro, but his ability took him only as far as a five handicap, and Kimber decided he did not want to be a shop pro booking tee times and selling Mars Bars. During a year spent on the greenkeeping crew at Cottesmore G&CC in Sussex, England, he considered a career in engineering, only to determine it was way too regimented. Kimber was impressed with the Edinburgh

College of Art's landscape architecture program, although the admissions gatekeepers were not as equally impressed with his portfolio filled with golf course drawings. Kimber went back to Cottesmore for two years then reapplied to Edinburgh College of Art, this time making no mention of golf, figuring it best to wait until after he'd actually been accepted. That did the trick, and in 1998 Kimber was awarded a master's in landscape architecture.

As a graduation gift Kimber treated himself to a weeklong vacation in Greece. Three months later he had parlayed his diploma into a job as a bartender, learned to sail, and acquired a taste for Metaxa, the Greek brandy. A friend back in England whose company was on the hunt for a person good with computers managed to track Kimber down, and while his heart said stay and play, his mind won out and Kimber traded a life of debauchery for a desk job as a CAD monkey.

It quickly became apparent that he was teaching his bosses, not learning from them, so Kimber struck out on his own, dubbing his solo concern the Digital Image Services Consultancy. Among his first gigs was volunteering at European Golf Design, a division of golf industry behemoth IMG. EGD was also among Kimber's last gigs, as shortly thereafter he attended the wedding where he heard about the DMK job. With each successive project, Kimber took more onto his plate, which meant more off Kidd's. At Powerscourt, Kimber was a grunt. At Nanea, he took direction from Kidd. At Fancourt in South Africa, where DMK redesigned the Montagu Course, Kimber required suggestion then relied on intuition. At No. 7, he gave the orders. Kimber had gained Kidd's respect; however, he would have to earn that from scratch with Mick McShane.

A ruddy, barrel-chested bloke with a salt-and-pepper (heavy on the salt) beard, mustache, and mane, lead shaper McShane, forty-seven, was Kidd's first draft pick. If Kidd were the owner of a sports team and Kimber the manager, McShane would be the captain on the field. A bear of a man, McShane is a grizzly to those who cross him and a teddy to those he trusts. His standard greeting upon first meeting is "You have *no right!*" He's the big kid who pushes the new kid to see if he'll rise up or run away. McShane is wholly committed to his craft, and he expects equal unconditional dedication from the rest of the team. That is precisely why Kidd had to have him.

McShane had no background in the game of golf, he simply found it more compelling to shape fairways than highways. Along with an older sister, Sylvia, and big brother, Jock, McShane was born in Mochrum, in an area of southwest Scotland near England known as The Borders. The family lived on dairy farms where their father worked as a laborer, but they were forced to move whenever the old man had a falling out, which was often. His mum left them, his father suffered a series of heart attacks, and by the time McShane was eleven years old the family was on the street. The kindly owner of a bed and breakfast took the family in, and Mick earned his keep washing dishes, cleaning bathrooms, feeding the dogs, and so on. On his own at age sixteen, he continued working odd jobs: tartan maker, sweater factory worker, furniture mover, and reservoir builder. Hooking onto the construction crew that built the Megget Dam between Selkirk and Moffat, McShane learned to drive a bulldozer by attrition. When others showed up too drunk to drive, McShane happily hopped into the cab, and when nobody wanted the night shift he made the most of the opportunity. McShane's first job as a muck shifter on a golf course was in the late 1980s, at the Edinburgh Course at Wentworth Golf Club in England. From there he went to work at Hambury Manor for contractor Southern Golf, where he met one of the company's up-and-coming young construction managers, David Kidd.

McShane's shaping prowess has earned him more money than he ever imagined and taken him places he never dreamed of; his passports boast stamps from France, Holland, Germany, Portugal, Spain, Sardinia, Italy, Hungary, Austria, Turkey, Slovenia, China, and the United States. But it was McShane's transformation of the bland dunes at Kingsbarns into a time-twisting, mind-bending golf wonderland, which appears to have existed in its setting for centuries, that earned McShane universal respect and admiration from his peers. Arnold Palmer is not a peer, though he is an admirer. McShane shaped The Golf Club at North Hampton in Fernandina Beach,

Florida, for Palmer in 2000, after which the boss offered high praise. "You may play golf to a twenty handicap," Palmer told McShane, "but you shape to scratch." Among McShane's most prized possessions is an eight-by-ten glossy of himself and golf's genteel King sharing a couple of cold ones.

David Kidd was a peer. He understood "the muck and the bullets," McShane's term for the down and dirty. Kidd's calluses came from working golf, not playing golf. McShane had nothing to prove to the golfers of St. Andrews, not after Kingsbarns, but he knew that Kidd did. From that first day Kidd rang McShane and invited him up from England for a few pints and a look at the site, McShane sensed Kidd's hunger. His passion to create a golf course that defied expectation and flaunted convention was infectious. Kidd was a rebel with a cause, which appealed to the rouser in McShane. It all sounded so good—and then he saw the site. McShane kicked the dirt off his boots and climbed back in Kidd's car harboring serious trepidations about blemishing his reputation. After all, unlike Kingsbarns's dunes, there seemed to be only so much one could do with flat farmland surrounding a sewage plant. But the draw of working with a fellow Scot in Scotland for the town of St. Andrews was strong. On the plane ride back Kidd made clear that McShane would be working with, not for, Kidd. He wanted a collaborator; Kidd did not want to be a dictator. He did not offer McShane creative freedom so much as he demanded it. "Create me the kind of landscape Old Tom might have had," said Kidd. He beseeched McShane to right the wrongs caused by centuries of cattle grazing and potato farming: "They killed the character of the place and buried it. You need to exhume it. Then we can go find ourselves a golf course." McShane signed up before the plane touched down.

Machinery, not compatibility, proved to be a bugaboo. Kidd envisioned No. 7 replete with tight, gnarly hummocks and hillocks. McShane scoffed with his own brand of blunt honesty: "Bollocks. Not with a D6." The industry standard D6 Caterpillar bulldozer, weighing twenty tons and sporting a thirteen-foot-wide blade, was too cumbersome and heavy, a cleaver compared to the paring knife Kidd sought.

"Describe your dream rig," said Kidd.

"The new D5N," answered McShane, "with an eleven-foot blade, low ground pressure, auto-shift and auto-kickdown, fingertip controls for gears and steering, and the air suspension seat." The D5N is a doozie of a dozer, five tons lighter than the D6 and exponentially more nimble given its tighter turning circle and compact blade. The fingertip-controlled joystick makes shaping like playing a video game.

"That's it?" asked Kidd.

"Right," McShane said, "and a kick-ass stereo."

Banking on the fact that he could lease the machine to the Links Trust for the duration of the project then put it on another site or sell it, Kidd stepped up, swallowed hard, and plunked down over £100,000 for McShane's dream mount. If nothing else, Kidd now had the tool to dig McShane's grave if he screwed this up.

• • •

The original construction schedule, starting in late March 2005 and running through the following October, looked to have been drafted in a perfect world by an eternal optimist wearing rose-colored glasses.

Topsoil Strip	*69 days*
Bulk Earthworks	*107 days*
Shaping	*103 days*
Drainage	*96 days*
Irrigation	*109 days*
Topsoil Respread	*83 days*
Green Construction	*80 days*
Tee Construction	*78 days*
Preparation & Seeding	*82 days*

It would be physically possible to sign, seal, and deliver No. 7 in just eight months if Murphy's Law magically inverted and whatever could go right did go right. In truth, ideal conditions do not occur in this business or in this place, and the schedule got shot to hell right out of the chute when, on March 24, 2005, Kimber slept through his alarm on the first day of construction and had to be rousted by Mc-Shane. They had not even started, and they were already behind.

Hole 9

• • •

Par-4
448 yards / 381 yards / 372 yards / 348 yards / 319 yards / 253 yards

Separating the eighth green and ninth tee are the water treatment works to the right, a deep ravine to the left, and a pathway through the middle. Paul and I often mused about putting a tee box on the far side of the ravine, which would require a ball-busting carry to reach the edge of the fairway. Not a shot I would want to play in a match, but I'd sure like to try it.

It reminded me of the ninth hole on the Ailsa course at Turnberry, where the very back tee shaves past the lighthouse. I've never played that tee, but I've always wanted to sneak over there and hit a ball just to see if I could make it to the other side.

We could not resist. We went ahead and built that sixth tee, which plays nearly seventy yards longer than the tips on the opposite side of the ravine. Who knows how often it will be used, but everyone will walk past it, and everyone will wonder. . . .

Standing on the regular tees at the ninth hole, golfers find a short par-4 that plays just 381 yards from the tips. Fully downhill and frequently downwind, there is a reasonable expectation that a big hitter could drive the green, but it could be a foolhardy try. The green is not terribly receptive. Unlike many of the others, where a golfer can run up a punch shot, chasing a ball into that green would be difficult, thanks especially to a greenside pot bunker set front right.

Hook the ball off the tee, and it is over the braes. Slice it, and it is in the driving range. We worried early on about the width of the ninth fairway given the range on the right-hand side, but it worked out quite nicely. The smart play is to pull whatever club a golfer is most confident with from 6-iron up. For me it probably is my 5-iron. A solid strike off the tee ought to leave a low-iron shot in. Golfers that properly place their drives on the left-hand side of that fairway, in the ample flat spot, will have a perfect lie for their approach.

The double green shared by holes nine and eighteen is the sweetest spot on the entire site. We had the chance to do something pretty special there on Kinkell Point, and we believe we made the most of our opportunity.

—David McLay Kidd

10

Premature Evaluation

Murphy's Law played true to form: things went from bad to worse, with epic rainfalls in April and May 2005, 155 percent above normal. One person who reveled in all the rain was Mark "Skippy" Lindsay, the proprietor of the New Inn. Located on St. Mary Street on the east edge of town, the New Inn became the equivalent of *Cheers* for the crew at No. 7, not only because it was the closest pub to the job site, but also because it was just far enough away from the tourist-laden center of town. When the rains drove the crew off-site, they often drove to see Skippy, who grilled a tasty bacon cheeseburger and kept pint glasses perpetually full. Between catering the Tuesday meetings, pub lunches, pints, the Red Bull–and–vodkas favored by McShane at the end of the evening, and the quid they pumped into the jukebox, the lads from No. 7 dropped £1,000 a month in Skippy's place. He wished it would never stop raining.

The depth and breadth of the design of the golf course depended largely on two factors: the weather and the budget. Less rain meant more time for more intricate shaping, while the more it poured the less McShane could add in the way of finishing touches. Kidd could do nothing about the weather, but he could stretch the already thin £2.5 million budget in his role as contractor. Some items on Kidd's wish list, including more gorse and fescue, enhanced water features, and additional drainage, would hopefully be added by the Links Trust at a later date. For now, Kidd avoided buying anything he could borrow by leveraging existing Links Trust's assets, from equipment to manpower and everything in between, in an effort to funnel as much money into the design.

Showing flashes of the boy who used to sock away half of his lunch money, Kidd figured to save a few bucks by moving his own furniture into the empty flat at 24 Hepburn Gardens that he and Kimber rented. (So as to give everyone their space and avoid regressing [deeper] into a fraternity mentality, DMK's crew bunked in separate digs.) Kidd's plan was brilliant in theory: please two constituencies—the bean counters at the Links Trust and his wife, Jill, who wanted to redo their home in Essex. One weekend Kidd flew home, rented a seven-ton truck, loaded it up, made the 450-mile drive back to St. Andrews, and then spent the balance of his time off hauling couches and beds and dressers and TVs up two and three flights of stairs. Not counting the lost weekend and near coronary Kidd endured, the cost of the truck rental and fuel was over £1,000, or about 1/100th of the hit Kidd took for agreeing to let Jill redecorate back home.

•   •   •

Décor is nothing more than frosting on a cake, be it in a house or on a golf course. If water collects beneath plush carpet or lush fairway the only way to fix it is to rip it up, an ugly and expensive proposition. Ask golfers what they believe architects base design decisions on, and the mixed bag of answers will include overused buzzwords like shot value, playability, or risk/reward. Ask golf architects what they actually base design decisions on and the majority will likely cite drainage. Put simply by Kimber: "If I were a raindrop, where would I land and where would I go?" There is no way to keep water off a golf course; the trick is to keep it moving, preferably in an orderly fashion, because water runoff inflicts increasing damage when it gains volume and velocity. A requirement to connect all golf course drainage to existing outfalls presented a dilemma at No. 7, most notably at holes nine and eighteen, where no outfall existed behind the massive double green, meaning water would have to be brought back onto the course before it could be redirected off.

Golf course construction typically begins at the lowest elevation because the low spot on the site is often the wettest, so the drains are dug from the low ground to the high ground, same as in any garden. Working up the slope allows construction to continue through the temperate seasons and move to higher, drier land when the weather turns inclement. Conventional wisdom would thus have called for breaking ground down by the brae tops then progressing upward and inland toward the Crail Road, except Kidd believes the weakest golf holes on any course are usually the first ones built, largely because individuals in any endeavor improve as they gain confidence. The holes along the braes promised to occupy the white-hot media spotlight. That was no place for trial or, God forbid, error. "The weather in springtime is shite, and if it is shite up high it is going to be doubly shite down low," Kidd said to the crew in explaining his decision to start up in the southeast corner, on holes twelve, thirteen, and fourteen. In truth, Kidd worried mightily about a new team that had not yet gelled and a plan that did not yet exist beyond the two-dimensional boundaries on which his routing plan was printed.

Designing in two dimensions eliminates the critical element of depth. The edges of a piece of paper or a computer screen become creative boundaries that, when reached, force the designer to stop and start anew. Working on paper or computers is like painting, whereas working in dirt is akin to sculpting. Over a strategy session that took place one Friday night in the pub at the Dunvegan, Kidd, Kimber, and McShane agreed that the first hole to be sculpted would be the thirteenth hole, a par-3 projected to play around two hundred yards. Under normal circumstances the three would have trod out armed with cans of paint, a flagstick, and a few golf clubs and balls; found a natural spot for a green; spray-painted an outline for the green and perhaps the form of a potential bunker; stuck the flag into the ground where a hole might go; marched back a couple hundred paces; kicked clear a patch of dirt; dropped a few balls; and had a whack to see what could be. Under these circumstances there was no natural spot for a green, no place Kidd could stand and squint and see in his mind's eye a suitable place to putt. There was nothing to frame his reference.

Kidd asked McShane to cut a valley and fill some mounds, nothing too "polished." That adjective sits atop Kidd's list of despised words. He cringes at the cookie-cutter courses on which so many PGA Tour events are played, with their immaculately manicured fairways, gently rolling mounds, neatly edged bunkers, flat tees, symmetrical greens. They are pretty. They are perfect. They are *polished*. They are fake. Designers who build pristine courses are, to Kidd's mind, the furthest thing from artists and more like Botox-happy plastic surgeons. Nature is not manicured or neat or symmetrical, and the pursuit of perfection comes at the expense and demise of distinctive features, inherent character, and true beauty.

Kidd knew that no matter what he did at No. 7 there would be those who would grouse. Not only was he fine with it, he relished it and used it as a battle cry. "People are going to throw stones," he told his troops, "so what say we give them something to throw stones at!" He demanded that the course ooze flavor, anything so long as it was not vanilla. "Häagen-Dazs makes the world's best vanilla," he is fond of saying, "but it is still just vanilla." Kidd favors strawberry cheesecake ice cream served up just like his golf courses: hard, lumpy, and full of surprises.

There is a scene in the wickedly funny mockumentary *This Is Spinal Tap* in which the band's lead guitarist, Nigel Tufnel, explains to filmmaker Marty DiBergi that while other rock groups have amplifiers with volume controls that top out at ten, Spinal Tap's crank to eleven. Kidd is fond of the volume analogy, as he contends most shapers turn it up to about three, and if they dare push it to four the designer begins to convulse. "Turn it up," Kidd challenged McShane. "Show me eleven."

While Kidd headed home to Essex for the weekend, McShane saddled up and dug in. What started out as flat as a freshly made bed looked as tousled and rumpled as the blankets after a right roll in the sack by the time Kidd returned to have a look—and a listen. "We may need a booster amp for your stereo," critiqued Kidd, "because it looks like you've only dialed it up to seven." Kidd noted McShane's benign bunkering and a putting green that was lackluster. "No one will be offended," Kidd carped, "and if no one will be offended at one end of the spectrum, no one will be inspired at the other end."

The bunkering was of particular concern to Kidd, who was convinced after this first pass that McShane was not the man to give the bunkers the jagged edge Kidd so desperately craved. The old saying "A good carpenter doesn't blame his tools" proved false in this case because Kidd argued that any bunker built with an eleven-foot bulldozer blade is bound to be too conforming, too *polished*. It's tough for a coach to yank a player when he is giving his all, but Kidd stood firm and pulled McShane off the bunkers. Not without a fight; however, McShane could not counter Kidd's argument that the D5's satellite-dish-shaped bunkers were neither offensive nor inspiring.

Kidd would make the kind of doctor you love to hate; he is quick to diagnose problems and decisive in prescribing effective remedies, but his bedside manner sucks. He is notorious among his shapers for a hand signal in which he holds aloft his left palm as if it were a slate then runs his right back and forth across his palm like an eraser. It means just that: doze it flat and start again. Kidd may have a hole shaped a half a dozen times before he's sorted the symptoms and discovered the cure. "It's just shifted muck until David says it's a golf hole," acknowledges McShane. Starting over, and in some cases over and over and over, sounds terribly inefficient and horribly expensive, but it is not. Kidd likens it to pottery, in that the clay can be molded and remolded over and over and over until the glaze gets added. Once that element is added, the design of the pot cannot be altered without throwing it out and starting over from scratch. The same goes for a golf course, in that the dirt can be shaped and reshaped over and over and over until infrastructure gets added. The cost is negligible if Kidd makes changes *at the right time*, but changes become expensive and arduous the moment they sink drainage and irrigation in the ground, because the design of the hole cannot be altered without tearing it up and starting over.

Despite the pounding rains, McShane managed the rough shaping of holes twelve, thirteen, and fourteen by the end of April. One month into construction one might expect the client to ask for a look about, and although McGregor and Moir had periodically popped in to check in, at no time had they or any of the Trustees or any member of the Links Management Committee requested a guided tour, offered a suggestion, or dropped so much as a hint indicating their impressions one way or the other. Kidd was used to *some* reaction, never total silence. On the bright side, Kidd appreciated the implied trust and enjoyed working without interference. On the flip side, client interaction is like a physical exam: dodging it only makes things worse, and sooner or later someone is going to poke around in your business.

Calling the client and requesting a walkthrough is akin to ringing the taxman and inviting him for an audit. Never once had Kidd made that call. He preferred to keep clients at bay, but a month of hearing nothing felt like singing a concert for an audience that neither cheers nor jeers. The Links Trust had been eminently professional and exceptionally trusting, a dream really, essentially telling Kidd, "We trust you, have at it," and then actually trusting him to have at it. Clients who are footing the multimillion-dollar tab are often overeager to chip in their two cents; however, first impressions can doom a golf course if a client passes judgment on a work in progress. Imagine a chef having to endure diners walking through the kitchen and critiquing the Baked Alaska before it has been flambéed. Alas, golf course designers can do little to prevent premature evaluation.

Sitting at the desk opposite Kimber's in the office trailer on-site, Kidd stared at the telephone and wondered whether he should let the sleeping dogs lie. Figuring he'd rather get bit now than mauled later, Kidd picked up the phone and made the call down to Pilmour House inviting up McGregor, Moir, and Allan Patterson, the recently appointed head greenkeeper for Course No. 7. Patterson, thirty-seven, started as an apprentice and spent a decade at Powfoot Golf Club in Dumfriesshire, after which he honed his craft under the same wing as Kidd. Prior to beating out nearly one hundred applicants for the head post at No. 7, Patterson spent eleven years under the tutelage of Jimmy Kidd at Gleneagles.

"If the Links Trust are going to get their tuppence worth in," Kidd told Kimber, "now is their chance."

The gathering was set for April 28 at 2:00 P.M. Kidd would've preferred to return to St. Andrews at least a day early to survey the progress, but horrendous weather and a half dozen other projects crying like teakettles on the back burner kept Kidd chained to his desk in Essex. Never far from his mind was an unsettling fear that the Links Trust did not completely comprehend that once pipe went in the ground that was it, the pot was fired. The incessant rains had turned the site into a quagmire.

"It's like tramping through baby poo," Kidd whispered to Kimber as they set out.

While the work they had done did not look nearly as good as it would have on a sunny day in the late afternoon when the sky is alive and shadows are long, there was a silver lining. With McGregor, Moir, and Patterson watching their steps so as to keep from getting their Wellies stuck in the mud, they could not give the course their undivided attention; thus any flaws should have been less obvious. To Kidd's trained eye, however, the flaws were glaring. Kidd began the tour at the twelfth hole, an uphill par-4. Aloud, he explained the visuals, addressed the drainage, and detailed the dimensions. Inside, Kidd hated it. The landforms behind the green displayed a symmetry that does not exist in nature, and the bunkers fronting the green looked too nice, too round, too *polished*. Walking a step behind the clients and kicking at the mud, Kidd's displeasure was not lost on Kimber. The bunkers and mounding were like an electric lime paint job—arresting yet fixable. Once they reached the twelfth green, Kidd's disposition brightened. It was exceptional, making the most of the highest point on the course and the 270-degree panoramic views across the firth to Carnoustie and back to town. McGregor, Moir, and Patterson's reactions to the twelfth remained theirs alone, as they did very little talking and a whole lot of nodding.

The par-3 thirteenth had come along nicely. McShane piled a huge knoll left of the green and cut a deep gulch in front of the tee, creating a dodgy carry to a green that sloped sharply from back to front. This, Kidd thought, resembled the natural imperfections he needed McShane to re-create. Expecting the clients to ask about the tiny tee boxes, Kimber prepared a homily on old-fashioned teeing grounds. Here again there were no questions, just more nodding. At the fourteenth, a downhill dogleg-right par-4, McShane proved Kidd's contention about getting better as you go. It was spot-on, with a landing area so chock-full of knobs it resembled a giant Baby Ruth candy bar. Standing on the tee Kidd glimpsed McGregor struggling to decipher where the fairway could possibly be. This pleased Kidd greatly. In and among the humps, lumps, and bumps Kidd suddenly had a dozen different sites for a green, not a one of which could have been designed on paper, given all the nooks, crannies, and nuances McShane had created.

At the end of their three-hole appetizer, Kidd took McGregor aside. "Are you happy?" Kidd asked. Over McGregor's shoulder he spied Kimber chatting with Moir. Hands were shaken and pleasantries exchanged; then the men who controlled David McLay Kidd's legacy climbed out of their Wellies and back into their car and motored down the Crail Road toward town.

"So?!" said Kidd, pumping Kimber for info like a schoolboy desperate to know if the girl he likes likes him or *likes him* likes him.

"'Carry on,'" reported Kimber. "That's all Gordon said, 'Carry on.'"

Kidd shared McGregor's feedback, which was similarly succinct. "Alan said, 'You have my trust.'"

"That's good," offered Kimber.

"That," said Kidd, "is brilliant."

Hole 10

• • •

Par-3
175 yards / 161 yards / 154 yards / 143 yards / 127 yards

The Links Trust's desire for two nine-hole loops, combined with our insistence on the par-3 seventeenth, par-5 eighteenth grand finale fairly dictated a routing plan that made the tenth hole a par-3. This presented any number of potential problems: opening with a par-3 invited pace-of-play issues, it was the shortest hole on the golf course, and it played uphill. Honestly, I have never played an uphill par-3 that I thought was truly exceptional. I have tried to create that hole many times, but it is extremely difficult to make work.

We all feared that the tenth could well be the weakest hole on the golf course, but everything turned around. We cut the green down about ten to fifteen feet, then we raised the tees about the same amount, and the net effect is a hole that appears flat. If it is uphill at all it is by an amount that a golfer is not going to perceive.

Mick shaped in some landforms, then he, Paul, and I set out with pin flags to try to figure out where we might put the green. I remember distinctly that none of us could agree on the best place for the putting surface within those landforms. We all had the middle of the green within twenty feet or so of one another, so we all flagged out where we thought the green should be, and then we painted in the dirt to the outer limits of all the flags and said, "Right, let's call all of that the green."

That happened more than once in the building of the seventh course, and the net effect for our client was increased costs for greens construction because many of the greens got bigger. However, that was all to the advantage of the golfer because everyone wants to hit the green.

Miss the green at the tenth, and the best play is to pray for par and hope for bogey. There is water running down the left side, which tends to turn golfers to the right, but missing right, especially short right, makes for a dodgy up and down.

Perhaps more than any other hole on the course, the tenth exemplifies the team's incredible talent and imagination. They turned a serious weakness into a genuine strength and truly made something out of nothing.

—David McLay Kidd

11

McShane & Walsh

*First class holes . . . at first sight
excite the most violent spirit of antagonism. . . .
Only after the holes have been played many times . . .
the feeling of resentment disappears.*

ALISTER MACKENZIE
The Spirit of St. Andrews

This sentiment encapsulates Kidd's guiding vision. Negative reaction is better than no reaction, because initial frustration often grows into appreciation. McShane's refrain "You have no right!" might well be directed at golfers for he, Kidd, and Kimber share a resolute mind-set that par is not a right but a privilege. (Among them the three represent all levels of golfers, as Kidd plays worse than his eight handicap, Kimber better than his six, and McShane pretty much right to his sixteen.) If they sound defensive, they unapologetically are. The designers are on defense and the golfers are on offense, and as in any sport, if the offense scores at will, then the defense has failed. Such is the logic in every sport where the hazards are arranged precisely where the player aims. Placing bunkers alongside a fairway to catch errant hooks and slices is as ludicrous as positioning baseball fielders outside the foul lines or a football goalie next to the net instead of in front of it.

Golfers habitually complain about hitting a perfect shot only to have it land in a hazard. "That wasn't a perfect shot then, was it?" Kidd will counter. "There are no misplaced hazards, only misplayed shots." Big believers in local knowledge, Kidd, Kimber, and McShane want that whiny golfer to think twice the next time around about taking a different club, or better yet a caddie.

Kidd's vision is also shaped by a match play mentality. In the United States, golfers are obsessed with posting a score, whereas in the UK their focus is winning a match. Yanks approach a par-4 and think driver. Scots approach a par-4 and think driver may not be the play. Double-bogey is depressing when trying to shoot a score but irrelevant when trying to best your mate, so long as your mate cards a triple. That mentality, plus maturity, plus necessity borne of No. 7's exceptional nothingness combined to give Kidd, at age thirty-seven, the confidence to match the creativity he had when he first laid eyes on Bandon at age twenty-seven.

In Old Tom's time, crews used shovels and spades and wheelbarrows. That was the extent of the earthmoving. Today, technology is such that even a mediocre shaper can fashion an Augusta-like *polish*, but what caught Kidd's eye was what McShane achieved going the opposite way at Kingsbarns: craggy, ancient, and organic, as if it had existed for eons. It sounds easy in theory—less polish, less work—but the truth is that it's more difficult and requires more talent to sculpt a landscape that looks like it was carved by the wind and the rain and centuries of Scottish winters than it is to whitewash two hundred acres with gently rolling mounds, neatly edged bunkers, flat tees, and symmetrical greens.

The greens at No. 7 would be generous and accommodate Kidd's ideal of six different pin placements. There would be varying numbers of teeing grounds but five sets of tee markers, more than the four found on the Old, New, and Jubilee. This speeds pace of play by moving mid- and high-handicappers who are blinded by hubris away from the tips and up to a more appropriate teeing ground without making them feel somehow emasculated. To Kidd's mind the first (farthest) tees should present a demanding task for men with low handicaps, while the fourth should offer like visuals and a similar challenge for top ladies. The second and third tees ought to make the experience variable and enjoyable for the rest of us, while the fifth tees up front are designed to appeal to golfers in their infancy or twilight. Bunkers that are not in play are by no means random. They might frame a hole visually, steer golfers in a desired direction, play tricks on their eyes, or just mess with their minds. Kidd's intention is not to penalize the golfer who hits in, but rather to punish the golfer who fails to hit out. Given that No. 7 is a seaside course, as opposed to the links courses, Kidd opted not to feature revetted, or stacked-sod, pot bunkers. "A gash in the face of a boxer," was the look Kidd described to Kimber. From a distance golfers don't always see sand in the bunker. It is much more unsettling to face deep, dark shadows that cloak a nefarious unknown.

• • •

The pub at One Golf Place became an instant favorite of the crew's, partly because the big-screen plasma TVs are continually tuned to sports, but more so because the understated upscale coziness attracts flocks of pretty birds from the university. Kimber might as well have been a scarecrow, what with his foul scowl, one otherwise lovely evening in early May 2005. Hunkered down with pints of Tennent's Tops (the popular Scottish lager topped with a shot of lemon-lime soda), Kimber, Kidd, and McShane watched the PGA Tour's Zurich Classic of New Orleans via satellite. The site was the Tournament Players Club of Louisiana, a new, $30 million venue designed by Pete Dye (with PGA Tour pro consultants Steve Elkington and Kelly Gibson). Dye is a respected elder statesman whose portfolio of renowned works includes the Stadium Course at the TPC at Sawgrass, located at PGA Tour headquarters in Ponte Vedra Beach, Florida. Hailed as revolutionary when it opened in 1980, for fan-friendly features like natural amphitheater seating, the most famous hole is the par-3 seventeenth with the island green. Where some see imagination, others see contrivance. Golfers either love it or hate it, though no one who plays it will ever forget it.

As Kimber watched the action from the TPC of Louisiana, itself a gentrified swamp, he grumbled into his beer about the tricked-up thirteenth hole, a 377-yard par-4 with a ninety-degree-angle dogleg, and the 490-yard, par-4 fifteenth hole, where a vast waste bunker that parallels the left side of the forward tees and the first part of the fairway only poses a threat, physical or visual, to rank amateurs. Kidd and McShane did not disagree, but they refused to allow Kimber to sponge their fun. Kidd dashed off to the loo, and McShane went to buy another round of pints.

Upstairs, Kidd popped outside onto the small second-floor terrace. Even in the dark of night there was a glow about St. Andrews, a luminescent energy from the ghosts of golfers past that enveloped the place. Scottish pride welled inside him, but before it could leak out his tear ducts Kidd ducked back inside. By pure happenstance, he looked up, and there it was.

Students at play in "Cheapes Bunker"
2nd hole Old Course 1857

Hanging in the stairwell was a sepia-toned poster print showing a dozen-plus blokes hanging in and around Cheapes Bunker, all sporting wool jackets and hats and one boasting serious muttonchops. It was not the two golf clubs lying crisscrossed in the sand or the fact that there were six guys standing in the bunker as one addressed his ball that caught Kidd's eye, but rather the ragged face of the bunker. It resembled a raptor scratch in a dune, deep and rutty and gnarly, like an envelope opened with one's thumb, versus the letter-opener precision of what Kidd derisively calls "Orlando bunkers." In the poster the golfer addressing his ball is turned sideways away from the sheer cliff before him, a graphic example of Kidd's desire for bunkers that punish the golfer who fails to hit out. Kidd beckoned Kimber and McShane. "That is what we want our bunkers to look like," instructed Kidd. "Scary."

There was, of course, no possible way to re-create that saw-toothed look with a dozer. So Kidd bought a digger. Not just any digger, but a six-figure, top-of-the-line Caterpillar 312CL hydraulic excavator with a turbocharged engine, adjustable pilot-operated joysticks, and a six-foot knuckle bucket that works like a cupped hand with sharp fingernails. The digger can stretch and dip and flick and flit about effortlessly, versus a dozer that treads as gingerly as a size-14 ski boot. However, his fancy new digger solved only half of Kidd's problem. He had a state-of-the-art cart but no horse.

Missing from the cast was a supporting actor, a second shaper who could work the digger in concert with and under the direction of McShane in the dozer. The catch-22 in hiring shapers is that anyone worth bringing on ought to be already working. There is usually a reason why an experienced shaper does not have a job come springtime, and rarely is it a good one.

McShane kept thinking about a young Scot with whom he had worked a few years back named Conor Walsh. After helping to build fourteen exquisite football pitches, priced at over £750,000 apiece, for the English national team in Burton-on-Trent, Walsh hooked on at Castleknock Country Club in Ireland, where McShane was the lead shaper. The two had last seen each other the previous November when McShane was helping Kidd rework four holes at the PGA Centenary course at Gleneagles. Walsh, twenty-six, drove from his home in Monifieth over to Auchterarder to hoist a few pints with McShane, who brought along Kidd. The three had a grand time and swapped war stories from Southern Golf, for whom Walsh had worked for three-and-a-half years.

A solid amateur golfer who once played to a four handicap, Walsh studied golf course management at Elmwood College in Cupar then spent three months in 1988 at Greywood Plantation in Lake Charles, Louisiana, digging by day and having a hot time on the bayou by night. Returning to Scotland, Walsh hooked on with the construction crew at St. Andrews Bay, which, despite his finding both courses decidedly bland, became the first golf project he saw through from start to finish. McShane lobbied Walsh hard to sign on for No. 7, but the young man was headed west. Shortly thereafter Walsh shipped out for seven months of fun in the sun in L.A., Hawaii, Fiji, New Zealand, and Australia.

DMK auditioned three hopefuls on the digger, but none possessed the right combination of talent and spark. McShane tracked down a phone number for Walsh, and Kidd ran him down in Sydney in June 2005. The offer to return home to Scotland and work in St. Andrews, complete with a ticket on the first flight back, still stood. This time it sounded more appealing, and not only because Walsh was sweeping concrete dust on the docks for rent and beer money at the time.

On June 11 Walsh hopped a plane off of Australia. On June 12 he stood, albeit a bit wobbly after a twenty-six-hour flight, in One Golf Place.

"Welcome back," said McShane as he passed Walsh and Kimber a couple of freshly poured pints.

"Cheers," replied Walsh.

"Want to have a look at what you'll be doing?" asked Kimber.

Walsh set down his pint. He hated wasting it, but he was eager to please and assumed Kimber meant for them to go have a walk about the site. Kimber handed back his beer then led Walsh with McShane in tow to the stairwell and the poster print of the students at play in Cheapes Bunker circa 1857.

"Bloody hell," murmured Walsh.

It was unclear whether Walsh meant that in a good way or a bad way. He was not DMK's last hope, but it was not a stretch to say that he was their last good hope. (Talent seemed to be an increasingly scarce commodity. For their No. 7 grounds crew the Links Trust made good faith efforts to work through the local job bank and made four hires: three no-showed and the fourth walked off the job two hours in without so much as a toodle-oo or a tip o' the cap.) Kidd's antennae came up anytime he encountered a shaper who was not working during the busy season, but in this case Walsh proved an exception to that rule. Kidd respected his desire to see the world, and the fact that Walsh was well traveled appealed to him. As did his being Scottish and a native of the linksland, experienced, accomplished, worldly, fond of pints, young, and single. In sum, the perfect potential employee.

Kimber and McShane waited and wondered what Walsh was thinking as he took a long look at the poster. Then he turned and faced them, his lips curled in a sadistic grin. They had their man.

• • •

Had Walsh required any additional proof that working on No. 7 would be a unique experience, he got it on the first day when he spotted the sandbox. Two feet wide by three feet long by four inches deep, the sandbox sat beside Kimber's desk in the site office and served as an ersatz drawing board/Zen garden. The sandbox, which McShane had employed in the past, allowed the designers to fiddle with 3-D ideas in the sand, which the shapers then formed in the dirt. The result need not be perfect. That was the point. Such esoteric execution can be intimidating for a shaper who is used to working from precise renderings on paper; however, the hope is that freedom begets ownership, which creates pride, which fosters creativity, which results in inspiration, which stifles convention, which quashes *polish*.

Walsh delivered the goods from his second day in the digger. On the first day he hauled three different buckets out to the twelfth hole. Like a painter mixing and matching his brushes, Walsh shaped his first bunker. It turned out perfect. Too perfect. Kidd held aloft his left palm as if it were a slate and ran his right hand back and forth across his palm as if it were an eraser. Walsh did not need to be told anything twice. When Kidd returned, it looked like a meteor had plowed into the ground. Now it was perfect.

Doing a job is one thing, but doing it right is something else altogether. Walsh proved so deft with the digger he looked to be able to pluck a ladybug off a dirt clod and deliver it safely to a flower petal. His eye matched his touch. Walsh picked and flicked at the dirt like a child adept at making it appear there are fewer vegetables on his plate than there really are.

Walsh's coming of age came on the pathway between the eighth green and the ninth tees. It was a critical bit of shaping because the alternate reality of this ancient landscape, which golfers would have bought into over the first eight holes, would be obliterated by the sudden, jarring appearance of the sewage plant. With no supervision from McShane and no direction from Kidd or Kimber—other than to make the damn thing disappear—Walsh took the look of the cliffs between the water and the brae tops and re-created it identically between the brae tops and the water works. When the gorse grows in, there will be no way to tell where nature stopped and Walsh started. It looks like one great landform with the only crafting by the hand of man being the pathway.

Kidd preached, "Less is more," and Walsh was thrilled to be part of the choir. McShane, too, was thrilled, not just to be working with his young friend again but also to have his attention undivided. Mc-Shane acknowledged that the kind of polished bunkers a dozer could create threatened to besmirch his work like welts on a swimsuit model. The arrival of Walsh settled McShane's stomach and allowed him to go back to driving his dozer. McShane harbors no aspirations to be a golf course designer, in part because he already effectively is, but also because he would be pulling his best shaper off the machine: himself. What separates the good shapers from the great ones, Mc-Shane contends, are vision and courage: the ability to see a great golf hole in a patch of dirt, and the chops to build it. "Shapers are egotistical, but architects are even worse," he'll tell you. "They think they are God. I *know* I am."

Kidd relishes the bravado. McShane is the best—he knows it, you know it, and he demands that anyone who is not the best had best get cracking. Having McShane on the job is like having an iron-willed team captain in the locker room. Kidd has no interest, much less time, to micromanage, and he alleviates the need by assembling teams that buy into his system. DMK Golf Design is no different than a successful sports team: the owner sets a level of high expectation and creates an atmosphere in which his people can succeed; the manager devises the strategy and inspires his charges to achieve greatness; the players work together, execute the game plan, and everybody wins. Along the way opinions and styles may differ, but the common goal remains the same. Total commitment is paramount. Anything less is tantamount to treason. Any person who is not fully on board is shown the plank.

Such was the case with an American chap who had been working in Ireland and came on to drive a D6 and help with the extraordinary earthmoving. He seemed so promising in the interview, but once he landed the job he sat back instead of stepping up. He lacked talent and displayed even less enthusiasm and was given the heave-ho by Kimber after one day. In a pinch, McShane suggested that if they couldn't find a muckshifter, perhaps they could make one, and he sold Kidd on investing in the future in the form of Clint McShane, Mick's twenty-one-year-old son. Kidd agreed to take Clint on, but he made it unequivocally clear that it was McShane's job to manage his boy. McShane gave his word that if Clint got out of line, Kidd would not have to worry about firing young McShane, because the old man would kick his ass eight ways till Sunday.

Working together proved tough enough without the added stress of living together—and drinking together. Weekend nights and rained-out days were spent in the pub, and pint after pint after pint was fuel on the fire after year after year of strained relations. McShane was twenty-two when he lost a four-week-old son; two-and-a-half years later he welcomed Clint; however, the boy was barely walking before his mum and McShane separated. Clint got his first exposure to dozers as a tot riding on his pappy's knee when McShane worked on the Channel Tunnel shortly before landing his first golf gig. Then, with Mick off building courses around the world, father and son were lucky to see each other a handful of days each month during Clint's formative years. Clint left school at sixteen and trained as an apprentice bricklayer, later working on golf courses as a jack of all grunt trades, but his first paying job in a dozer came at No. 7, where his role was to move what Mick said where Mick said when Mick said.

Clint proved to be proficient but not efficient. Like all twenty-one-year-olds, he was easily distracted. He wanted to learn and he

wanted to have fun, but he could not seem to decide which he wanted
more. On the job Clint worked slowly and predictably. His work was
polished. He focused on making a good impression, and while that
does not sound like a bad thing, DMK needed someone whose work
was good *and* fast. They were working against the calendar, cranking
to make up lost time. By the first week of June construction was 40
percent behind schedule. Of the fifty-five working days since the
start of the job in late March, thirteen days had been partially
scrubbed and seventeen completely washed out.

Brad Russell was no stranger to rugged weather or hard work. A
physically fit, curly-haired, blond, and blue-eyed twenty-four-year-
old Canadian, he was finishing up his final term in the golf course architecture program at Edinburgh College of Art when, in the spring
of 2005, he spotted a bulletin board posting for a summer internship.
It paid a pittance, but it beat the hell out of his past summer jobs.

Russell hailed from Flin Flon, Manitoba. Legend has it that the
town drew its name from a dime-store science fiction novel titled *The
Sunless City,* in which a character named Josiah Flintabbattey Flonatin
discovers a city rich in gold deep in a bottomless lake. Flin Flon sits
on a nearly two-billion-year-old volcanic belt rich in gold, silver,
copper, and zinc. The area's largest employer is the Hudson Bay
Mining and Smelting Company, where Russell hooked a blue-collar
gig following his freshman year at the University of Saskatchewan.
Toiling sixty hours a week for the equivalent of $10.75 USD per
hour, Russell carried out the inglorious task of extracting molten
metal from a furnace that melted copper at temperatures exceeding
2,000 degrees Fahrenheit.

Once the smelting crews had extracted as much of the molten
copper as possible, they shut off the burners and left the remains to
cool for three or four days, cleaning up around the furnace in the
meantime. Rule No. 1 was keep water away from the molten metal,
because it would vaporize on contact and turn to hot steam. When a
crust formed atop the remnants, some thirty-six to forty-eight hours
after shutting off the burners, the crews could carefully begin working with water, hosing down the platforms around and above the

brick furnace. As more time passed, the crews became more relaxed, and it was not unusual for a foot or so of water to pool atop the crust, which was thought to help the cooling process.

Russell had just come on shift one otherwise ordinary summer day and was washing down an area directly in front of the furnace when the crust cracked. The blast of scalding steam knocked Russell off his feet, tossing him onto his back. Faceup and staring at the opening in the furnace, he was enveloped in the explosion.

Ten to twelve. Russell kept hearing doctors and nurses bandying about the numbers ten to twelve. It was the number of workers feared injured in the blast. It was also the number of months Russell was expected to remain in the burn ward at University of Alberta Hospital in Edmonton. Nineteen years old at the time, Russell was one of four men listed in critical condition. Two were badly burned, one with devastating injuries to his hands. Another friend inhaled the blast, torched his innards, and died within weeks. Lying in a hospital bed with excruciating second- and third-degree burns covering 65 percent of his body, Russell could not help but wonder whether that man was the lucky one.

Just ten weeks into his sentence, Russell was released from the burn ward. Youth and determination trumped laughter as the best medicine. Mercifully, his hands and face were spared, his bright smile unscathed. Following three weeks in a residential rehab facility and a month at home, Russell returned to university in Saskatoon. The accident that for no good reason did not cost Russell his life wound up costing him only one semester of school.

Upon his graduation from the University of Saskatchewan with a degree in civil engineering, Russell received a job offer from Vancouver-based BCG Engineering, a multinational firm specializing in applied earth sciences for the mining, transportation, and natural resource industries. In search of a career with a bit more pizzazz, Russell, a keen golfer, surfed the Web for *golf course architecture college*. The only program that popped up offered a master's degree through Edinburgh College of Art. So he went.

Russell was weeks shy of graduating from the two-year program when, in the spring of 2005, he spotted the bulletin board posting for a summer internship. He answered the ad, sending an e-mail that went to DMK HQ in Essex and was then forwarded to Kimber, who called Russell and invited him up to the site for a visit. "We are just past the caravan park," said Kimber. His wording was intentionally ambiguous, a tactic learned from Kidd, so that Kimber could judge whether Russell possessed the initiative to find the site. Russell borrowed a friend's car and drove up for the interview, which essentially consisted of a walk in the mud. Kimber offered him the job on the spot: two days a week until the end of the school term then full-time through the summer. Getting the job was easy. Getting *to* the job was the hard part.

Russell had no car, no place to stay, and no deep stash of cash. For the two months that school was still in session, twice a week, Russell would catch the 6:20 p.m. bus out of Edinburgh, arrive in St. Andrews around 8:30 p.m., and plunk down £15 for a bed at the youth hostel. The following morning he'd catch the 6:30 a.m. bus heading east, but because there was no bus stop anywhere near the site, Russell had to cajole the driver into dropping him off on the side of the Crail Road.

Anything DMK needed at No. 7, Russell did: laying out drains, checking grades on greens and fairways, laser-measuring yardages, inspecting irrigation, directing traffic for the respreading of topsoil. Not only did he do it all, he did it all well and willingly and in spite of being dog tired from grinding to finish his master's degree. Come quitting time, Russell would catch a lift to the bus station for the long ride back.

Kidd is big on initiative, and Russell made a huge impression on the boss. Here was a guy who was lucky to be alive and acted like it. He picked up and moved all the way to Scotland to pursue a master's degree in golf course architecture, hustled to land an internship, got to work on time, was always ready to go, and never bitched about what a pain in the arse it was just to get to work. Russell was worldly, fond of pints, young, and single. In sum, another perfect potential employee.

The nearly simultaneous hiring of Conor Walsh and Brad Russell was fortuitous for Kidd for reasons far beyond No. 7. In Walsh, Kidd saw an ambitious and willing talent that he hoped to groom and bring along from job to job to job. Russell was different. He wanted to design golf courses, and he seemed to want it badly. In Russell, Kidd saw more than a protégé. He saw a younger version of himself.

DMK satellite offices around St. Andrews: The New Inn, The Dunvegan, One Golf Place, The Clubhouse, The Central

The Band (left to right)—
Paul Kimber, Mick McShane,
Conor Walsh, and David Kidd.

Pictured at the DMK holiday party 2006,
the last time (ever?) they all played together.

Hole 11

• • •

Par-4
424 yards / 421 yards / 396 yards / 349 yards / 290 yards

The eleventh hole is not the longest par-4 on the course—but it is going to feel like it. The tee shot is a little bit uphill, and the approach is a lot uphill. Even the best players will likely be hitting driver off the tee and a long iron into the green.

We had a major problem constructing that green. The entire hillside is rotten rock, which crumbles nicely and drains brilliantly, so we cut into the seam and started using the rotten rock to build all the pathways around the golf course. Unfortunately, that happened to run under the middle of the eleventh green. We had it all ready for final construction when we noticed water leaking out the side of the green for no apparent reason.

The reason was we had cut into the seam beneath the green, so we had to scramble and do a total rework of the entire green to fortify it and make sure it drained properly. It was like putting Humpty Dumpty back together again. It took a couple of months, but we got it fixed. It was the kind of unpleasant surprise we inevitably encounter during the construction process, but golfers will never know the difference.

A draw will come in very handy on the approach to the eleventh green. Everything falls off to the right. If the supposed prevailing wind is in the golfer's face, a fade is going to end up short, ugly, and nowhere near the green. The good news is that the eleventh has a large green with a big backstop. Given that the hole plays pretty long as it is, we were keen not to punish players who go big. If a golfer has the gumption to take his biggest club and rip it, we felt he ought not be penalized for hitting it a bit long or with a touch of a draw, so the green really pitches up at the back.

When in doubt, air it out. Go a club or two clubs bigger here because the chances of it going through the green are next to nil.

—David McLay Kidd

12

In Reality . . .

Paul and I had a good meeting with Fraser Smart.
Fraser seems like a good chap, easy to get along with
and like-minded in terms of traditionalism with a contem-
porary twist.

DAVID MCLAY KIDD IN A LETTER TO ALAN MCGREGOR
November 28, 2002

Among the players the Links Trust brought to the party was Fraser Smart, the architect responsible for all the non-golf construction on the site, including the clubhouse, car park, maintenance yard, management offices, buggy storage, employee facilities, utilities, and so on. A native of Kinglassie, a small village in central Fife, Smart, fifty-nine, lives and works in Leven, fifteen miles south of St. Andrews, on the Firth of Forth. An alumnus of Duncan of Jordanstone College of Art and Design, part of the University of Dundee, Smart started out designing hospital and health care facilities before refocusing on residential projects when he hung out his shingle in 1984. In 1992 he earned a commission from the Links Trust to design the Golf Practice Center, a modest facility consisting of twelve covered hitting bays, six open-air bays, and a lounge. Smart subsequently took on a number of projects for the Links Trust: the caddie pavilion, the retail shop behind the eighteenth green of the Old Course, the new starter's box at the Old (after the previous one was auctioned off to a group of Yanks in 2001 for £60,000), the Eden greenkeeping facility, the Jubilee greenkeeping facility, the Eden Clubhouse, and Pilmour House.

Smart did not take up the game of golf until his involvement in No. 7 sparked his interest. He did not seek golf-related work so much as he happened upon it. Smart was used to a traditional structure, a separation of powers. Having the course designer serve as the general contractor was unusual, like having a player-coach. Only instead of executing plans from a playbook, this was seat-of-your-pants school-yard ball where the plays were drawn in the dirt, or in this case a sand-box. Strict interpretation gave way to intuitive improvisation. Kimber was an alarmingly efficient quarterback, but for Smart it was like switching gears from a grind-it-out running game to a run-and-shoot passing attack. Working from a blank slate was Smart's greatest challenge at No. 7. Everything would be conceived whole cloth, whereas prior to this commission Smart's work for the Links Trust consisted of fitting new pieces into an established puzzle. On the links, there already existed a look, a feel, a space and dimension. No. 7 was removed from the links not just physically but also metaphysically.

Smart seemed flustered from the get-go. The hiccups were chronic and often borderline calamitous. In late June 2005 the utility company was to bring power to the site, a critical requirement for nearly every facet and function of the operation, not the least of which was running the well and the high-pressure pumps that moved water across the entire golf course. Months in advance Kimber asked Smart what needed to be done prior to the utility company's arrival. Smart noted a couple of minor details, but nothing significant. Weeks in advance Kimber again asked Smart what needed to be done. Bits and bobs, but it was covered. Then on the Monday night before the weekly construction meeting held every Tuesday, Gordon Moir discovered a letter from the utility company, on which Smart was cc'd, that detailed a list of prep work, all of which was mandatory but none of which was done.

To call the silence at the weekly meeting uncomfortable would be to call the temperature of the North Sea brisk. They were now staring down a three-month delay. No power meant no pumps; no pumps, no water; no water, no seed; no seed, no grass; no grass, no golf. "You all got the letter," said Smart at the meeting. "I copied you." Indeed he had; however, the ball was in his court, and he sat on it. In less than a week crews yanked off other tasks, erected the requisite building, dug the necessary trenches, and saved Smart's bacon.

It became something of a game in the weekly meetings to chart how many times Smart began a sentence with his catch phrase qualifier, "In reality . . ." The record was fourteen. McShane was especially contemptuous of Smart and thought seriously about bulldozing Smart right off the edge of the braes the day he tried to take a shortcut across the first fairway. McShane had shaped the opening hole starting at the tees and was working up near the green when he spied Smart in his Land Rover Discovery coming around a mound of topsoil. There had been a road for trucks there until McShane blocked it off with big rocks to keep vehicles off his finished work. McShane motioned for Smart to go the long way around and use the main road to the clubhouse site. Smart turned tail, but instead of going back to the main road, he pulled behind the other side of the topsoil mound and tried to cut in front of the finished first tees. Livid, McShane blasted his horn and jumped out of the D5, waving his arms and screaming at Smart, "Any blind man with shite in his eyes can see that is a fairway and the road is over there!" Smart wisely backed out in reverse, like a golfer retracing his steps out of a bunker.

• • •

Peter Mason's business card was already squeezed for space. His trifecta of titles included external relations manager for the St. Andrews Links Trust, director of St. Andrews Links Golf Shops Ltd. (the retail division), and director of St. Andrews Links Ltd. (the licensing arm). In July 2005, at the age of sixty-three, Mason added the title of project manager, Course No. 7. Prior to joining the Links Trust in 1994, his résumé featured high-level public relations and marketing posts, though nothing related to managing the construction of a golf course. In this role Mason was ostensibly the Links Trust's point person in charge of the budget, media and public relations, and overall coordination and cooperation for Course No. 7. In truth, Mason was put on the job largely to keep Fraser Smart in line.

Smart is a good man and a fine architect; he simply had taken on a workload that proved more than he could carry. The Links Trust shouldered part of the responsibility for Smart being scattered, as they admittedly ought not have bestowed upon him the whole of Course No. 7 at the same time they had him designing an extension to the golf practice center that included the addition of a new golf academy. The size, scope, and services of the original facility, built in 1993, had tipped woefully out of balance with the advances in technology and demand, and so the Links Trust undertook a £750,000 upgrade. The new and improved practice center boasts a floodlit driving range with twenty-two covered bays and twenty-nine open bays, air-cushioned mats, choice Callaway balls, Power Tee automated ball teeing, and a short game area featuring putting, pitching, and chipping areas and multiple bunkers, including a replica of the infamous Road Hole Bunker. Housed within the practice center is the St. Andrews Links Golf Academy, home to three swing analysis studios and a separate custom club-fitting studio that utilizes New Age gizmos with space-age names like the Dartfish digital analysis system, which enables an instructor to analyze a golfer's swing on a computer and e-mail swing tips to the golfer anywhere in the world. The TrackMan ball flight monitor, employing a Doppler radar device originally developed to track missiles, tells golfers everything they wanted to know about their ball flight and then some, including height, speed, direction, spin rate, and smash rate. There is also a SAM PuttLab system that uses ultrasound scanning to check twenty-eight different parameters of the putting stroke that can go awry. After a visit to the golf academy, if it's still broke, you can't fix it.

Some of the problems Smart encountered at the practice center were unquestionably beyond his control, like the steel fabricator who was a month late delivering materials for the roof of the academy. Other issues fell squarely on the shoulders of the architect. The extension to the practice center and creation of an equipment testing center for the R&A were two separate projects, and Smart assumed that the contractor who won the bid to build the practice center extension would also build the adjoining test center. However, because the R&A controlled the building of the test center, they required that their project go out to competitive bid separately from the practice center extension. Smart had to go through the whole rigmarole all over again, and while the same contractor ultimately won both bids the process caused a delay, which in turn caused a delay in the process of Smart getting the Course No. 7 maintenance facilities out to bid. That project was key not simply to get Allan Patterson and his growing crew suitable digs, but also to avoid the doubling up of deliveries between Kidd's course and Smart's buildings. Fife Council's approval came contingent with a limited number of truck movements, a lesson learned the hard way with St. Andrews Bay. The Links Trust's plan called for the six-month facilities build to commence in autumn of 2005 and continue over the winter while golf course construction went on hiatus, so that the new maintenance compound would be complete when DMK returned in full force come spring of 2006. But when the usual suspects gathered on Tuesday, October 18, for the final weekly construction meeting of 2005, the maintenance facility had not gone out to bid.

Nor would it, not for a good long while.

• • •

From the trailer office on-site Kidd could see the putting green at the fourteenth hole. He did not need to peer out the window, however, for it was indelibly etched in his mind's eye. Were it paved instead of grassed, the fourteenth green would make one helluva skate park. The first golfing grounds visitors encountered, the green served as an eye-opening first impression of the radical augmentation practiced here, rather like parking Pamela Anderson in the lobby of her plastic surgeon's office. Kidd did not mind that golfers might stomp to the fifteenth tee cursing under their breath; his match play mentality liked the timing of the toughest green on No. 7 coming in the middle of the back nine (not unlike the match-swinging fifteenth green on the New Course). However, while the fourteenth green exemplified Kidd's dictum about cranking up the volume, it also threw his design/construction/maintenance/operation matrix out of whack because the sharp contours would be hard to mow.

"The finest movements of soil on a flat piece of land I have seen," said Jimmy Kidd upon his first visit to No. 7. The greenkeeper in him could not help but add, "The greens will be hard to putt but even harder to maintain."

Building a putting green is a painstaking exercise. The mold is shaped ten inches lower than the surroundings; then the drainage is installed and topped by four inches of gravel. Twelve inches of rootzone is spread on top of that and across the exact contour of the shaping. Rootzone consists of 90 percent sand and 10 percent peat and costs roughly £22 per ton, which adds up to £400,000, given an average of one thousand tons per green, times eighteen greens. Once the rootzone is spread, the laborious task of "dipping" begins, wherein the point of a steel rod is poked into the rootzone to ensure uniform depth of eleven-and-a-half to thirteen inches, so as to meet USGA specs, an accepted standard for nearly half a century. Dip, move a few inches, dip, move a few inches, dip, move a few inches, dip, and so it goes across the entire surface of the green. One of the crew typically took the first stabs at it before Kimber came in to double-check and sometimes triple-check areas where the grade changed significantly, because a low spot too near a high spot could render an entire section of a green unpinable. Dipping the gigantic, climactic double green shared by holes nine and eighteen took Kimber an excruciating eleven straight hours.

Prepping fairways for seeding is no walk in the park either. Once the topsoil is respread, workers canvass the fairways with machines called stone buriers, which punch stones deep into the soil. Smooth fairways would appear incongruous with the rough-hewn teeing grounds, aggressive bunkering, and malevolent greens, so quirks like ripples and crags and outcroppings were added. However, because these accents could not be effectively or efficiently created with a bulldozer blade or a digger bucket, sand was trucked in and added strategically—to the extent that the budget would allow. DMK's bespoke methods took time, which required money beyond the materials cost, and on a budget as tight at No. 7's the team constantly found itself teetering on a tightrope between everything they wanted to do and only those things they could do.

As a rule, the majority of golfers tend to miss short and right, which played right into the design at the seventeenth hole. Destined to become the most photographed hole on the course, the long par-3 plays over a crescent-shaped cove that looks into the center of town. Right is wet. Short left funnels down to the green, while long left leaves a confidence-killing second shot from a cavernous bunker or the nasty grassy mounds that surround it. McShane's first pass at shaping the green left Kimber questioning whether the back left corner was too severe. Kidd agreed it needed tweaking. McShane's second attempt worked for Kimber, and while Kidd gave Kimber the green light to go ahead and drain it, Kimber sensed that Kidd was not won over. Their dialogue became heated—Kidd's frustrations were less with the shaping than with Kimber's defensiveness—though it never reached a boiling point. McShane took a third crack at it, then stood with Kidd and Kimber as they judged the results. Kimber nodded his head approvingly.

"Doze it," said Kidd. "Start from scratch."

Kimber glared at Kidd, flummoxed.

"He's right," concurred McShane. "It's shite."

Kimber let fly an unprintable retort. Kidd and McShane high-fived and doubled over laughing. The only thing more perfect than the green was their gag to dupe Kimber and wind him into a twist.

With the seventeenth green set on the west side of the cove and the double green at eighteenth locked onto Kinkell Point, the design for the home hole called for a sharp dogleg right that hugged the braes. Ideally the architect would present a safe three-shot line and an aggressive two-shot option; however, golfers could not be allowed to cut the corner off the dogleg because of the walking path below, which sat in the line of fire for shots missed short and right. The solution for how to make golfers play the two legs of the triangle instead of blasting across the hypotenuse vexed Kidd and Kimber. They agreed that the landing area alongside the braes had to be so uninviting that no one dared tread there; however, in the absence of mature vegetation, a caddie, or local knowledge, golfers on the eighteenth tee might not grasp the inhospitableness and bomb away, which would surely result in slowing the pace of play. The essential visual intimidation came at the suggestion of McShane, who proposed dozing a vertical face into the landing area along the braes, a muckshift Green Monster like the thirty-seven-foot left field wall in Boston's Fenway Park. From the tees golfers would clearly see that the play is away from the braes and left of the barrier to a plateau. Local knowledge or a good caddie would tell golfers that a downslope on the backside of the plateau could add another fifty yards of roll to a well-struck drive.

By mid-July McShane had finished shaping the eighteenth hole. Rainfall since mid-June had totaled all of one inch, and the relatively cooperative weather allowed the crews to pick up the pace. Walsh was cranking on the bunkers at twelve and thirteen, Russell had taken on managing the drainage crews, and Kimber was making headway staking the front nine with his cut-and-fill flags (red flag means dig it out, blue flag means fill it in). Meanwhile, newcomer Ian Hamilton, whom the Links Trust brought on as project administrator, set about the critical task of organizing the office pool for the Open Championship.

Hole 12

• • •

Par-4
479 yards / 454 yards / 417 yards / 403 yards / 379 yards

The twelfth was one of the very first holes we built. We were finding our way, but the team was so gifted at making everything so seamless I guarantee there is not a person who could come in and order the sequence in which we built the golf holes.

Here is a hole where taking a caddie really pays off. The twelfth is another long, difficult par-4. From the tee golfers see a hole that bends to the left and bunkering that ought to be easy to fly. What they don't see is peril lurking on the other side. A good caddie will take his man the longer way, wide right but clear of the trouble.

Approaching the green from the left-hand side appears to be the shortest distance between the fairway and the flagstick; however, that is coming at it from completely the wrong direction. Hook the ball from there, and there is a good chance it will be lost in the gorse and tall grass. Slice it, and there is an excellent chance of winding up with a horrible chip shot.

Also, there is a bunker in the middle of the approach, some seventy yards short of the green. A lot of golfers may think it is not in play, but we think a lot of golfers will get overly ambitious with their approach and skull their second shot straight into that bunker.

Par is relative, especially at the twelfth hole, and even more especially for golfers playing a match. Mid- and high-handicappers would do well to aim for a safe bogey rather than flirt with disaster shooting for par.

The golfer who hits a halfway decent drive out to the right might want to pull a 3-wood and go for that green, but he'd be wise to take the 7-iron his caddie offers, get past that center bunker, and leave himself a chip. Maybe he gets lucky and makes a putt for par, but chances are that unless an opponent makes a sterling play, most golfers will escape unscathed with a bogey.

The eleventh and twelfth are going to feel like the hardest back-to-back holes out there. Any golfer that makes it through those two without dropping any shots is carding one helluva score.

—David McLay Kidd

13

Open Week

Every five years the circus that is the Open Championship returns to St. Andrews. The 2005 edition promised to be especially electric as Jack Nicklaus's rounds around the Old Course marked his farewell from tournament golf. Kidd agreed to act as tour guide for the journalists that the Links Trust planned to bring up to the site; however, Communications Manager Mike Woodcock's best efforts to fill the shuttle bus were mostly in vain, as all but a few scribes passed on the opportunity to view shifted muck at No. 7, in favor of Jack's swan song and the Tiger vs. Phil show. Since the press was not coming to him, Kidd went to the press, logging long hours hanging in and around the media tent.

Among those who did drop by the site during Open Week was a local environmental volunteer who arrived unannounced in the office and invoked his self-appointed right to monitor the tender loving care DMK was providing for the Maiden Pinks. Had McShane been in the office instead of on his dozer, he surely would have relished the opportunity to bellow, "You have no right!" at the bloke, who was escorted to the cordoned-off patch of flowers so he could see that no harm had been done before he was escorted right back to the security gate.

Another unexpected guest was Alan Barron, a retired schoolteacher who owns two, and lives in one, of the three cottages that sit just off the Crail Road at the southwest corner of the site boundary closest to the tees at the sixth hole. Flustered and a bit red in the face, Barron explained that he had lost something: the view of the sea that he'd enjoyed from his kitchen window for the past thirty years. Indeed, that morning the bulk earthworks crew had begun building the mounding that would enclose the putting green at the fifth hole so as to keep golfers' attention turned away from the road and toward the scenic blue waters beyond the braes. In the process Barron lost the sea and gained a mountain of dirt. Kidd was more conciliatory than Kimber, whose sole focus was what was best for his golf course. Barron conceded that he had no legal right to his view, but he hoped they might knock the mounding down to more of a molehill. Kidd explained that the crew was merely moving earth at the moment and that its current form did not represent the final shaping. Placated, the neighbor shook hands then toddled off.

Later that afternoon Kidd and Kimber drove out to check the progress at the fifth hole in the bucket-of-bolts Isuzu Trooper site vehicle that Kimber had picked up for the princely sum of £500. They watched a thirty-five-ton dump truck heap load upon load of earth atop the landform designed to conceal the Crail Road and the cottages from the golfers' view. If the golfers could not see the cottages, then the cottages could not see the golfers—or the sea. Kidd and Kimber could, however, see Barron pacing up and down his driveway as the heap outside his home grew larger and larger.

On Thursday night following the first round, Kidd and Kimber attended the Chairman's Dinner hosted by Links Trust top dog Alastair Dempster. It was a perfectly lovely soiree, immediately after which the two changed into more comfortable clothes and headed for the Gin House. A popular watering hole in the heart of town, the Gin House had been rented for the week by *Golf Punk*, the British lad mag known for splashy pictorials of scantily clad "Bunker Babes." The place was buzzing like a beehive. Kimber waltzed right through to the VIP section, while right behind him Kidd got the cold shoulder. As Kimber disappeared into the sea of debauchery, Kidd pleaded his case to the bouncer, who seemed bent on cutting off the number of Y chromosomes inside but ultimately relented and let Kidd slide. What happened in the Gin House stayed in the Gin House, but suffice it to say that the early morning wake-up calls that week were not made any easier by the late night carousing.

Kidd never turned in before three o'clock in the morning. One night, maybe Wednesday, could've been Saturday, in the wee hours outside the Dunvegan, or perhaps One Golf Place, Kidd struck up a conversation with an affable Yank who may or may not have introduced himself as *Sports Illustrated* magazine writer Gary Van Sickle. They tipped a pint and had a chat, and that was that until Van Sickle's story appeared. In part, it read:

> *What could be bigger in the Home of Golf than a new golf course? It's still early in the construction process. Only about eight holes are shaped. Nothing is grassed. That was supposed to happen later this year but heavy rains in June, followed by a dry spell and the heat wave that coincided with the Open Championship at the Old Course, has delayed the construction schedule.*
>
> *David McLay Kidd, the personable Scotsman who is designing No. 7, said that 2008 is a more realistic estimate of when the course will be grassed and ready for play.*

Kidd spoke the truth; however, that particular truth about the course not being ready to open in full until 2008 had not been officially cleared by the Links Trust press office. Peter Mason, the external relations manager, was none too pleased when Kidd's quote landed on his desk. Kidd did not view his act as seditious. There was no significant financial downside to a soft opening in 2007 followed by full play the following spring, no tournament that would have to be rescheduled, no frothing lather of anticipation among the townsfolk.

Mason paid Kidd a visit on-site to address his having spoken too freely about an issue that had not yet been agreed to by the Working Party, and Kidd apologized for speaking out of turn.

"We need to stay on message," reiterated Mason at the next construction meeting. "We need to watch what we say outside the pubs at one-thirty in the morning, and we need to present a consistent message announced at the proper time in the proper manner."

"That is fine," replied Kidd, "but that consistent message should be that the course will open for full play in 2008."

"Yes, yes," concurred Mason, "but we need to ease that message out to the locals."

"The same locals you referred to as 'loonies' in *Golf Digest?*"

In its Open Championship preview issue *Golf Digest* ran a story titled, "A Scalping at St. Andrews." The title alone set the tone for a five-page ripping of the Links Trust over the Keith Prowse *Old Course Experience* deal:

> *The animosity between some St. Andrews townspeople and the Links Trust senior management isn't helping matters. Many locals are suspicious of anybody connected with the Trust. . . . There is little love lost on the Links Trust side. Mason told* Golf Digest *last December that he considered many local critics "loonies."*

Mason did not call the faction of Links Trust critics "loonies." He called them "bampots," Scottish slang for "loonies." And despite Kidd's good-natured ribbing Mason maintained his insistence that a consistent message be approved by the Working Party before being communicated to the media.

The media storm that preceded the departure hearing had largely petered out once Fife Council granted approval, and construction on No. 7 began. Select journalists, industry insiders, and opinion leaders had been invited to tour the site, but the Links Trust did not encourage locals to go up to have a look at No. 7 for fear that untrained eyes might view the work in progress and make, or worse yet share, a premature and uninformed judgment. The ripple effect could be devastating, like a radio disc jockey hearing a song after only the drum track was laid down then lambasting the song to his listeners. Until all the layers were added and all the dots connected, it was nigh impossible for a layman to see the bigger picture. Only after grow-in had begun later that fall did the light go off for Alan McGregor: the germinating of the grass seed added the color and texture that at last allowed him to truly see what beforehand he'd merely been viewing.

"I've always taken care of you, Fredo."

"Taken care of me? You're my kid brother!
You take care of me?"

The Godfather: Part II

Jock McShane is the Scottish Fredo to Mick's Michael Corleone. Mick, one year younger, helped out Jock at every turn, getting him on the Megget Dam crew and later into golf course construction. Big brother made the scene during Open Week, having spent his recent past splitting time between Morocco, where he worked more off than on as a shaper, and Spain, where he was living off the kindness of a prostitute.

It is telling that Jock roots for Celtic and Mick for Rangers in Scottish football. More telling is the fact that Mick roots for Rangers *because* Jock roots for Celtic. Collectively known as the "Old Firm," Rangers and Celtic are one of the best and most bitter rivalries in all of sport. Since first squaring off on May 28, 1888, the two teams have dominated Scottish football, claiming sixty-three Scottish Cups and ninety-one League championships between them. This rivalry makes the Yankees and Red Sox look like Paris and Nicole. The enmity is complex, as it is rooted in religion and politics: Celtic have a historic relation to Catholics and Ireland, while Rangers have traditionally been associated with the Protestants of Scotland. Close quarters are also a contributing factor, as both teams hail from Glasgow, a city smaller than Baltimore, with Celtic from the east end and Rangers from southwest. The hostility is so ingrained and the passion so intense that lives have been lost due to violence sparked by Celtic vs. Rangers. There is even a Web site devoted to the mutual repulsion, rangersfansvcelticfans.com, which comes with the warning, "If you are easily offended, do not enter this site."

The McShane boys were no strangers to local law enforcement growing up. Most weekends saw the lads start out in separate pubs and end up sharing a cell in the Selkirk pokey. After a night of heavy drinking they would inevitably encounter each other at the chip shop looking for a late night snack. The brothers traded roles but the dialogue usually went something like:

"You think you're tough?"

"Tougher than you."

"Looks like someone's got a bellyful of brave juice."

"Let's go."

A street brawl would ensue, full-on fisticuffs, no punches pulled, no holds barred. Mick earned his fake teeth on the night Jock kicked his baby brother in the kisser with a Doc Marten boot. When they were hauled off to the police station, the desk sergeant would shake his head and sigh and then, without having to ask, pick up the phone and ring the British Legion Hall, where old man McShane was a fixture on bingo nights. If Dad was winning—and feeling charitable— the boys might make bail. More often than not they cooled their heels in the hoosegow, overnight if it was Friday, as they'd be sprung Saturday morning. Saturday night dustups meant two nights in the klink.

During his stay in St. Andrews, Jock asked Mick if he could stay on and help out at No. 7. Mick was understandably reluctant. He'd already stuck his neck out for Clint, but there was more work to be done than there were workers to do it, so any muck that Jock could shift while Kimber continued searching for reliable dozer drivers was gravy. Kimber turned Jock loose respreading topsoil, and he worked out well—for about two weeks, at which point Jock succumbed to a chronic medical condition: acute hypochondria brought on by comfort. It never failed; once Jock settled in to cozy digs and a steady gig, he started taking ill from work. First it was his pesky stomach, then his recurring gout. Jock had a good heart, metaphorically speaking, but he was not the picture of health, and his lack of dependability became a liability. Within six weeks Jock had moved on.

Kimber subsequently brought on a man named Graham Foster, who proved to be the ideal hire. All Kimber had to say was "There is the dozer, there is the topsoil, there is the hole, have at it." Have at it he did. Whereas Jock logged thirty-two loads between 7:00 A.M. and 6:00 P.M., Foster clocked the same amount by 4:00 P.M. even though he didn't get started until 10:00 A.M.

• • •

Kidd was home in Oregon the first weekend in August. His thick skin was wearing thin from the rash of criticism over his redesigned seventh hole at Gleneagles' PGA Centenary Course. The complaints came courtesy of a handful of European Tour pros at the resort to contest the 2005 Johnnie Walker Championship. In the field for the Wednesday pro-am was a gent steeped in local knowledge: Jimmy Kidd. His pro was Brett Rumford, a twenty-eight-year-old Australian who'd won a Euro Tour event in France as well as the 2004 Irish Open. Also in the group was Bevan Tattersall, a man who knew of what he spoke when it came to golf course conditioning. As golf courses manager at the Belfry in Sutton Coldfield, England, Tattersall prepared the Brabazon Course for the Ryder Cup in 2001 and again in 2002 after the former was postponed due to 9/11.

The conditions and the company were both perfectly pleasant. The amiable Aussie engaged his amateur playing partners, and the opening holes proved easy prey for Rumford. Then they came to the seventh hole. David Kidd had been hired by Gleneagles to toughen up the course for the 2014 Ryder Cup. The work would be done slowly but surely, and by the start of the 2005 Johnnie Walker event Kidd had completed remodeling holes four, six, seven, and eight. Most of the tweaks involved putting hazards back in play for today's— and tomorrow's—monster drivers; however, the seventh hole received an entirely new green on a natural plateau that transformed a previously innocuous straightforward par-4 into a vexing dogleg right.

True to his belief that par is a privilege and not a right, Kidd took what was an easy birdie hole and brought bogey firmly into play.

Just prior to the start of the Wednesday pro-am, Jimmy was stunned to learn of the decision by tournament organizers to rope off Nicklaus's old seventh hole and debut the new, adjacent seventh designed by David McLay Kidd. To Jimmy's mind the green was far too new, given that construction had taken place during the winter and grow-in over the spring. It was like moving into a house with wet paint on the walls. The green proved to be the least of Rumford's worries. Off the tee his drive failed to clear the corner of the dogleg, finding the bottom of a deep pot bunker.

"How bloody unfair is this bunker?" Rumford grumbled from the depths of his misery. "There is no way anyone can reach the green from this pit!" In fact, Rumford's ball found one of Jack Nicklaus's original bunkers, around which Kidd created the dogleg. Unaware whether Rumford was aware that his son was responsible for the Ryder Cup redesign, Jimmy held his tongue as he watched Rumford pop out sideways, his only play. Rumford continued to rail to his caddie, until Jimmy had heard quite enough.

"If your tee ball found the bunker faced by railway ties at the twelfth hole at Royal St. George's in the Open Championship, would you have said the same thing?" Jimmy questioned Rumford. "Or say your ball came to rest against the face in the Cardinals at Prestwick, or beside the stacked sod in the Road Hole Bunker, what then?"

"I expect," answered the Aussie, "to have a chance to make the green from a fairway bunker on any course."

Jimmy and Bevan Tattersall enjoyed a right laugh at this, which only served to reinforce Jimmy's belief that even journeyman pros today are spoiled prima donnas. Rumford seemed to Jimmy more than a bit aggrieved by the amateurs' jaundiced view of the pro's opinion, and the cheery mood turned suddenly chilly. Unfortunately that would not be the end of it, as Rumford struck his approach boldly at the pin, only to see it catch the contour that slides off the left side of the green. Under different circumstances Jimmy would have conceded that the pin position was indeed poor on a green that had only just grown in; however, Jimmy withheld his condolences as Rumford and his caddie blasted every element of the hole save for the tee markers. When they finally took a breath between spewing venom, Jimmy shared some perspective.

"It is most probably prudent that you be advised my son is responsible for the redesign of this golf course, including that last hole," Jimmy said in the clipped tongue he affects when his blood roils. "The concepts are to incorporate a strategic design that will test not just you in 2005, chum, but the very best golfers in the world in the Ryder Cup come 2014."

The group played the remainder of the round quietly, and Rumford opted neither to sit with his group for a post-round beer nor to join the championship banquet that evening. Rumford was by no means alone in his criticism, as former Scottish Ryder Cupper Andrew Coltart lodged a formal complaint with tournament organizers about the seventh hole. No doubt the cries of the pros contributed to the decision on Thursday morning to reroute the gallery ropes and revert to Nicklaus's old seventh hole for the tournament.

As the media fanned the flames of the brouhaha, Kidd sat and stirred in Oregon, wishing he was there to defend himself and his work but also knowing his quick tongue and acid wit would just make matters worse. Kidd's fear was that St. Andreans who were home watching the Johnnie Walker on the telly would get so hot and bothered over what was being unfairly painted as an unfair golf hole designed by David McLay Kidd that they would ring up the Links Trust and complain about the degree of difficulty at No. 7. Fortunately the cloud of controversy dissipated and no storm ever developed.

The sun continued to shine in St. Andrews, and work at No. 7 pressed on into August. Kimber took a much needed break, jaunting up to Aberdeen to visit friends for a weekend. He played the Balgownie Links at Royal Aberdeen Golf Club then took in a thrilling football match between Aberdeen and Rangers, with the home team notching its first league victory over Rangers in seven years by the slim margin of 3–2, after striker Jamie Smith buried a rocket from twenty-five yards out just two minutes before the end of regulation.

Relaxed, reenergized, and excited about a dinner date that Sunday night, Kimber sailed down the A90 back to St. Andrews. With a spring in his step he bounded up the stairs of 24 Hepburn Gardens.

A haze of cigarette smoke wafted about Mick, Jock, Clint, Clint's girlfriend Laura, and a mate whose name escaped Kimber as he gawked slack-jawed at the McShane family reunion organized by Jock, who'd made himself right at home after Kimber had hospitably allowed him to bunk in a spare bedroom. Few things irked Kimber more than cigarette smoke, but having his space invaded was definitely one of them. It wasn't the fact that they'd been drinking that peeved Kimber, it was the *amount* that they'd been drinking, combined with the insidious smoke that Kimber so detests. Early on Kimber learned that there was no talking to Mick when he was three sheets to the wind. Some people turn into happy drunks or angry drunks, but McShane turns into a bipolar drunk, combative one moment then cuddly the next. To his credit McShane's extracurricular activities never once interfered with his work or caused him to miss a shift. What he did on his time was his business, so long as he did it anywhere other than in Kimber's flat.

Kimber did not throw the lot of them out on their keesters; rather he made clear his distinct displeasure by seething. Also on the list of things Kimber eschews is confrontation. He does not run from it, but neither does he court it the way Kidd seems to.

Kidd enjoys pushing people's buttons to see what kind of reaction he might elicit. He has no time or use for shrinking violets, and he wastes little time sussing out the mousy. He has a superiority complex, though not as it relates to class or wealth or anything material, rather in terms of fortitude. Kidd encounters countless people who want to be in his shoes, but he's met precious few who might be able to match his drive, who have the will to do whatever it takes, who have the chops to walk the walk. Kidd is only too happy to enlighten the clueless. Playing Bandon Dunes once with a wealthy potential investor and his two college student sons, Kidd trod the length of the first fairway listening to one child of privilege prattle on about his grand plans of becoming a golf course architect backed by daddy's greenbacks.

With the father out of earshot, Kidd pulled the lad aside and chipped in his own two cents. He chided the brat. "You just want to swan about and play golf. If you were serious, you'd bin your Foot-Joys, buy yourself a pair of work boots, and get your arse in an ag class."

Likening them to martinis, Kidd is shaken and Kimber is stirred. It's the same drink, just a different style. Kimber's commitment is absolute, and his investment is so complete that criticism, sometimes even a mere difference of opinion, cuts Kimber deeply. That makes it hard on Kidd when it comes time to overrule Kimber (as Kidd suspected he might eventually have to do over the fourteenth green); however, Kimber has made it easy for Kidd to share the load. As Kidd likes to say, "I have absolute veto power, though on this project, thankfully, I rarely had to use it."

Kidd and Kimber's individual strengths balance out their respective weaknesses. Each knows and accepts his role. They bring different perspectives to a shared vision. Issues are confronted, not buried. They take time to make time. They talk a lot. They laugh a lot. They genuinely like each other and sincerely respect each other. Theirs is, professionally speaking, a happy marriage. Kidd has offered Kimber first pick of any job on the DMK docket, but to entertain speculation is to invite distraction, and Kimber abhors distraction above confrontation. When the time comes that No. 7 is at last lush and green and actually has a proper name, Kimber will have a decision to make. He may one day choose to spread his wings, but for his part Kidd aims to make the decision to leave the nest excruciatingly difficult for any of his employees. Professionally and personally, he wants them to feel the weight on their shoulders and the lump in their throats and the knot in their stomachs.

Kidd wants Kimber to stay, but he needs Kimber to want to stay.

Hole 13

• • •

Par-3
183 yards / 179 yards / 157 yards / 144 yards / 129 yards

From the summit of the thirteenth tees golfers get a panoramic view of the course and the sea. The Links Trust originally envisioned a pond in this section of the site, a bit lower than the thirteenth green. We were told it was to be used for irrigation storage. Operationally, it made sense. Environmentally, people liked the idea. Philosophically, I absolutely hated it.

Our goal was to re-create a landscape that might have existed centuries ago, back when Old Tom Morris tended to the Old Course or Kinkell Castle graced the braes. A body of water sitting on-site could not have been more unnatural. We weren't creating a style golf course that suited open water—other than the North Sea.

Fortunately the lake disappeared from the plans. So, too, did another uphill par-3 at the thirteenth. As with the tenth hole, we cut the thirteenth green way down and lifted the tees way up and created a hole that now plays downhill. Not a lot, but maybe six feet from tee to green.

This is a hole that requires concentration and courage because we've dressed it up with all manner of visual intimidation. Two big pot bunkers front the green, and there is a wicked bunker on the middle left, and then another short of that. There is more room at the front of that green than most golfers will think, at least their first time around. Most balls hit long will come to rest amid the spill-offs backing the green. From there it all depends on the lie, and there won't be many fun ones.

I will aim for the middle left on this green every time regardless of where the pin is. With the bunkers in front and the spill-offs through the back, trying to hang a ball out to a right-side pin placement is masochistic. Those are sucker pins. A golfer would have to be yard perfect to hit and hold a tee ball anywhere to the right, and I for one am just not good enough for that. I am happy to land one middle left, take my two putts, and move along.

Given the style of design we've picked, knowing how best to play any given hole is going to take a number of rounds—if not a number of years.

—David McLay Kidd

14

Buried Treasure

Tom Morris had the solution . . .
sand, and more sand,
and when you have done that
more sand, was what he pleaded for.

By spreading sand and keeping the surface open,
only the hardy grasses will survive and the
seaside turf will for long dominate the scene.
Nature's wheels may not move back, but their progress
may be slowed down by putting sand in them.

Professor R. J. D. Graham
The University, St. Andrews, "The Golf Links,"
The Scottish Journal of Agriculture, July 1938

The fact that No. 7 was built on dirt as opposed to sand was a good thing in that it largely spared Kidd the inevitable comparisons of his seaside course to the town's existing links layouts. On the other hand, the absence of sand hamstrung Kidd like a bartender trying to make margaritas without limes. Sand is the key ingredient for growing the kinds of tall, wispy fescue grasses Kidd envisioned lining the fairways and covering the craggy landforms. Sand allows fescues to grow unencumbered, whereas topsoil, such as that present at No. 7, contains seeds, which compete for nutrients and can choke out the fescues. Other than tons of clay mud and occasional patches of pain-in-the-arse sandstone found underground, the only surprise discovery to date at No. 7 was some rotten rock, which was used to fortify some key drainage areas and stockpiled for later use on foot and buggy paths. There was nothing, unfortunately, like that which was found at Kingsbarns.

During the Napoleonic battles of the early 1800s French prisoners of war held captive in the area are believed to have used thick tablets to cap an extensive network of cundies, or stone-lined channels. Earth was then piled high atop the tablets to create more farmable land, and that was that for two hundred years, until a digger excavating around the tenth tee at Kingsbarns discovered the maze of ancient waterways, which was unearthed and incorporated into the design. In addition to their visual impact and fascinating backstory, the cundies are memorably in play on a handful of holes, most notably between the sixth and sixteenth greens, originally intended to be a shared double green, and fronting the home hole.

There is a flip side to finding buried treasure, as evidenced by events at The Carrick at Loch Lomond. Located less than a half hour north of Glasgow, the original plan called for an Englishman to develop an exclusive private golf course on the bonnie banks of the scenic loch, then add a resort course and a hotel. That went awry, and American developer Lyle Anderson stepped in and saw to the completion of the private Tom Weiskopf/Jay Morrish–designed Loch Lomond Golf Club, which opened in 1994 and since 1996 has hosted the Scottish Open, considered by many to be Britain's second most prestigious golf tournament after The Open. Anderson later sold his other interests to DeVere Hotels, which operates Cameron House, an eighteenth-century baronial mansion turned luxury hotel that overlooks the loch. DeVere subsequently commissioned Canadian Doug Carrick to design a parkland course for the resort just down the road from Anderson's private club.

Construction at The Carrick course began in the spring of 2004 and experienced only the usual hiccups until the day in July 2005 when crews working in the ninth fairway unearthed a single glass bead. Following protocol, the Glasgow University Archaeological Research Division was alerted, and before long the West of Scotland Archaeology Service and Loch Lomond National Park Authority were on the case. Painstaking excavations ensued and confirmed that significant archaeological remains existed right smack in the middle of the golf course.

Researchers eventually uncovered a blacksmith's iron smelting workshop, as well as multiple, sizeable ruins believed to be relics of Iron Age hut circles dating from the second millennium B.C. to the first millennium A.D. Four thousand-year-old Bronze Age urn burials, possibly Viking or Norse, shed light on prehistoric funerary practices that saw cremated remains placed in pots and buried in pits upside down. Had the golf course developers been allowed to keep any of the artifacts, they might have considered selling them on eBay to recoup their losses: related delays pushed the project back fifteen months, and the original £47,000 budgeted for archaeology ballooned to a staggering £1.3 million.

Kimber was well aware of the costly travails at Loch Lomond. Kimber was well aware of everything, despite appearances to the contrary. His desk at DMK headquarters looked to have been turned upside down and inside out by someone who became increasingly frustrated looking long and hard for something he could not find. Kimber's coworkers knew better than to burrow through the haystack of papers and cords and mail and hats and catalogs and this and that and the other things. Yet if Kidd were to ask Kimber for, say, last April's construction budget meeting minutes, Kimber could produce them in seconds, pulling them seemingly out of thin air. What is more, he could probably ballpark any item on the spreadsheet within 10 percent off the top of his head.

Kimber was also well aware that there was no line item in the No. 7 budget for archaeology, so when he was told that his crew had found something underneath the car park, Kimber's mind immediately flashed to a passage in the *Archaeological Assessment* commissioned by the Links Trust:

> *The area of Kinkell has long associations with St.*
> *Andrews. . . . Standing on the brae above Kinkell Harbour*
> *there was a castle, chapel, and dovecot of the middle ages.*
> *Records show that by the 18th century it was in a ruinous*
> *state and in 1883 the remains were still there. . . . Today no*
> *remains can be seen, however earthworks and the building*
> *of the clubhouse and car park may reveal remains of founda-*
> *tions and associated structures.*

"Please don't let it be Kinkell Castle," Kimber mumbled under his breath as he pulled on his neon reflective vest and hard hat. The havoc caused at The Carrick by the discovery of one tiny glass bead was bad, but that was nothing compared to the horror stories Kimber heard while building Nanea, about how questions over ancestral burial grounds contributed to a five-year legal battle at Hokuli'a, Lyle Anderson's super-swanky golf community, also on the Big Island, which managed to survive a frighteningly costly court-ordered shutdown of development *after* the Jack Nicklaus Signature Course was finished, 190 home sites were sold, and $350 million was invested in the project. Now Kimber's mind flashed to a disturbing image of the top of a turret lying exposed in the car park. What if this were just the tip of the proverbial iceberg?

• • •

With his client happy, his crew having gelled, his vision for the shaping crystallized, and his second-in-command firmly and confidently in charge, Kidd enjoyed peace of mind and increasing freedom to focus on other matters, most notably new business. The only other DMK project under construction at that time was a private course called Stonebrae in the San Francisco Bay Area, where senior design associate Tom Cushnahan and lead shaper/general contractor Jim Haley were cast in the roles Kimber and McShane played in the St. Andrews production. Kidd took seriously the responsibility of keeping his employees employed, and questions loomed over what Kimber, McShane, Walsh, and Russell would do over the coming winter. Plus, the St. Andrews commission had, as hoped, generated serious buzz for DMK. Kidd's BlackBerry rattled and hummed with incessant requests to please come and see for yourself the natural beauty and magnificent site ideally suited for a golf course in/on the desert/mountains/island/lake/coast. *P.S. LOVE Bandon Dunes!*

In addition to the PGA Centenary Course redesign at Gleneagles in advance of the 2014 Ryder Cup, Kidd, along with Kyle Phillips of Kingsbarns, was a finalist for Gleneagles West, an amenity at a planned playground for the superrich adjacent to the resort, where homes are expected to fetch upward of £5 million. Kidd had also inked a deal to design a course and take first pick of the home sites at Tetherow, a new resort community in central Oregon near Bend, where he and Jill planned to relocate from Bandon. He'd verbally committed to create a Scottish links course in the dunes at Macrahanish Bay, pending funding that was just days away for over a year, and he'd made similar promises to projects in Lake Tahoe and San Diego. Kidd had accepted an invitation to meet with Donald Trump's golf handlers regarding the eponymous opulence that one day may be Trump International Golf Links near Aberdeen, should The Donald's grand plans pass muster with the imperious Scottish Natural Heritage.

Every time Kidd's phone rang or his BlackBerry chimed, it could be opportunity knocking. One day in the summer of 2005 the associate of a reclusive billionaire came calling. It seemed the associate's employer had bought a private island in Fiji, and he was keen to have his own private golf course. Kidd accepted the invitation to have a look-see; however, the remote location made the prospect prohibitive. Getting there required an eleven-hour nonstop flight from Los Angeles to Nadi that arrived at 3:00 A.M., a quick catnap at the nearby Mocambo Hotel, an 8:00 A.M. puddle jumper to Taveuni, which made a brief stop in Savusavu, followed by a forty-five-minute bilechurning boat ride in a rowboat fitted with an outboard motor.

Kidd walked the lush jungle site, after which he suggested in all honesty that the owner could save a bundle of money and still have a great golf course with nine holes and multiple tee boxes. It was a reasonable option, especially considering that the owner of the island did not play golf and the course was strictly for his friends. He wanted eighteen holes, and he wanted to know what it would cost to have David McLay Kidd design it. Kidd aimed high, half-hoping the billionaire would say no so that Kidd could focus his efforts closer to home.

The billionaire said yes.

• • •

There was no castle in the car park. There was no rainbow either, but what the crew found might as well have been a pot of gold as far as Kimber was concerned: sand. Not as valuable on the open market as bullion, but the discovery of a juicy underground vein of sand that would ultimately yield some ten thousand tons instantly changed both the complexion and the complexity of the course. Mining, sifting, and stockpiling it would impact both the budget and the schedule, but it was well worth it, given the plethora of possible applications. Adding sand to the landforms insured the growth of healthy fescues that, while wild and wooly, would allow golfers a better than average chance of not only finding their ball but potentially getting a club on it. The sand added layers of intricacy and levels of detail that could not be achieved with topsoil alone. Perhaps most importantly, the discovery of sand meant more widespread usage of the bump-and-run.

The most potent and necessary weapon in links golf would have been rendered all but obsolete at No. 7 due to the fact that the fairways were made of topsoil, an organic matter that gets spongy and soft when wet. Putting greens, on the other hand, are built with rootzone, which is 90 percent sand. In the absence of this sort of transition between the fairway and the green, the traditional bump-and-run shot is likely to hit and stick instead of hit and roll. However, from the outset DMK intended to create that transition by dressing the approaches with rootzone, and this newfound trove of sand would only aid in the cause of ensuring that golfers who know and favor the bump-and-run would have the option of employing it at No. 7.

First there would have to be actual grass, and on August 27, 2005, the first seed was spread on the green at the twelfth hole, seven-and-a-half years after the seed of the idea for a seventh course was first planted. The timing came two weeks later than Allan Patterson had hoped, for he had learned from Jimmy Kidd at Gleneagles that the ideal days for seeding in Scotland are the two weeks beginning August 15, give or take a day. Planting a seed in the ground is no different than planting one in a womb. There exists an optimal time frame when conditions are most receptive, and in the case of a golf course this occurs when ground temperatures are at their highest and there is a reasonable expectation that for at least six weeks after seeding there will be no ground frost to hamper germination. Also, most seed mixes in the UK include some fescue, which, once germinated, must "tiller," or sprout at least three leaves per seed, in order to survive the winter. As such, Jimmy is adamant that he will flatly refuse to seed in Scotland before May 15 or after September 15 unless the client guarantees they will cover the cost to overseed again the following spring.

A key factor in the equation at No. 7 was the wind, which made life miserable for the grounds crew as they struggled not only to keep sprinkler water hitting its intended targets, but also to keep the seed that was not watered down from blowing away. On that first day of seeding, Patterson sloshed back into the trailer with his rain gear and boots so thoroughly soaked that he'd have been better off wearing a wet suit and flippers.

Hole 14

• • •

Par-4
414 yards / 403 yards / 383 yards / 347 yards / 318 yards

One of the few landforms we inherited on the otherwise flat site was a large mound at the fourteenth hole created ages ago when a previous owner mined the rotten rock. When we came across that mound, it was all gnarled up and covered in gorse and whin bushes. We recognized a striking similarity between the braes and that landform, and that crystallized our vision to stretch that look across the entire 220 acres.

We talked about taking the fairway wide left of the mound and paralleling the Crail Road, but ultimately we agreed that bringing the road into the picture introduced reality and shattered the facade. It also brought into play the prospect of shattered windshields on passing autos.

The fourteenth hole was the first place we started to play with the spill-offs in a big way, pushing them into the fairways and tight up against the greens. Thankfully this revelation came very early on in the project—the fourteenth was the third hole we built. Whereas Kingsbarns has wild shaping in the rough and gently rippling fairways, we wanted to do just the opposite. We put our defenders in the field of play, not on the sidelines.

It was perfectly unpolished. Immediately, we all loved it. Mick's shaping looked different and wild and fantastic, but most of all it looked natural. It was exquisitely anti-Orlando.

By adding one of these spill-offs pretty much right in the line of play between the landing area and the putting green, we managed to take a fairway that could have been relatively uninteresting and add real strategy to it. Now a golfer may hit what appears to be a spot-on drive, only to walk up and find a blind second into the green. The better play off the tee is to get inside right of that landform where there is a clear sight line into the green. However, a ball that skips through the green from the right is wet, as a burn wraps around the left of the approach and behind the backside of the green.

I locked horns with Paul and Mick over this one, but it achieves our objective of catapulting golfers toward a memorable finish. Many a match will take a dramatic twist at the fourteenth green. It is an adventure that cannot be described; it must be experienced.

—David McLay Kidd

15

Icarus

Jill Kidd is an Oregon girl. Born and raised on the coast in Coos Bay, she was a star sprinter at Marshfield High School. For the past three years her running has been confined largely to chasing after Ailsa, an angelic toddler who has her mother's flaxen locks and crystal blue eyes. Angelic, that is, until she does not get her way. In addition to her irresistibly pinchable cheeks, Ailsa inherited her daddy's stubborn streak.

In the entryway of their home in Essex hangs a framed picture taken on February 15, 2003, the day David and Jill were married on Hawaii. He looks crossculturally dashing in a kilt and lei, while she radiates the kind of mesmerizing glow that gets other guys at a wedding elbowed in the ribs by their dates for staring too long. Jill got plenty of stares—and phone numbers and propositions—as a bartender at Bandon Dunes; however, having recently extricated herself from a failed marriage in Florida, she was looking to simplify her life, not complicate it. Perhaps that is why the guy who paid her no attention is the one who caught Jill's eye.

It was not that Kidd had not noticed her. He was, after all, human. It was more that Kidd already carried heavy enough baggage. Alone, far from his home, family, and friends, leaking confidence, and enduring long-distance divorce proceedings, Kidd's cup runneth empty. He was content to sit back, sip his gin and tonics, and enjoy the show as Jill swatted guy after guy after guy like flies with no wings. The harder they tried, the less chance they had. Kidd took a different tack. He ignored her. He did not talk to the pretty bartender, not a word for months other than "Gin and tonic, please" and "Thank you," not even after she'd make his cocktails extra stiff in an effort to loosen his lips. Then one night he broke the ice.

"I'll have the meat loaf, please" was Kidd's opening line.

"You don't look like a meat loaf kinda guy" was Jill's comeback.

She recommended the steak, and he bit. Soon after, the two connected at a party at a mutual friend's house and wound up talking into the wee hours. She asked him out on their official first date: her mother's sixtieth birthday bash.

Kidd was taken by Jill's bright, easy smile, her infectious laugh, her love of the outdoors, and her willingness to try new things, like travel. Jill had never been out of the country, and in fact had to expedite her application for her first passport when Kidd asked her to join him on a trip to the UK. Six months later she returned home after circling the globe with Kidd. For her part, Jill was smitten by his lust for life, his spontaneity, his passion for his work, and his accent. It was, she told her mother, like dating 007.

The wedding picture in the Essex entryway is a reminder of an easier time, back when Kidd's travel schedule was merely crazy and not totally insane, when Jill could walk onto an airplane with just a carry-on, instead of packing the stroller and the car seat and the mountain of cumbersome accoutrements that come with parenthood. Kidd helped out with the heavy lifting in the summer of 2005 when, using his hoard of Virgin Atlantic frequent flyer miles, he flew his wife and baby daughter over to the UK for a planned three- to six-month stay. Between busy Miss Ailsa and the renovation and redecoration of the house, Jill was not lacking for things to do; still Essex was a long ways from Oregon. The village of Tiptree where they lived was small and sleepy, not entirely unlike Coos Bay, only without Jill's mother and brother and friends, the *Oregonian* newspaper, *People* magazine, Safeway, Starbucks, and her daily dose of *The Young and the Restless*.

Essex felt especially otherworldly when Jill was alone with Ailsa and her husband was away. Kidd's trips to St. Andrews weren't so bad, as he'd be gone just a few days and they could talk anytime, given that they were in the same time zone. Toward the end of August 2005 Kidd made a grueling trip that took him from London nonstop to Los Angeles nonstop to Fiji for three days then back to L.A. for a connection up to San Francisco and a day trip to the Stonebrae site before shuttling back to LAX and catching an overnight flight home. The detour to Stonebrae had massive financial implications, as only after Kidd had reviewed and approved the seeding of the initial hole did a clause kick in that allowed the developer to begin selling home sites.

On August 26, 2005, the first seed was spread on Stonebrae's third hole, one day before seeding began at Course No. 7. Taking in the view of the San Francisco Bay, Kidd's mind drifted to St. Andrews Bay. He felt fortunate. He felt thankful. He felt unworthy. What had he done right? What good karma had he engendered?

Why me?

Why not me!

Kidd's cell phone rang, rousting him back to reality. Perhaps it was opportunity knocking once again, he thought. Maybe another billionaire in need of a golf course?

It was Jill.

•   •   •

When the Kidds were away, Jill's brother Bob would keep an eye on things. He'd swing by the house, bring in the newspaper, collect the mail, turn off some lights and turn on others, put out the garbage cans, maybe grab one of Kidd's spare drivers and a couple of range balls from the tub in the garage and tee it up near the stone yardage marker Kidd sunk in his front lawn. On warm summer nights when Kidd was home, the brothers-in-law liked to knock back a few beers, fire up a couple cigars, and pound range balls deep into the adjoining canyon, where an old salmon eagle liked to perch on a snag atop a Douglas fir tree. Never once had either succeeded in making the bird so much as flinch.

In that summer of 2005, Jill arrived from Oregon in Essex to find a notice in the mail from her doctor in England stating that she was overdue for her routine exams. As she had just been to her ob-gyn in Oregon before leaving for the UK, Jill called the doctor's office in Essex and asked if she could have the doctor in Oregon fax over her recent results. No problem—until she called Oregon.

The receptionist back home sounded curiously anxious as she told Jill that the doctor had been trying to reach her. He had left messages for Jill at home and on her cell phone and even gone so far as to send a letter to the house asking her to please call the office. Jill explained that she had not checked messages since arriving in England. The receptionist took down the phone number for the house in Essex and said she would have the doctor call Jill right back. Odd.

The moment she hung up with the doctor's office in Oregon, Jill immediately called Kidd at Stonebrae.

"Dr. Carlson is going to call you in England?" Kidd asked his wife quizzically.

"Something is not right," Jill sighed.

"I know he is a keen golfer, but I don't suppose he's calling to arrange a tee time," said Kidd, hoping to inject a little levity.

Jill's call waiting beeped.

"That's him," she said.

"Call me as soon . . . ," he shouted over Jill's voice before she clicked and was gone, ". . . as you know."

The most excruciating wait Kidd had ever endured came when he was working on the redesign of the Montagu Course at the Fancourt resort on the south coast of South Africa and Jill went into labor with Ailsa in Oregon six weeks early. The aggregate flying time from George to Johannesburg to London to San Francisco to Portland to North Bend is over twenty-six hours. Tack on the time spent in lines, layovers, security checkpoints, customs, taxi, and takeoff, and the actual travel time is probably double that. When Kidd finally arrived at North Bend Medical Center, he was knackered, stinky, bleary-eyed, and too late to witness the delivery. That hurt, but that ordeal seemed a cakewalk compared to what Kidd endured waiting for Jill to call back.

In the famous sixteenth-century painting *Landscape with the Fall of Icarus,* Flemish artist Pieter Brueghel the Elder depicts the scene surrounding Greek mythology's Icarus as he crashes back to Earth only moments after having flown so high he felt he could touch the sun. Alas, the heat melted the wax that held together his homemade wings, and as Icarus nosedives, a farmer, a shepherd, and a fisherman all go on about their business unwittingly (pessimists say indifferently). The scene at Stonebrae's third hole bore a striking resemblance to Brueghel's tableau: one moment Kidd was soaring and the next he was spiraling out of control, while around him everybody went about their business. Life marched on, but for Kidd, as for Icarus, time stopped.

A half hour later Kidd's phone finally rang. He could barely make out the syllables between Jill's heaving sobs.

"*Ag . . . gres . . . sive can . . . cer*" was all she could eke out.

Kidd felt numb. He felt helpless. He felt sick to his stomach. What could Jill have done wrong, what bad karma could such a sweet soul have possibly engendered?

Why Jill?

Why not Jill? Cancer knows no charity. It does not play favorites. It is the malevolent dictator that picks on people indiscriminately. Eeny, Meeny, Miney, Mo, You, Get, *It.* Kidd could not bear the thought of Jill being there, in a foreign country, alone except for a two-year-old baby, with no one to talk to, no shoulder to cry on, no husband or mother or brother or friend to hold, and no flights home until the following day.

Kidd wallowed for all of about a minute before springing into action. He called Virgin Atlantic, which responded brilliantly, waiving the usual blackout restrictions so that he could cash in seventy-two thousand frequent flyer miles for two Upper Class tickets for Jill and Ailsa on the 11:00 A.M. flight from Heathrow to San Francisco the next morning. Next he called the car service DMK Golf Design uses and arranged for a driver to pick up Jill and Ailsa at the house, take them to the office, where Kidd had their passports, then deliver them to the airport. Kidd then called Alaska Airlines to book passage for the three of them from San Francisco through Portland to North Bend.

Ailsa was asleep and Jill was collected when Kidd called with the details for their trip. He instructed Jill on how to turn off the alarm at the office and pinpointed the location of the passports in his desk drawer. Trying his best to sound like he believed it himself, Kidd reassured Jill that everything was going to be fine. He told his wife to get some rest, gave her a long-distance kiss good night, and whispered, "I love you." Then Kidd hung up and immediately dialed a well-connected friend and member at Nanea, Sara Duryea, who lived across the bay from Stonebrae, in San Francisco. If needed, Duryea pledged to get Jill to the very best doctors at Stanford Hospital straightaway.

Kidd told himself there was nothing more he could do, but it turned out there was. Jill needed space and comfort, not a protracted shuffle from San Francisco to Portland then Portland to North Bend. There would likely be locals on the puddle jump to North Bend that he and Jill knew. She would be in no mood to talk, but she would not want to be rude. If Jill did talk, she would likely get upset, and then she would have to explain why, but then she did not want people talking about her condition, at least until Jill knew herself what her condition was. Kidd knew his wife would be exhausted, emotional, and fragile, and all he wanted to do was get her home peacefully, quietly, and quickly.

The proliferation of private air travel and fractional jets had afforded Kidd increasing opportunities to avoid commercial flights. His dance card had become so full that he found himself having to turn down projects sight unseen simply because he physically could not get to some sites to have a look in any reasonable time frame. One option was for prospective clients with private planes to fly Kidd in, tour him round their site, then fly him back. Kidd was bold, but he was not gauche. He did not demand this, but if he could not get to a site reasonably on a commercial flight, he would explain that quite honestly. If a client with the will and the wherewithal wanted to solve the problem by sending a private plane, then it was probably money well spent.

Kidd called information and got the number for a charter service based at North Bend Airport. He could charter a plane to pick them up at SFO and bring them back for $5,000, which Kidd deemed bearably reasonable—until the agent just happened to mention that the plane doubled as a medical transport and sported big red crosses on the wings and the tail. Wanting the private plane to be a *pleasant* surprise for Jill, Kidd asked what else they had. A ride in a sleek, cozy Lear 35 was precisely what Kidd envisioned. The $7,500 bill was not.

"Here's a chance for you to do something meaningful with the money you've made," counseled Jimmy. Kidd had a hard time pulling the trigger on any major purchase without first consulting his father. This, felt Jimmy, was a no-brainer. Kidd wholeheartedly agreed, but he harbored an underlying fear that Jill might have an equally opposite reaction, viewing his chartering a private plane for her as an unnecessary extravagance.

•   •   •

Kidd's first thought the following morning was that he hoped Ailsa was being good for Jill on the airplane. Their flight left at 11:00 a.m., so the baby would be wide awake, unlike Jill, Kidd suspected. He'd had a fitful night's sleep, and he imagined Jill's had to have been even worse.

The plane was due into SFO at 1:50 p.m. Jim Haley, the lead shaper at Stonebrae, drove Kidd from the job site across the Hayward Bridge and up the Bayshore Freeway, arriving at the airport well in advance of the flight. While Haley circled the terminal, Kidd sat on the edge of a seat near the flight status display in the international arrivals hall. At last.

Virgin Atlantic VS019	*On Time*	**ARRIVED**

Kidd hurried to the very front of the greeting area, an arena in which the spectrum of human emotion is on display every day: the glee of lovers reuniting, the grief of relatives gathering to pay their last respects, the trepidation of transplants in a new environment, the self-absorption of chatterboxes who blather into their cell phones oblivious to their invasion of others' privacy, the pie-eyed wonder of a child who has never seen anything quite like it all. Bobbing and weaving like a boxer, Kidd struggled to catch a glimpse of Jill or Ailsa through the river of people clearing customs.

A half hour passed. Kidd tried Jill's cell phone, but it went straight into voice mail. Forty-five minutes. The flow from customs slowed to a trickle. An hour. Haley called from the car as he made loop after loop around the airport. One hour and ten minutes. Kidd could not fathom where they could be. One hour twenty. Had she missed her flight? She would have called. Had something gone wrong in the night? On the plane? Kidd caught himself straining to hear ambulance sirens, when his cell phone rang.

"Hi," said Jill, perfectly calmly. "Where are you?"

"I'm at international arrivals outside customs," replied Kidd, a little less calmly, "wondering what's happened to *you*!"

"We cleared customs then took the walkway over here to Alaska Airlines."

Kidd grimaced. He'd completely spaced that connecting passengers do not exit all the way out into the arrivals hall, but rather follow internal passages to the domestic terminals. Kidd hung up and started running—no easy jaunt for a slightly overweight, out-of-shape bloke wearing work boots. As he pounded the pavement, Kidd kept telling himself, *I cannot cry, I cannot cry, I cannot cry.* His eyes were not entirely dry when he finally spotted Jill. Wrapping his arms around his best girls, Kidd felt all his pent-up dread drain away.

"I have a surprise for you two," he said, as he led his wife and daughter out of the terminal to the car where Haley was waiting.

Kidd had guessed right. Chartering the Lear 35 turned out to be money incredibly well spent. Following a peaceful, quiet, and quick flight up to North Bend, Jill took a long, hot shower and pulled on her coziest sweats. Jill's mother played with Ailsa, while her brother cracked open a couple of ice-cold beers. He passed one to Kidd, who tended to the thick, sizzling steaks on the barbecue. Stepping away, Kidd ducked into the garage and emerged moments later with one of his spare drivers and a handful of range balls. Teeing it up on his front lawn, Kidd reared back and uncorked two days of raw emotion. The old salmon eagle perched atop the tree did not so much as flinch as Kidd's ball sailed high over its head.

——Original Message——
From: David McLay Kidd
Sent: Monday, August 29, 2005
To: Brad R Russell; Elaine Alabaster; Paul C Kimber; Tom A Cushnahan
Subject: Change of plans

Dear All,

Just to let you all know I got back from Fiji to San Francisco when I got a call from Jill, she has been diagnosed with a potentially serious cancer so I immediately arranged for her and Ailsa to return from the UK to Oregon where we all are now.

She has some further tests this week to establish exactly what is wrong so until further notice I'm AWOL.

I am sure you all understand what my priorities need to be at the moment. I am tentatively holding tickets to return on September 3, but it depends on events this week.

Hole 15

• • •

Par-5
610 yards / 592 yards / 559 yards / 525 yards / 468 yards

Paul had drawn inspiration from an Alister MacKenzie drawing of the Elysian Fields between The Beardies and Hell Bunker on the fourteenth hole at the Old Course. He suggested the idea of doing something with a split fairway, and my feeling, having dabbled with design elements like that before, was that we had to be especially mindful of what we did with that bit in the middle.

My caveat was that the separation feature contouring, not deep rough. We could really piss the golfers off if they hit drives to the middle of the fairway only to lose their ball.

What Paul came up with was a tight line down the left-hand side, a very narrow landing strip that to my eye looks to be no more than twenty yards wide. The potential payoff is a shorter, better line into the green, but if I were standing on that tee on the top of that hill with my driver in my hand, I would have to be way up or way down in my match to go for it. Under normal conditions and circumstances, the only way I hit that left fairway is if I yank my drive off the tee. Most golfers, myself included, will take the safer three-shot route to the right.

The burn in front of the green is Conor's handiwork. That was the first streambed he had done on his own, start to finish, without direction, and it is absolutely amazing. The way he placed the rocks and the shapes he made, it is such a gorgeous composition. I want to take a photograph of that brook when the water is running and frame it.

In addition to a split fairway, another thing Paul and I talked about was a plateau green. A number of the putting surfaces on the course sit in a bowl or are surrounded by shapes that feed onto the green, so we saw a chance at the fifteenth to build something in the shape of an upturned saucer, Pinehurst-style.

Go big anywhere around that green and the ball will fall off. Play to the area before the burn, where most golfers will hit a low iron for their third shot, and the fairway pitches right to left, a natural hook stance, which should help draw the ball into the green. Nothing to it.

—David McLay Kidd

16

Batten Down the Hatches

Kidd did not return to St. Andrews on September 3. Instead, he was with Jill in Eugene at the office of Dr. Deborah Dotters, one of the most respected gynecological oncologists on the West Coast. A routine test performed by Jill's ob-gyn in Coos Bay before she left for the UK had come back with red flags. Upon her hasty return, subsequent tests performed by a local pathologist showed questionable cells that appeared to be cancerous. The opinion they received in Coos Bay for a total hysterectomy seemed radical, if not premature, so Kidd pressed to get Jill referred to Dr. Dotters, who ordered yet another battery of invasive, scary tests.

Staying in Oregon meant missing the bash Kidd and Kimber were to cohost for the crew at No. 7. Typically they would have thrown a cast party sooner so as to get the different players—shapers, drainage guys, irrigation crew, muck shifters, greenkeepers—acquainted; however, timing, weather, and circumstances had conspired against such a gathering until early September. With the ice long since broken and the crew getting on swimmingly, everyone got down to the business of getting very drunk. McShane was in an especially celebratory mood, having just finished shaping the green at the first hole earlier that day. He did not laugh when Kimber jokingly pointed toward the freshly minted green and asked whose car was parked on it, though McShane did find humor in the garish clown cake some of the lads brought as a belated birthday gift. The biggest cake in the display case at the Morrison's grocery store, the cherry-cheeked clown with the blond frosting curls did bear a curious resemblance to McShane.

As Kimber grilled burgers on a portable grill set up on the pad of the car park, the partygoers teed it up in the dirt and took their whacks in a closest-to-the-pin contest to the double green at the ninth and eighteenth. Drinking and driving did not mix well. Most of the shots were atrocious, while the others were downright dangerous. No one remembers who won. Clambering up onto the hood of his site vehicle, Kimber quieted the crowd and made a sincere, if slurred, toast. "Thanks to each and every one of you, this is going to be a phenomenal golf course," he said, "enjoyed by many, hopefully for centuries." Kimber raised his bottle high. "Our names won't be known, but we'll know. We will know." The revelers clanked bottles and drank deep. "Now, please do this one thing for me," Kimber told his charges. "Go get drunk!"

Long, full days working out in the elements exhausted Kimber, who spent most of his September evenings crunching numbers in anticipation of an important budget meeting of the Course No. 7 Working Party at the end of the month. Midnight usually found Kimber snoring on the couch in the living room with his feet propped on the coffee table next to half-eaten takeout and his face lit by the glow of the spreadsheets on the screen of his laptop. Kimber's progress chart projected that roughly half of the work at Course No. 7 would be completed by mid-October 2005, when construction went on hiatus for the winter. Realistically that meant the course would not be finished until the fall of 2006, weather permitting. The original construction schedule, which overeagerly had No. 7 signed, sealed, and delivered in eight months, had long since been tossed, but the additional time meant additional money, which needed to be reviewed by the Working Party then approved by the Trustees. *How much more money?* was the question keeping Kimber up at night. Optimistically, half the work was done and half or less of the budget was spent. Pessimistically, half the work was done and more than half of the budget was spent. The latter seemed to be the case, as it looked from Kimber's first pass like upward of 80 percent of the kitty was shot. If that were true, Kimber would be shot.

• • •

The results were much more promising after Jill's visit to the specialist in Eugene, who suggested that Jill come back in for biannual biopsies. Kidd got the green light to travel and attended the weekly construction meeting on Tuesday, September 20, but he could not stay through for the gathering of the Working Party, which took place September 26 at 12:30 P.M. in Pilmour House. Kimber was in attendance, as was the architect, Fraser Smart. After a brief update by Alan McGregor on the status of negotiations with the farmer Sandy Fyfe and Scottish Natural Heritage regarding the fence line along the braes, Kimber brought the Working Party up to speed on the progress of construction.

- *Site clearance—complete*

- *Topsoil strip—complete*

- *Bulk earthworks—85% complete, another 5% expected before winter*

- *Topsoil and bulk earthworks—complete in 2006*

- *Shaping—65% complete*

- *Drainage—60% complete, another 15% expected before winter*

- *Irrigation—45% complete, another 15% expected before winter*

- *Topsoil respread—30% complete, another 5% expected before winter*

- *Greens and tees preparation and seeding—20% complete, another 5% expected before winter*

No one raised a stink over that or the plans Kimber presented for the coming winter:

- *Allan Patterson to maintain holes already completed*

- *Shaping to continue until the end of November, weather permitting*

- *Irrigation to move forward as weather allows*

- *Paul Kimber to make sure the site is sealed up and not holding water anywhere*

The next item on the agenda was "Budget and Costs." Kimber had submitted his budget to McGregor, who was pleased to report that with roughly half of the work done a commensurate half of the budget had been spent. Kimber's initial results showing upward of 80 percent spent proved to be skewed after he re-crunched every number this way and sideways until everything added up. That said, the estimate of additional monies required came in at a not-so-measly 31 percent above the original budget. After much discussion about the likely delay of opening the course for paid play until 2008 and the prospect of a soft opening in the summer of 2007, the chairman of the Working Party asked McGregor to prepare a revised business plan to be presented at a future meeting of the Trustees.

Kimber escaped unscathed. Fraser Smart, not so much. The architect reported that drawings for the maintenance facility were being done at present and the tender process was imminent. Smart targeted December 2005 for the start of construction and the following April for completion. (In reality, come December, not only had construction not begun on the maintenance facility, but the job had still not gone out to tender.) As for the clubhouse, with the work not even close to beginning and the dates being bandied about so far into the future, one member of the Working Party earnestly suggested scrapping the grand clubhouse altogether in favor of a more modest building. The Eden Clubhouse, for example, was nothing fancy, and yet it served a golfer's every need.

Kimber loved the idea. Smart, not so much. The expression on the architect's face upon hearing this suggestion was such that Kimber feared Smart might have a coronary and Kimber might be called upon to administer mouth-to-mouth resuscitation. Luckily for Smart (and Kimber) it proved to be a fleeting fancy. The clubhouse would live another day.

Later that week, on Friday afternoon, Tom Doak turned up on-site. Kidd's friendly rival was over playing in the Dunhill Links Championship, a coveted pro-am invite contested on the Old Course, Carnoustie, and Kingsbarns. Peter Mason showed Doak around. Kimber was already gone for the day, but McShane ran into Doak outside the office trailer. "Looks like you guys are having fun," Doak offered, which McShane took as a cop-out bordering on an insult. Mason later relayed to Kimber Doak's comment that "No. 7 far exceeded his expectations." It was a backhanded compliment, to Kimber's mind, as if Doak had thought they would screw it up, but they hadn't. As for Kidd, he would have appreciated, and in fact expected, a call from Doak. Regardless, Kidd is from the sticks-and-stones school; what Doak said about No. 7 was not of consequence—though Kidd would have loved to see the look in his eyes.

• • •

When the skies opened on Monday, October 10, construction at No. 7 closed for the winter. As of that date a total of 2.3 inches of rain had fallen over the previous seventy-two days; over the next seventy-two hours that same amount drenched St. Andrews. Kimber was not able to get out and survey the damage until the following Thursday. He and Patterson trekked out to the far northeast corner of the site and were setting out defenses to try to slow the water down when project manager Mason arrived at the trailer office. He reached Kimber by cell phone but was not up for the slog all the way out to the sixteenth hole, so he headed down the hill back to Pilmour House. Not that Kimber expected Mason to haul hay bales, but Kimber was peeved Mason did not come see the extent of the damage firsthand.

That Friday Clint McShane left St. Andrews headed for a job driving equipment on a golf project in Edinburgh. Russell relocated to headquarters in Essex, where Kidd set him up with the keys to his house and his car. Kimber came to the States to inspect a site near Lake Tahoe and catch the Rolling Stones in San Francisco. McShane and Walsh had hoped to spend the winter building Macrahanish Bay, but the funding never came through. Kidd was especially disappointed. Macrahanish was one of his favorite places on Earth; when he was a boy, his family had had a caravan there and spent countless weekends camping at the beach. Kidd would be keeping good company, with his course near Old Tom Morris's classic Macrahanish layout, plus it would provide a welcome return to working in sand dunes, which meant no stripping of topsoil, no bulk earthworks, no drainage, no trenching, no need to create landforms, because they were already there. Mostly, though, Kidd was bummed because Macrahanish Bay would have allowed him to keep his shapers engaged and in Scotland over the winter.

Walsh went to Gleneagles the last week in October to continue the Ryder Cup redesign work on the PGA Centenary Course. Kidd needn't be concerned about Walsh coming back to No. 7, as he had signed on as a DMK employee. McShane, on the other hand, preferred to remain an independent contractor. With McShane's profile high and the temperature in Scotland low, Kidd feared that he might opt to seek out sunnier climes for the winter—and beyond, if the right location, situation, or woman came along. However, McShane had eyes only for St. Andrews. He knew from experience gleaned while building Kingsbarns that winter in the East Neuk of Fife could be downright pleasant. Indeed, St. Andrews touts itself as the sunniest and driest location in the United Kingdom, with average annual precipitation that is the same as Rome and less than New York, Chicago, Dallas, Atlanta, or Miami. This is thanks to the North Atlantic Drift, a powerful ocean current that brings warm water to the northernmost reaches of any ocean. Its strong westerlies deliver warm, moist air to the UK, which dumps copious amounts of rain across northern and western Scotland; however, the mountain ranges of the majestic Highlands and the central part of the country provide a rain shadow effect, whereby the mountains act like a dam blocking the majority of the precipitation so that only a relatively small amount trickles over to the eastern half of Scotland, and most of that dissipates before it reaches the east coast where St. Andrews sits.

When the weather whips around and blows in from the east then all bets are off, but McShane knew that if he stayed in St. Andrews over the winter he would work more often than he would not. After a few weeks at Gleneagles with Walsh, McShane returned to St. Andrews and settled into his new digs in one of the cottages near the sixth tees, the cottages owned by Alan Barron, the forgiving neighbor whose view of the sea was spoiled by the earthworks at Course No. 7.

Any progress McShane made over the winter would pay dividends the following spring because the drainage and irrigation guys cannot get in and do their jobs until McShane is finished shaping a hole. Had he worked elsewhere for the winter, those crews would have had nothing to do come late March and early April while waiting on McShane to shape ahead. McShane did not mind being the only guy on the job. In fact, he rather enjoyed the solitude. The biggest adjustment was knocking off work early and parking his D5 at 4:00 P.M. due to short days when it got dark before supper. The upside, of course, was more time in the pubs.

Kimber shuttled up from Essex to check in periodically, and Kidd visited in mid-December. Both were pleased with the strides McShane made thanks to a run of good weather and lighter than usual rainfall. Kidd did request significant changes to the green at the par-3 eighth hole, where the back right pitched away from a tee shot that plays downhill and downwind. McShane argued for a more minor tweak, but Kidd was adamant. At Powerscourt and at Nanea he'd similar problems on par-3 holes, and Kidd did not aim to make the same mistake again. The request did not rile McShane as much as an underlying softening he sensed in Kidd, whose feedback this time focused on dialing things back instead of cranking them up. "I am going to buy David some balls for Christmas," McShane told a friend before the holidays. "And I don't mean golf balls."

Hole 16

• • •

Par-4
437 yards / 411 yards / 392 yards / 365 yards / 350 yards

The sixteenth hole returns golfers to the water on the northeast corner of the site. The first order of business was convincing the Links Trust to purchase the plot of land on the brae tops where the green now sits. That was literally like finding the missing corner piece to a giant puzzle.

Getting golfers to look at the sea was easy. Keeping golfers from seeing the neighbors was not. Had we left the hole at its original elevation, the view to the east would have looked over a stone wall to Sandy Fyfe's 4×4 track backed by the St. Andrews Bay Hotel, which I personally think resembles something in the federal penitentiary system. Talk about shattering the facade.

To remedy that, we dug out the sixteenth fairway so it sits well below the level of the wall. Now as golfers play the sixteenth hole, they can look to their right and see only the stone wall and the sky above it. There remains, of course, the distraction to the left of the seventeenth hole, which exists in a state of suspended anticipation as golfers make their way around the golf course.

We intentionally made the sixteenth fairway big and wide, in part to benefit recreational golfers but also to taunt long hitters. With the putting green set on the far side of a deep swale, the hole sets up so that unwitting bombers can get in more trouble than average players. Lace a big drive here, and it may well find a slot in the fairway that deposits balls in a nasty little bowl in front of the green. Getting up and down requires the kind of creativity and touch usually reserved for people who make a living playing this game.

For everyone else, a well-struck, well-placed tee shot leaves a full wedge or maybe as much as an 8-iron into that green. There is no running a ball up to the sixteenth green, as all shots have to clear the swale. The best line in is from the right, although a slight miscalculation may see approach shots disappear into a set of bunkers that can quickly dash any hope of par.

—David McLay Kidd

An Unexpected Loss

Brad Russell returned to Flin Flon for Christmas with his family. He was happy to be home and thrilled to be out of the office. Deskwork in Essex proved a rude awakening after six months spent in his element, working outdoors, getting his hands dirty, and breathing fresh air with St. Andrews Bay as his backdrop. Meanwhile, Old Man Winter seemed to be have taken a holiday from St. Andrews, as the total recorded rainfall for the month of January was three-quarters of one inch, 73 percent below average. McShane spent nary one day rained off and tipping "lager tops" with Skippy at the New Inn. With no weather delays or other distractions, McShane could knock out an entire hole in about two weeks. By the middle of January the eighth hole was shaped, including the changes Kidd ordered for the green.

In town, the Trustees gathered at Pilmour House on the morning of January 13. Course No. 7 project manager Peter Mason walked through the requested increases and detailed the reasoning behind them, notably the cyclical upswing that saw construction costs across Scotland shoot up 25 percent in the three years since the drafting of the original project budget. The provost of Fife, Councillor John Simpson, encapsulated the disposition of the Trustees when he stated that in his experience in public works he often encountered projects that had to be built to budget even at the expense of quality; however, in the case of Course No. 7 it was imperative that the project be done right—within reason. The Trustees approved the new budget, but, as the meeting minutes showed, not without issuing a parental warning:

> *The Chairman emphasized the importance of tight cost con-*
> *trol during the remainder of the project. The Trustees would*
> *wish to see the course completed within the revised budget.*

Back home in Oregon, Kidd was happy to hear the good news. He did not doubt they would get their increased funding, as they had made it this far without the Links Trust freaking out. However, the events of the three years since he got the St. Andrews gig had taught Kidd that the only thing he knew for sure was that nothing was for sure.

• • •

One of Ailsa's favorite pastimes is toppling towers of blocks built by her daddy on the family room floor. Kidd lay sprawled across the carpet nursing a bottle of Mirror Pond Ale, half-watching the evening news on TV, and restacking his baby girl's tower, when the telephone rang. Like most husbands, he instinctively looked for his wife to answer it, even though the handset sat within arm's reach on the coffee table. Jill was upstairs. After two rings he knew she was not going to get it. Kidd spent the third ring wondering whether he should let it go through to the answering machine. After the fourth ring, he finally grabbed it. The Caller ID flashed a UK number. Kidd did not have to do the math to know it was the middle of the night.

His heart sank.

Various worst-case scenarios flooded Kidd's mind. Something had happened to his son, or perhaps his mum, who had suffered painful complications after slipping and falling in a restaurant in Barbados and shattering her knee. Maybe it was work-related. Kimber could be calling to say the sewage plant had exploded and the site was knee-deep in shite. It could just as well be McShane calling with a bellyful of brave juice, or Walsh, notorious for drinking and dialing when he's feeling no pain on champagne.

"David," sighed the caller. "It's Brad."

"It's the middle of the night there," said Kidd. "Is everything all right?"

"I've got to talk to you about something."

Russell sat on the cushy leather couch in Kidd's home in Essex watching Kidd's flat-screen TV and holding Kidd's telephone in one hand and his TV remote in the other. Russell had been parked there for hours, dialing a few numbers before hanging up the phone and changing channels with the remote. "After this show," he told himself. "After the next show," he vowed. Finally Russell took a deep breath, dialed Kidd at home in Oregon, and let the call go through.

"What's wrong, Brad?"

"It's not working out for me."

"What's not? The house? The job?"

"The house, the job, the lifestyle. I see how much Paul and Tom travel, and then I look at you. You travel so much."

For once Kidd was at a loss for words.

"Have you met a girl?"

"No," said Russell. "I really just don't want your lifestyle."

"I don't understand," Kidd admitted. "You moved to Scotland, studied, trained, earned a master's degree in golf course architecture, and caught what many in your position would consider to be a nice break in the business."

Russell had no answer.

"I like and respect you, Brad."

"I like and respect you, and I appreciate everything you've done for me."

"You have a bright future."

"It's just not working out for me."

"Is there anything I can do?"

"No," said Russell. "I've made up my mind."

"Why don't you take twenty-four hours to think about it, and let's talk tomorrow," Kidd suggested. Russell agreed.

Kimber had noticed that Russell had something on his mind earlier in the day. He seemed unusually quiet around the office, somewhat solemn. Kimber asked if anything was the matter.

"The golf thing isn't working for me," answered Russell.

Kimber was floored. Russell was not easily replaced, and not just because of his initiative but also because of his engineering background. It would be no small feat finding a construction guy who knew design or a design guy who knew construction, and the harsh reality for Kimber was that it would take him more time and effort to find and train a new guy to take on Russell's myriad duties than it would for Kimber to take on the extra workload himself.

As promised, Russell called back the next day. As Kidd suspected, he had not changed his mind. Kidd offered him one last chance to stay, but Russell was resolved and Kidd was not going to beg.

"I don't want to waste my time or your time waiting for you to figure out that this is not for you," said Kidd.

Russell offered to stay on for up to six weeks, but Kidd gave him two days to be out of the office and out of the house. This caught Russell off guard. He thought he was being generous offering to stay and help transition someone in, but Kidd wanted a clean break. Russell felt that Kidd had taken it personally, and to an extent he did, but in truth two days was generous on Kidd's part, as most companies, especially those that trade in intellectual property, usher departing employees out the door and deposit them at the curb.

Russell took his eye off the prize. He lifted his nose from the grindstone, looked around, and questioned what he saw. Most people in that position would look back, and they would talk themselves into sticking it out at least a little while longer after having moved across an ocean and committed such time and money on schooling and training. Russell, however, refused to look back. That motivation, Kidd sensed in hindsight, fueled not only Russell's decision to pick up and come to Scotland but also his decision to pack up and leave. Cheating death taught him to look forward, to consider what is as opposed to what may be. Whether that made Russell impulsive or enlightened was irrelevant. Kidd did not begrudge his decision to change careers—it was unfortunate but understandable—however, Kidd did not want or need Russell's second thoughts polluting the office air or clouding the minds of Kimber and other DMK employees. They were all on board. The golf thing worked for them. The job, the travel—they wanted the lifestyle.

That comment "I really just don't want your lifestyle" stuck in Kidd's craw. Russell meant nothing by it; the guy was born without the mean gene, but in losing Russell, Kidd lost more than a protégé and a friend. For Kidd it felt like being rejected by the little brother who used to look up to you but has now decided you're not all that. The two have not talked or e-mailed since parting ways, though more so due to time, distance, and circumstance than any ill will. Russell was deeply and sincerely appreciative of Kidd's generosity, but the conflict was internal and the solution not material. For his part, Kidd succeeded in making Russell's decision excruciatingly difficult. He'd felt the weight on his shoulders and the lump in his throat and the knot in his stomach, though not over whether to leave but how to tell Kidd.

Kidd wanted Russell to stay, but Russell needed to want to stay. Try as he might, he just didn't.

• • •

Epochs ago, a mighty glacier cut a swath across Scotland from the northwest to the southeast and created in its wake the valley of Strathallan—*strath* is Gaelic for valley, and the *Allan Water* is the name of a river that flows past what is now the Gleneagles estate. The catawampus landscape that marks Gleneagles Kings and Queens golf courses occurred naturally thanks to eskers and kames, or gravel and sand deposits formed in inverted riverbeds under the melting glacier. On a sunny day, the resort and surrounding glen are a scenic dreamland. But when the skies turn dark and the foul weather blows over the Grampian Mountains and down that same glacial path, it can feel like the Ice Age cometh again when the valley gets walloped with bone-chilling winds, merciless rain, and frigid sleet and snow. Such were the conditions Walsh slogged through at Gleneagles while the weather was alarmingly cooperative on the other side of the hills in St. Andrews (just one-and-a-half inches of rain in January and February *combined*, better than 60 percent below average). Kimber was able to bring in a guy known as "D8 Davey." An experienced dozer driver from Arbroath, Davey and his mammoth Caterpillar D8 bulldozer lent an invaluable hand ripping the hard sandstone McShane encountered on holes seven and eight.

Walsh was called back to active duty in St. Andrews by the first of February 2006, and by the end of the first week McShane had made such headway that he had essentially dozed himself into a corner. He had the par-3 third hole and the par-4 seventh looking shipshape and the greens all ready to drain, but it was all just shifted muck until Kidd said it was a golf hole, and Kidd was not there to make that call.

Jill's condition had taken a turn for the better with the news that the extent of her treatment was the biannual biopsies. The middle of a deep, dark February in Oregon seemed the ideal time for an overdue family vacation, so Kidd rented a house for two weeks at Keauhou Estates overlooking Kahaluu Bay on the Big Island, where the sun shone as bright as the memories of premarital bliss that Kidd and Jill shared (save for his nearly getting killed by that wave on Christmas Day). A few days before taking off, Kidd received an e-mail from Kimber that touched on a laundry list of topics, including a cottage he proposed to rent, the unresolved and contentious issue of farmer Sandy Fyfe's cattle route, and plans to finish draining the seventh green then start the process at the third, which Kidd addressed in his reply:

——Original Message——
From: David McLay Kidd
Sent: 09 February 2006
To: Paul Kimber
Subject: RE: Bovines

Paul,

Thanks for the update, sorry you are going through the wars with Sandy Fyfe.

I am a little disappointed that you are planning to drain two greens I haven't had the chance to have any input on, 3 & 7. Is there any way you can delay or at least send me some pics?

I am working from home until next Wednesday then off to Hawaii. See you later.

Kimber e-mailed Kidd the digital pictures he requested, but they were useless. There was no sense of three-dimensional depth, shadows, contrast, or the grades of the greens. The bunkering was outside the frame, and Kidd could not see the bigger picture of what different kinds of shots golfers might hit into the greens. It wasn't that Kidd did not trust Kimber and McShane, but given the changes Kidd had ordered at the eighth green and his lingering concerns over the fourteenth, he was understandably weary of sinking pipes into the ground before having a firsthand look. Nor was it that Kimber and McShane were trying to add infrastructure so as to make it more difficult for Kidd to make changes when he eventually did see the greens; they simply wanted to stay a step ahead of the weather.

The grounds crew would have been better equipped had they a maintenance facility, unfortunately Fraser Smart's revised deadline to put the job out to tender by January 27 came and went, as did his re-revised deadline of February 24. The word Kimber heard was three more weeks. Project manager Mason was disconsolate, and head greenkeeper Patterson had all but given up hope that his men would ever enjoy suitable workspace, but on Friday, March 3, Smart put the egregiously overdue job out for bid. There would be consequences, as Smart's project could not feasibly begin work before early April, which augured not only confusion over concurrent deliveries to both the golf course and the maintenance facility, but also a potential violation of provisions in Section 75 of Scotland's Town and Country Planning Act of 1997, which limited the number of vehicle movements during the construction phase of the development to "a maximum of 12 heavy goods vehicle trips per day."

Kimber was irked over Kidd's e-mail, but McShane was downright bent. "If you can build a green in the winter in Scotland," he bellowed to Kimber, "you bloody well better get the drains in before the rains come!" They managed to finish draining the seventh green but stopped short of starting the process at the third. The rains soon came, and with a vengeance. March rainfall was off the charts with almost four inches, nearly double the monthly average. The temperature plummeted to the point where daily highs were below freezing, and snow blanketed the site on more than one occasion. The snowmelt combined with the rains put all hands on the defensive to repair the myriad damage: drains were washed out on the tenth, fifteenth, sixteenth, and seventeenth holes; extensive erosion appeared on the sixteenth fairway; a new washout poured onto the site from Sandy Fyfe's farm; silt covered greens at the seventh, eighth, and eleventh despite preventative measures including straw bales and silt fencing. The most significant problem occurred behind the seventeenth green, where a large catch basin overflowed and jumped the cart path immediately behind the eighteenth tee, causing a wash over the edge of the braes. On the bright side, the damage was mostly cosmetic and largely within non-golf areas that were beyond the fields of play. That said, the green at the third hole would likely have fared better had it been drained before the rains.

• • •

In the hierarchy of shapers, dozer drivers rate higher than digger drivers. Conor Walsh knew his place at No. 7 was in the digger, but he also knew he could do more, and he kept after Kidd and Kimber to give him a crack at the dozer. As a general rule dozers stick to shaping and diggers dig, respread topsoil, and apply gravel and rootzone to a green. No. 7 was an exception in that Walsh shaped with the digger and McShane spread the rootzone with his dozer. With McShane's blessing, and the keys to the D5, Walsh finally got his shot while McShane blew town and headed home to southern England for a long weekend. For Walsh it was like a call-up to the big leagues, and not just during garbage time at the tail end of a game.

Walsh wanted the hot seat, so Kimber threw him into the fire with orders to shape the green at the second hole.

Kimber and Walsh discussed strategy in advance, but Kimber wanted to give Walsh more freedom to improvise than direction to execute. He spent all day Friday and all day Saturday sculpting the green, and at the end of the second day Kimber's lone criticism was purely constructive: the green would hold water in one low spot, but that was an easy fix that Walsh saw to Monday morning when McShane returned.

Seeing McShane coming, Allan Patterson grabbed a fat red marker, snatched a piece of white paper from the fax machine, and made a sign bearing a big letter "L," which in Scotland is called an L-plate and signifies a learner. Patterson taped the learner's badge to the digger in time for all the lads to have a good laugh at McShane's expense. He could not have been more supportive of Walsh, but there was no way he was setting foot in the digger. McShane tore off the L-plate, grabbed a pen from his pocket, scribbled on the other side of the page, then reposted the sign on the digger:

FOR SALE
One Owner
Call Paul Kimber

Hole 17

• • •

Par-3
236 yards / 206 yards / 178 yards / 146 yards / 110 yards

Ask any golf course architect to sit down and sketch his dream golf hole and he will sketch a par-3 across a chasm with the beach below. That is the hole all golfers love and all golf course architects love to have on their résumé.

The moment we saw that chasm we saw the hole: a par-3 playing completely across a vast expanse on the edge of the North Sea. Not only was it the dream golf hole, it set up the perfect par-5 finishing hole hugging the braes all the way to Kinkell Point. This hole just had to be.

We all pictured it in our minds, but when it came time to actually build it, there seemed a collective nervousness over knowing that we'd only get one shot at it and we had best not muck it up. We spent a fair amount of time and effort sculpting the tees, though it was as if they were always there; we simply unearthed them.

On the other side of the gap the putting green poured in from the left, so we had to be careful when shaping against the braes to make sure we could create an ample green that would receive tee shots and accommodate multiple pin placements. That is exponentially easier said than done.

Paul and I knew how talented Mick was. He had the best résumé on the project. Even with Bandon Dunes on mine, I'd defer to Mick's. He went in there with the D5 and shaped in a green and an amazing set of bunkers that make the seventeenth hole as sympathetic to a modest shot as possible. A good shot is always going to hold the green, but the way he set it up, a golfer can hit a tee ball well left of the pin and the contours are such that the ball might funnel and run 150 feet right to the pin.

If the golfer can manage to safely cross the chasm, Mick's genius will allow that ball to stop somewhere where par is in play. That seventeenth hole gave me a newfound appreciation for the art and science of golf course shaping. It's really quite something to behold an artist who is driving a machine that weighs fourteen tons but is driven by a golf ball that weighs an ounce and a half.

—David McLay Kidd

18

Believe in Yourself, Buddy

A Scotsman is driving by himself down a deserted road through a dark glen when his car gets a flat tire.

He gets out to have a look, and by the wee light of the moon he sees that, sure enough, he's popped his tire. He opens the trunk and lifts out the spare tire, only to discover that he has no jack.

"Shite," the Scotsman mutters to himself, but as luck would have it he spies a lone cottage across the glen with a light flickering in an upstairs window.

"I will go knock on the door and ask those nice people if I can borrow their jack," says the Scotsman. He lifts the spare tire back into the trunk and tells himself, "Surely they will lend me their jack."

But as he closes the trunk, he wonders, "What if I go knock on the door and they don't have a jack?"

"Bollocks," he tells himself. "Right, then, onward." The Scotsman locks his car and strikes out toward the cottage.

"But what if they are sleeping?" he wonders. "Maybe I shouldn't go."

He stumbles in the moonlight and cuts his trousers on some gorse, but he presses on. "I'm stuck. I have to go," he tells himself.

"But what if they are awake but do not answer their door? I don't want to bother them."

He steps in a puddle, soaking his shoes and socks, but he presses on. "I have to find a jack," he tells himself.

"But what if they think I am a burglar? I don't want to scare them."

He trips and falls into a shallow burn but gets up and presses on. "I'll catch my death of cold out here," he tells himself.

"It cannot hurt to ask."

As he approaches the cottage, he smacks his head on a low-lying branch.

"But what if they are not nice people?"

Suddenly it begins pissing down rain.

"What if they have a jack but won't lend it to me?"

The Scotsman raps thrice on the door of the cottage but does not receive an immediate response.

"Well, if that's the way they are going to be about it!" scoffs the Scotsman as he pounds on the cottage door three times more.

After a few moments he hears feet shuffling inside. The latch unlocks, the door opens, and an elderly gentleman greets the stranger.

"What can I do for you?" says the old man.

"I'll tell you what you can do for me," barks the Scotsman. "You can take your bloody jack and shove it right up your arse!"

Left untended, the tiniest cut can deteriorate into a nasty wound. McShane absorbed the blows from the one-two punch of having to soften the eighth green and halt drainage at the seventh, but instead of clearing the air with Kidd, McShane let those scrapes fester. When Kidd returned to St. Andrews in early March his most pressing concern was quashing the Links Trust's concerted effort to save a few quid on the energy bill by installing wind turbines.

Windmills are usually reserved for miniature golf courses, but Peter Mason had learned of the Scottish Community and Householder Renewables Initiative and seized on the idea of harnessing one of No. 7's primary "assets" to generate electricity. An assessment of alternative energy sources by a SCHRI consultant compared the cost benefits of solar panels, ground source heat pumps, biomass boilers, and wind turbines, which proved to be by far the most economical. With the aid of a government grant to offset installation, the entire program could pay for itself in just five years. Plus, the Links Trust could offset one-quarter of their projected energy needs at No. 7 with the power generated by ten turbines.

"As if the sewage plant were not enough of a distraction," Kimber bemoaned when he shared the news with Kidd. "Now the Links Trust is talking about a windmill farm!"

Kimber damn near soiled himself when Mason first broached the idea. Mason assured Kimber, whose flabbergasted expression must have given him away, that the Links Trust was not considering the really big, unwieldy, garish sort of turbines, but rather the relatively compact WT2500 model, which came in two heights: twenty-one feet or thirty-six feet. Aesthetically, ten three-story windmills simply could not be left exposed on the golf course. Practically, any earthworks employed to hide them would be counterproductive to their ability to harness the wind that generates the electricity. The idea was ultimately tabled, in large measure due to the daunting prospect of trying to secure Fife Council planning approval for an unsightly windmill farm on Kinkell braes.

Kidd was due back in St. Andrews on the afternoon of Wednesday, March 8, and he asked Kimber to make a dinner reservation that evening at Nahm-Jim, an upscale Thai restaurant in town, for the two of them, Walsh, and McShane. Walsh and McShane were both anxious to see Kidd, though in opposite ways. Walsh was excited, while McShane was on edge.

The two were now roomies, with Walsh having taken up residence in the cottage's second bedroom. He and McShane got on famously and shared a mutual addiction for the American TV show *24*. That Wednesday was a rain-out, and they had spent the morning working their way through season one on DVD when DMK senior design associate Tom Cushnahan called from the home office in Essex. Cushnahan had served the same role on the Gleneagles job that Kimber did at No. 7, and he rang Walsh questioning the mileage allowance he had submitted on his expense report. Cushnahan had the drive down as forty-six miles from St. Andrews, but Walsh had put in for fifty-five miles. A couple of months had passed and Walsh did not recall the exact specifics, so he asked McShane. Cushnahan got an unexpected earful when McShane grabbed the phone.

"It may say forty-six [expletive] miles from point A to point B on the [expletive] Internet," groused McShane, "but if Conor said he drove fifty-five [expletive] miles then he drove fifty-five [expletive] miles!"

McShane thought Cushnahan was being petty over a discrepancy of nine miles, but more than that he was pissed because he felt Cushnahan was flexing rank over Walsh, something he knew better than to try with McShane. Nor did McShane appreciate Cushnahan's comment to Walsh intimating that Kidd would surely make loads of changes to the work that had been done at No. 7 during his three-month absence. The truth hurt. Not the bit about Kidd making changes, but about his three-month absence. McShane was sympathetic to Kidd's situation, having recently lost his own ladylove to cancer. He knew that the forty-seven days Kidd spent on-site in 2005 were more than any designer of his standing would likely devote, and yet McShane locked like a pit bull onto the eighty-three days Kidd had been away.

Cushnahan had opened a festering wound, and McShane decided to medicate it at the Red Reiver, a pub favored by locals. It took but a half a pint before he got into it with a bloke who, to McShane's mind, acted like he owned the place. Words were exchanged, none of them kind. The chap was younger, taller, and heavier, but when McShane drained his pint and then stood to head-butt the bloke, he must have seen the fire in McShane's eyes, because he backed off. McShane returned to his bar stool and ordered another. Then another. And another.

Kidd got sidetracked in the office and switched his reservation from the morning flight to the afternoon flight, which was delayed due to weather, which put him into Edinburgh at around 6:00 P.M. By that time Walsh had picked up Kimber and headed to The Central, a pub where they were to meet up with McShane, who was still busy self-medicating at the Red Reiver.

With each sip, McShane took another step deeper into the glen, like the Scotsman with the flat tire.

David will come and see what we've done and love it.

Sip.

Surely he will love it.

Sip.

But what if David comes and sees what we've done and doesn't love it?

Sip.

Bollocks.

Sip.

But what if he does make loads of changes?

Sip.

David's not like that. He trusts us.

Sip.

Then why did he keep us from draining the third green?

Gulp.

A load of changes could take as long to fix as it did to do the work in the first place!

Gulp.

David shoulda been here.

Gulp, gulp.

He should be here, not off on holiday in Hawaii, or in Oregon, or Fiji, because this is what matters!

Gulp, gulp, gulp.

Well, if that's the way David's gonna be about it, he can take bloody DMK and shove it right up his arse!

Having talked himself into the worst-case scenario of what Kidd could say, as opposed to what he should or would say, McShane blew out of the Red Reiver. Had this been a John Wayne movie, McShane would've been the drunken gunslinger who kicks open the doors to the saloon and ambles down Main Street looking for the man who done him wrong. If The Duke is feeling charitable, he will sober up the impetuous pilgrim with a dunk in a water trough. If not, he'll punch the ornery bastard's one-way ticket to Boot Hill. Either way, it never ends well.

McShane had staked himself to a six-pint lead when he finally joined Kimber and Walsh at The Central. Whatever conversation they were enjoying abruptly ended as McShane railed on about how "David shoulda been here" because, he said, "this is all that matters." With McShane spiraling and their dinner reservation at hand, Kimber and Walsh finished their pints then walked to Nahm-Jim, while McShane stayed behind and ordered another. Then another.

For all his bluster, McShane craved approval. As a boy he had longed to be tossed scraps of affection, and as a shaper he sought similar affirmation. He would not get so bent if Kidd's validation did not mean so much, and the reasons it did mean so much were rooted partly in McShane's respect for Kidd but also in the fact that, after a lifetime spent flitting from gig to gig, McShane had finally found a band he really wanted to stick with.

Kidd drove straight from the Edinburgh airport to Nahm-Jim, where the lads were all gathered. Kidd was bushed, but he was glad to be back, happy to see his friends, and excited to see No. 7. Kimber was confident. He knew Kidd would be pleasantly stunned by the progress. Walsh was giddy. He was absolutely itching to show off his shaping at the second green. McShane was thirsty. He ordered wine, a carafe of red and another of white, neither of which anyone at the table really needed, least of all McShane.

Kimber brought Kidd up to speed on recent developments at No. 7. The par-3 eighth hole was indeed more receptive to tee shots with the pitch now changed so that the green sloped back to front instead of front to back. Conor had shaped a green in the dozer, though they would not say which one because they wanted Kidd to see for himself. The bed of the seventh green had been raised to create a flatter landing pad and . . .

"You've been away too long," McShane interjected.

Kimber and Walsh had hoped that if they kept talking about all the good work that had been done, McShane might either give it a rest or not be able to get a word in edgewise. No such luck.

"Where have you been these past three months, David?"

"Working on new business," answered Kidd. "Traveling. Family holiday."

"You shoulda been here."

"I didn't expect so much to get done over the winter."

Who could have? Any normal winter in Scotland would have seen the team scatter like baseball players between the World Series and Spring Training. When McShane suggested the weather in the East Neuk could be workable during winter, even he could never have predicted it would be phenomenal. By all rights Kidd ought to have returned after three months to find a few nips and tucks, not an extreme makeover. McShane would hear none of it.

"This is what matters. The muck and the bullets are here," said McShane. "We talk about bespoke, but we can't do it without you. You need to be here."

Kidd opened his mouth to respond, but McShane was not finished.

"This is what's happening. This is where it is. Not Hawaii or Oregon or Fiji. Why is this on the back burner?"

"Because it was winter in Scotland," answered Kidd.

"Bollocks. We said we were going to do something unique, something special, layers upon layers, bespoke. The only way is all the way, hands on, full-time, here, on-site, in St. Andrews."

The fact of the matter was that Kidd wanted to be in St. Andrews, but he needed to be in Hawaii with his family, and in Oregon and Fiji setting up those jobs, and in the Bay Area checking on Stonebrae, and here, there, and seemingly everywhere drumming up new business so that the likes of McShane had a job to go to when No. 7 was finished. Kidd let McShane rant. Not that he could have stopped him, but Kidd respected McShane's passion and his opinion—to a point.

"You can't have it both ways," chided McShane. "If you trust us, trust us all the way, but don't not be here then tell us to stop till you get here."

McShane sat back and polished off the Chianti, seemingly sated after nibbling, if not quite biting, the hand that fed him. Kidd had half a mind to take that hand and punch the ornery bastard, but he decided to let the impetuous pilgrim sober up and see what he had to say for himself in the morning. Kimber paid the bill then McShane ordered more wine.

Kidd and Kimber left McShane with that carafe and called it a night. Walsh drove McShane back to their cottage in McShane's car, but as Walsh turned the key in the door McShane grabbed him and turned him around.

"What do you see?" asked McShane, presenting a pitch-black expanse.

"What do you mean?" said Walsh.

"What do you see?"

"Night?"

"No."

"The lights of Carnoustie?"

"No!" growled McShane.

"What do you see, Mick?"

"Nothing . . . ," McShane answered with a wink, ". . . yet!"

"Right, then, off to bed!" said Walsh as he danced around McShane and ducked inside.

"What say we listen to some music, Conor?"

"No, thanks, Mick."

"Shall we finish that episode of *24*?"

"No, it's late."

"Am I bugging you?"

"Never, Mick."

"Did I upset you?"

"Not at all."

"Did I offend David?"

Walsh did not dare touch that one and retired to his bedroom.

"You are the best at what you do!" McShane yelled from the living room.

"Thanks, Mick."

"I always told you that the day would come when someone would knock me off my Ivory Tower."

"Right you did."

"It hasn't happened yet, but the day is coming."

"You let me know, Mick."

Walsh moved to shut his door, but McShane swung it back open.

"Oh, you'll know," said McShane, "because that someone is *you!*"

Walsh turned out the light, shut his door, crawled into bed, flipped open his cell phone, and called his girlfriend. Speaking in a barely audible whisper, he recounted the night's events. Suddenly his bedroom door blew open. Backlit by the hall light, McShane stood at the foot of Walsh's bed wearing nothing but his skivvies.

"You," bellowed the hairy bear in his underwear. "You have to believe in yourself, buddy!"

"Cheers, Mick."

•   •   •

The following morning dawned clear but brutally cold. Kidd and Kimber arrived on-site shortly after 7:00 A.M. On any other morning Kimber might have wondered why McShane's car was not parked in its usual spot. He was always in early, reading a newspaper and brewing tea in the canteen, but after last night Kimber joked to Kidd that he wondered whether they would see McShane at all that day.

Walsh pulled in around 7:30 A.M., slightly earlier than usual for him, but he was up and at 'em and raring to show Kidd the green he'd shaped. As he locked the door on the way out of the cottage, he wondered why McShane's car was still parked in its usual spot, but after last night Walsh expected McShane could use a few extra winks.

Just after 8:00 A.M. Kidd, Kimber, and Walsh were about to set out for a walk on-site when McShane's BMW sped into the compound. The windows were steamed, and so was the driver. McShane pulled in, idled a moment, then whipped a U-turn and left as fast as he came, spitting gravel from his tires as he drove off. Kidd wondered aloud whether that would be the last they ever saw of Mick McShane. Walsh hopped into his car and drove back to their cottage. McShane's car was parked outside. Inside, McShane was seething. It turned out that when Walsh locked the door on his way out he'd locked McShane in. The old-fashioned lock required a key from both the outside and the inside, and with each passing minute that he could not locate his keys, McShane took another step deeper into the glen like that Scotsman with the flat tire. A proclivity for winding himself up combined with too many conspiracy-rich episodes of *24* had McShane wondering whether Walsh could have hid McShane's keys and then locked him in on purpose so that Walsh could show off his shaping at the second green and talk Kidd into giving him more time in the dozer.

Walsh talked McShane off the ledge and convinced him into returning to work. When he did, McShane bolted straight to the canteen and made a cup of tea, but when Kidd and Walsh walked in, McShane marched out without a word. Kimber ran him down.

"I need you to come on a walkabout," said Kimber. "I need you to hear what David has to say firsthand."

"I'll do it," McShane conceded, "but only for you."

Kidd's time in the sun in Hawaii and Fiji must have warmed his blood, because he had to pull on three fleece tops for the outing, while McShane appeared no worse for wear in but one wool sweater. They started with a loop at holes twelve, thirteen, and fourteen. Everyone puckered as they made their way down the fourteenth hole, but Kidd had nothing but positive things to say, focusing his praise primarily on the wicked cragginess of the burn that runs the length of the left side of the approach. Kidd bit his tongue when they came to the green, deciding he was better off waiting a few months until conditions allowed Allan Patterson to mow it down to playing length so that they could hit shots into and roll putts across the nefarious green.

After crossing the road behind the wastewater treatment works (where the mounding was at once so extensive but so natural-looking that the sewage plant was no longer an eyesore), Kidd, Kimber, McShane, and Walsh walked the length of the second hole, checked out the third, and then came back along the braes that flank the left side of the seventh. Again, Kidd could not have been more pleased. The execution was right on strategy, and what few tweaks he did request were small fixes with big impacts, like extending the front of the seventh green some fifteen feet to add a friendlier approach and additional pin placements. In happier times McShane would say that one of the things he appreciated most about working with Kidd was that every comment he made, made the golf course better.

It was not Kidd's style to make loads of suggestions after the fact, and not because he was afraid of offending anyone but because he made certain he communicated his vision before muck got shifted. Unlike many absentee designers, Kidd felt no need to request changes simply to put his stamp on the project and thereby justify his existence and his payday. He was confident enough to let his players play. Moreover, because he kept a close eye on things along the way, as one can do when spending forty-seven days on-site during the first half of construction, little problems never had a chance to mushroom into big problems.

"So, which one was it?" Kimber asked Kidd.

"Which one was what?"

"Conor's green," said Kimber. "He shaped one of those three greens. Which one was it?"

"I honestly did not notice any difference," answered Kidd. Walsh's wind-whipped rosy cheeks parted in a big smile.

"Was it the seventh?" Kidd asked. Kimber shook his head. Walsh's smile widened.

"The third, then," said Kidd. Again Kimber shook his head, but

Walsh's frozen face could smile no further. The fact that Kidd could not tell his green apart from McShane's was validation aplenty for Walsh.

Afterward, the four retired to the New Inn for lunch. By the time Skippy served up their burgers, the chill had thawed. Bygones.

Hole 18

· · ·

Par-5
564 yards / 546 yards / 513 yards / 496 yards / 289 yards

Like the hole before it, the eighteenth hole was predestined: a par-5 finishing hole that hugs the braes all the way from the tee to a green set on Kinkell Point.

The desire to place the eighteenth tees hard against the edge of the braes and set up a drive across the corner of the dogleg was almost overpowering. Even though our desire as golfers was to pound a drive across that corner, we had to respect that we could not do it without endangering people on the coastal footpath.

With that corner off-limits like an out-of-order ride at an amusement park, we had to conceive an exciting alternative, something that would set the heart racing and the mind spinning. Mick came up with the idea for a wall that runs perpendicular to play. Though he's never been to Bandon Dunes, it reminded me of our design at the sixteenth hole, where a ridge in the fairway is extremely effective at scaring away the kittens and enticing the tigers.

Here now, the decision off the tee is whether to go big or go left. Our intent is for average golfers to stay left and play the eighteenth as a full three-shotter, while only the very best players try to hit one over the wall. Fail to carry the ridge and the ball might as well be in a big, deep bunker, because the only play from there is a short iron back into play, leaving a long iron into the green.

Most players will aim thirty yards left of the ridge, put their drive in play, then hit their longest, safest club in order to set up a final approach into the shared green. There is a nest of nasty bunkers on the right-hand side of the second shot. I contend that Paul and Conor must've gotten really drunk the night before those were shaped, because they are downright evil.

The green is more receptive coming in on the eighteenth than it is on the ninth hole. It is possible to run a ball in—in fact it is advisable considering that from this angle the green is not very deep and falls off at the back.

There you are. It is our sincere hope that you walk off Kinkell Point feeling satisfied, invigorated, and anxious to go round again.

—David McLay Kidd

19

Back at the Rockpile

The Working Party reconvened on March 17, 2006. The assemblage was thrilled with the progress made over the winter; however, plenty remained to be done. Kimber outlined the program for the spring, including the crucial months of May and June when, knock on wood, shaping would be complete, green construction and topsoil respread would restart, and seeding would resume. Alan McGregor posed the question to Kidd whether plans for opening the course in the spring of 2008 were realistic.

"Realistic to optimistic," answered Kidd. With the seeding of the last green on the last hole targeted for September 2006, the youngest hole would have seven months' grow-in before the spring, and ten months before golf's bright spotlight returned in the summer of 2007. Not only would the Open Championship return to nearby Carnoustie in July (because of the town's dearth of accommodations, a good number of media and Open-goers lodged in St. Andrews during the 1999 Open, ferrying by hovercraft twenty minutes across the firth to the golf course), but also the Women's British Open would grace the Old Course that August. The Links Trust hoped to host a soft opening for No. 7 around those events; however there existed a very real fear that a cold autumn in 2006 followed by a cold spring could jeopardize those plans to showcase the sparkling new golf course. The Links Trust wanted to maximize press coverage while the media was back in the neighborhood, but they needed, Kidd reasoned, to temper their enthusiasm with opinion makers until the course was good and ready. Besides, every golf writer in the world would be angling for a freebie soon enough.

Peter Mason was positively chuffed to report that the maintenance facility was at last out to tender. His smile belied deep-seated concerns over an overworked Fraser Smart, who had become bogged down by the extension to the practice center, the addition of the golf academy, and renovations to the office space inside Pilmour House. In hindsight the Links Trust wished they had divvied up the architectural duties, but Smart owed a deep debt of gratitude to Mother Nature. The delays caused by the horrendous weather endured at the onset of golf course construction had bought the architect precious time on the maintenance facility, the road construction, and the clubhouse, all of which were in turn delayed. Regardless, bids on the maintenance facility were due by the end of March, with building to begin by the end of April. (Clachan Construction from Perth ultimately won the bid.) Furthermore, Mason cited a start date for construction on the clubhouse in November once the roads were all built.

On April 30, construction began on the access road to the site of the maintenance yard. Curiously, Smart was nowhere to be found. Supervision fell to Kimber, who informed project manager Mason that, for the record, Kimber had no qualifications as a road builder and as such would not and could not be held responsible. A week later an increasingly frustrated Kimber fired an e-mail to Kidd saying, "Still no sign of Clachan on-site!"

• • •

There is a manifest difference between coming back for your sophomore year versus coming in as a freshman. As the workers returned to No. 7 for the start of the second season, the learning curve had flattened considerably, which allowed for a quick start to 2006. The drainage and irrigations crews got busy on the holes shaped over the winter, and McShane and Walsh kept pace ahead of them. Kimber ticked the boxes on his to do list at a feverish pace. April showers never materialized. Rainfall was down nearly 90 percent, with a scant two-tenths of one inch for the entire month. Every Tuesday the construction meetings seemed to focus more on what was finished than what needed to be finished. Kimber trotted out a spiffy progress chart spreadsheet he'd created on his laptop that listed each hole in the order it was being created opposite the remaining tasks: bulk earthworks, shaping, drainage, irrigation, topsoil respread, prep, and seeding. By the end of the first week in May holes thirteen, twelve, fourteen, sixteen, and seventeen were finished. Holes ten, eighteen, nine, one, seven, three, and eight were completely shaped. The first grass seed germinated on Wednesday, May 10, and the following Friday the crew celebrated with a seeding party.

Finishing up a week on-site, Kidd stayed at the bash long enough to barbecue for the lads and knock back a few beers but short enough (before catching a flight home to Essex) to avoid the scrap that broke out in a spirited pickup game of drunken football. Tempers cooled when the rains returned around 7:00 P.M., at which point the party moved inside to the pubs, where goodwill was restored over countless pints. The highlight of the party was the sendoff the crew gave D8 Davey. Three weeks past his sixty-fifth birthday, David Ramsay had logged better than thirty thousand hours on his trusty D8. The muck shifting he'd done over the winter at No. 7, to transform the west side of the site, was critical, but his low-maintenance, high-productivity work ethic was especially invaluable. As a token of thanks on behalf of the crew, Kimber presented Davey with a die-cast model of a bulldozer engraved "Happy Retirement" and a cool CAT jacket embroidered with the DMK and Links Trust logos.

Good help can be discouragingly hard to find in the golf course design business. There is no shortage of the ready and willing. It's the able that are in short supply. Able bodies who want responsibility and do not need constant supervision are a borderline endangered species, but Kimber had found one such rare bird in Graham Foster. A thirty-six-year-old heavy equipment operator from Skipton, North Yorkshire, in England, Foster had twenty years in the heavy engineering trade working on pipelines, motorways, river diversions, football pitches, and assorted other projects. In the summer of 2005 he was on holiday in Greece when he got a call for a job on a gas project. Not twenty minutes later a friend rang Foster with a tip that there was work on a new golf course in St. Andrews. He had just come off an enjoyable job at the Normanton Golf Club in West Yorkshire driving a D5 to fill an old coal pit, then shape a driving range and pitch-and-putt. The pipeline never had a chance, as Foster opted for the gypsy life working in golf. Amenable to running a dozer or a digger (or a backhoe, scraper box, grader, dump truck, pipe layer, or anything else that burns diesel), Foster deftly jumped between machines depending on DMK's needs on any given day. Later in the summer when the majority of the earthworks were buttoned up in St. Andrews, Foster shipped out to shape down in Fiji.

Kidd plucked a plum hire in Niall Glen to replace Brad Russell. Raised in North Ayrshire, near the links at Troon and Prestwick, on the southwest coast of Scotland, Glen earned a master's in golf course architecture in the same program developed by Edinburgh College of Art that Russell later completed. During three years spent in the United Arab Emirates working for an outfit called Harradine Golf, Glen clocked time in five of the seven emirates (Abu Dhabi, Sharjah, Ras al-Khaimah, Fujairah, and Dubai, where he was based), as well as Russia, Bulgaria, Bahrain, Qatar, India, Morocco, Egypt, Kuwait, Pakistan, and Iran. It was with understandable enthusiasm that he answered a DMK Golf Design ad in *Golf Course Architecture* magazine seeking a design associate back home in the UK. The youngest associate member of the European Institute of Golf Course Architects, Glen competed extensively on the Scottish and UAE amateur circuits and played to a plus-two handicap, which made him, at least on paper, the best golfer in the office. More importantly he was, like Conor Walsh, Scottish, a native of the linksland, experienced, accomplished, worldly, fond of pints, just twenty-seven years old, and single. In sum, yet another perfect potential employee.

Another key pickup for DMK Golf Design was Jimmy Kidd. After three years Jimmy and June decided they'd had enough fun in the sun at Sandy Lane in Barbados, so Jimmy resigned his post and finally took his son up on his standing offer to sign on as the company's official goodwill ambassador and gatekeeper. Kidd wanted to grow the business, but he needed help. Adding Jimmy's eyes, experience, and instinct would afford Kidd the luxury of knowing that the prospective sites and clients he chose to visit were all worth his while.

With three-year-old Ailsa inching toward kindergarten, and Jill and Kidd having agreed that she would attend school in Oregon, Kidd hoped to focus a fair share of his future on projects Stateside. In an ideal scenario Kimber might grow into a role that would see him oversee the UK operation while Kidd ran the US office. In the meantime Kidd continued to bank frequent flyer miles at a staggering clip; however, one commission he would not get was the fourth course at Bandon Dunes.

In addition to his three existing golf courses, Bandon impresario Mike Keiser has room and plans for two more tracks on the 2,700 acres of Oregon coast he owns. The questions of *When?* and *Who?* are the source of lively debate and conjecture in golf magazines and Internet chat rooms. Two of the names most commonly floated are Kyle Phillips and Mark Parsinen, the designer and developer-cum-designer of Kingsbarns. Parsinen, who made his money in Silicon Valley, hired Phillips, a longtime Robert Trent Jones, Jr., associate, to design the Granite Bay Golf Club near Sacramento, which opened in 1994. Some years later Phillips approached Parsinen with the idea to develop the dunes outside of St. Andrews on which Kingsbarns now sits. The collaboration that had proved so successful could not be re-created at Bandon Dunes because Parsinen and Phillips suffered an acrimonious falling out over who'd done what and who deserved credit at Kingsbarns.

Keiser picked a complete unknown and a relative unknown in selecting Kidd and Doak, respectively, to design his first two courses, and the choice of Ben Crenshaw and Bill Coore for the third course, Bandon Trails, fit the mold of a "less is more" mind-set wherein the golf holes are not *created* by the architects inasmuch as they are discovered in their natural setting. (Of course, should the architect discover that he has no natural setting, he must then create one, as was the case for Kidd at No. 7.) *Travel+Leisure Golf* reported back in 2004 that Parsinen and Keiser had "already shaken hands on the fourth course at Bandon," however that was not the word Kidd heard when he answered his phone in Essex one chilly spring night.

The patch of grass between Kidd's back patio and the swimming pool stretches some fifty-odd yards, perfect for practicing chipping while heating up a frozen pizza. This night Kidd took a full swing with his wedge and airmailed his ball over the grass, over the pool, over the vacant horse stalls, and into the pasture. Kidd could use the pasture to exercise the horses he could keep in the stable if he liked horses, which he does not particularly. He'd prefer to put the pasture to good use. Kidd tried to acquire the four acres that sit empty behind his property, with an eye toward roughing out a couple of tees and greens for a pair of par-3s, but the neighbor wants to build houses on it.

When the fading daylight made it impossible to find his ball in the woodpile Kidd had stacked with his son, Campbell, the weekend before, and which the two planned to torch in a big bonfire the following weekend, Kidd headed inside. Flipping channels on the telly and nursing a Carlsberg beer, Kidd was munching a bite of still-frozen pizza when he answered the phone and heard from a friend back in Oregon that Tom Doak had nabbed the fourth course at Bandon Dunes.

(Mike Keiser made the announcement official in October 2006: Bandon Dunes' fourth course, targeted to open in 2010, will be called "Old MacDonald" in honor of revered golf course designer C. B. MacDonald. Doak and his senior associate, Jim Urbina, will lead the effort in conjunction with input from other architects who are familiar with the design style of MacDonald and Seth Raynor, the apprentice who went on to achieve great acclaim in his own right.)

Kidd felt stung. Not that he was surprised. He'd heard the whispers, and he acknowledged that he was not as tight with Keiser as Doak was. Doak might have *more*, but Kidd would always have *first*. The thing Kidd had found most enticing about the opportunity was working close to home, not the piece of land. He would like to have been approached; however, Kidd almost surely would have respectfully declined. He had very intentionally never done two courses in one place because, he believed, that save for *The Godfather: Part II*, the sequel is never as good as the original, and his original design at Bandon Dunes would be tough to top, especially given Old MacDonald's inland plot, which Kidd considered significantly less compelling than the parcels on which Bandon and Pacific were built. No, the sting simply came from knowing the gig was going to Doak.

For Kidd, there exists a psychotic dichotomy. He perceives Doak to be his chief competition but senses that Doak does not view him in the same regard. He considers Doak an equal but feels Doak considers himself something of a mentor. He likes Doak but bristles at losing to him. Still, just as Tiger wants Phil in the hunt on Sunday, Kidd wants Doak in the game because it makes winning that much sweeter.

• • •

On Wednesday, July 5, McShane finished the fourth green, the last green to be shaped. The happiest bloke in the New Inn that night was not McShane but Skippy the publican, whose beer taps flowed like Niagara Falls well into the wee hours. The forecast for the following morning was stormy with a chance of shite, and sure enough Thursday was a rain off. A few of the lads were going golfing, but Kimber holed up and caught up on a rising tide of paperwork. He was enjoying a cup of tea and comparing the relative benefits of different bunker sands when he got a call from McShane.

"Conor's hurt," he said.

The first thought that flashed into Kimber's mind was of mild-mannered Conor Walsh flying Superman-style down a flight of stairs at the hands of some drunk son of a bitch that McShane offended in the pub.

"How bad is it?" asked Kimber.

"Not so bad."

"What happened?" Kimber said, "And please tell me his last words weren't, 'I've got your back, Mick!' "

"No, but it is his back he's hurt."

"How?"

"He was lifting his golf clubs out the boot of his car."

From the initial sound of McShane's voice, Kimber had thought Walsh was actually hurt. Only later did Kimber learn how badly Walsh actually was hurt: he wound up laid up for two full weeks. On the bright side, Walsh missed McShaneapalooza, the three-day pint-a-thon staged the following weekend and starring Mick, Jock—who flew in from Spain—and Clint, who was paying his dues driving a dozer for Southern Golf in Ireland. As it turned out, Walsh's back injury probably spared him more serious liver damage.

Interlopers

One might think that choosing sand for a bunker is like selecting fabric for a couch. Pick a color, pick a texture, done. "Pink chintz, please." However, the balance golf designers need to achieve is aesthetic, mathematic, scientific, functional, and financial. The variables in the equation include cost, color, kind, shape, size, distribution, drainability, and wear and care.

Microscopically speaking, the roundness of the grains of sand has a significant impact on the way a bunker plays. Especially round sand tends to swallow balls, resulting in buried lies. It also provides less stable footing for golfers. The preferred shape for bunker sand is jagged and angular. The sharp edges hold the slope of a bunker face better, and they inhibit movement when a golf ball hits it, keeping the ball afloat. It is the same principle with the ball pits in which children play; were the pits filled with flat stars instead of round balls, kids would not sink below the surface. The size of the grains also affects play. Coarse sand requires players to pick the ball, while fine grains call for an explosion shot. In areas that experience high winds, coarser grains help keep the sand from blowing away.

Among the most common kinds of bunker sand are limestone and silica. Limestone can be made into a coarse sand or ground down to a fine powder. It is more susceptible to weather, and the minute silt and clay elements can glob or crust if limestone is not consistently raked. Sand made of limestone usually allows for greater backspin than silica sand, which is harder and typically rounder, thus presenting golfers with more buried lies. One of the key reasons designers favor silica is that it stands up better to weather and holds its shape and characteristics longer. Also, bright white sands made of high-grade silica present a stark contrast to green grass and give courses an Augusta-like look.

Heineken beer bottles may soon find their way into golf course bunkers, not strewn by impolite litterbugs but crushed by recyclers. In 2005 three golf courses in northwest England took part in a six-month trial that demonstrated that fine sand made of glass bottles offered a legitimate alternative for bunker sand. With the primary demand in the UK being for recycled clear glass, the experiment hoped to find alternative uses for green glass. The sand boasts an emerald tinge, but it works and has been approved for use by Britain's Sports Turf Research Institute.

The STRI recommended specs call for bunker sands to meet certain criteria:

- *The sand must not be so hard that the ball bounces out of the hazard, nor too soft so that the ball plugs to an excessive depth.*

- *The sand must provide a stable footing.*

- *The sand must be stable on high angles of slope to reduce the maintenance requirements.*

- *The sand must be free draining and not be susceptible to wind movement.*

- *Sand chipped onto the green must not interfere with the fineness of the putting surface nor contain a high lime content. (Sands containing more than 0.5% lime are best reserved for bunkers on the fairways or away from fine turf areas such as greens or tees.)*

- *The color of the sand must be aesthetically appealing.*

Course No. 7 required a medium-weight sand, not so heavy that it would sop up the rain but not so light that it would blow away with the wind. Compatibility with the rootzone used to build the greens was critical for greenside bunkers, as every time a golfer blasts out of a bunker and showers the green with sand he is effectively topdressing that portion of the putting surface. If the bunker sand and the rootzone are mismatched, then the sand can cake spots on the green and make it hard for water to drain through those spots.

Kidd preferred light-colored sand to dark, and Kimber liked a soft yellowish-orange. Any darker would make the bunkers appear filled with mud, and bright white would be too in-your-face. Whichever way they went, neither Kidd nor Kimber expected any compliments, considering that most golfers are too steamed about being in the bunker in the first place to stop and ponder the time and effort that went into decorating it.

• • •

Sunny skies across Great Britain absolutely baked Royal Liverpool Golf Club for the 2006 Open Championship, so much so that the crispy greens looked nearly as brown as the dirt at No. 7. The warm weather combined with the lack of the distraction of having the Open just down the Crail Road made this July decidedly more productive than the last. After he finished dipping the first green the evening before, Kimber spent an otherwise quiet morning overseeing the seeding of the green, the approach, and the fairway at the first hole. That afternoon Allan Patterson's crew was irrigating the green when the flow of water slowed to a trickle. It was as if a hose got a kink in it; only these were unkinkable two-inch-diameter plastic PVC pipes. There was no shortage of potential bad news—a burst valve, a power outage, an underground leak—but the scenario neither Patterson nor Kimber could have guessed was that the site had run out of water.

Buried in the ground at the top of the site, between the fifth tees and the Crail Road, were two forty-thousand-gallon tanks, both of which were running on empty. Patterson and Kimber knew they had put out a lot of water over the past few days due to the unseasonable warmth, but they couldn't believe they could've used eighty thousand gallons of water and run the tanks dry. Whenever the tanks drain to a certain level, the pump on the well is supposed to kick on and refill them, and with the first hole only partially seeded, Patterson decided to shut off the overnight irrigation system to allow the tanks to refill fully.

Only they didn't. The following morning Patterson and Kimber arrived to find the tanks at less than half of capacity. That told Patterson and Kimber that the problem was most likely with the well or the pump. After a fruitless morning spent on the phone and the Internet trying to figure out a solution, someone thought to ask Phil Langdon, the consultant who'd overseen the installation of the irrigation system, who nonchalantly suggested they check the wiring on the pump. Sure enough, the pump was haywired, an easy fix that saw the pump jump-started to life, and by the next morning their tanks were back to full.

The Links Trust continued to operate on a "less news is good news" basis when it came to local interest in the progress at No. 7. They kept a low profile, posting bits and bobs on their Web site and in their monthly newsletter about how things were coming right along, but by no means encouraging townsfolk to stop up and have a look. Still, despite the Links Trust's best efforts to control access, they simply could not keep everyone out.

Divots discovered in the tees at the seventeenth hole one Monday morning suggested that over the weekend a few overeager golfers had climbed up from the coastal path and taken a few Sunday whacks at the par-3. On another occasion an Indian family was found to be enjoying a perfectly pleasant picnic and an impromptu football game on the eighteenth tees. Having grown tired of watching walkers cut across his farm to get to the coastal path, Sandy Fyfe swung open a gate and put out a sign redirecting foot traffic along a trail between his farm and the east side of the golf course. With Fyfe's gate open, walkers had a hard time spotting Kimber's *"CONSTRUCTION SITE—KEEP OUT"* sign, so when the family spied an inviting patch of grass, they plopped down and busted out a picnic.

Those folks happily obliged when asked nicely to move along, but that was far from the case when another group of interlopers made itself right at home: rabbits. Like moths to a light, ants to a picnic, and shapers to a pub, rabbits in St. Andrews seem to have an incurable attraction to golf courses. At the first signs of the scratching that confirmed the infernal critters had discovered a new playground, rabbit fencing was placed around the greens and other sandy spots. However, the vermin did not take the hint, so a local exterminator named Ian Duncan was called in to assist Roger Waldron, a member of the Links greenkeeping staff nicknamed "Roger Rabbit" thanks to his expertise in the eradication of *Oryctolagus cuniculus*, commonly known as the European rabbit. Elmer Fudd could learn a thing or three from these two, as in short order they removed some two dozen wascally wabbits from the site. Permanently.

The damage that can be done to a putting green by a rabbit is nothing compared to what can be done by a coastguard Land Rover. Kimber arrived on-site one Monday morning to find tire ruts scribbled across the big double green on Kinkell Point. The story, relayed by Peter Mason, who had been called to the scene in the dead of the night before, had five lads out for a late Sunday stroll on the coastal path. One of the friends slipped and fell in the dark, injuring his ankle badly enough that he could not continue on. One of his mates used his mobile phone to call emergency services, and the coastguard and police were scrambled posthaste. Finding the fallen hiker was not easy in the dark. When they did reach him, in an area below the seventh green, they found him stuck at the bottom of a sheer cliff, so responders called in air support to lift the lad to safety. While awaiting the helicopter's arrival, the officers searched for a suitable clearing where the chopper could land and transfer the victim to an ambulance. The concrete pad for the maintenance facility was deemed to have too much debris in the vicinity, and while the dirt pad for the clubhouse (where concrete had not yet been poured) should have been more than adequate, someone had the bright idea to land on a level spot on the double green shared by the ninth and eighteenth holes. As the emergency vehicles repositioned to illuminate the landing site, the helicopter got the green light to take the victim straight to the hospital, which not only rendered the repositioning of the emergency vehicles moot but also left the putting green looking like the rutty, crusty top of an apple pie.

In an effort to avoid a repeat of the emergency services' follies, as it would surely not be the last time a hiker will get hurt on the coastal path, Kimber toured the site with an official from the coastguard to discuss the best routes and access points to the braes, a mutually agreeable helicopter landing site (most likely on the practice area), and perhaps some sort of markers along the coastal path to help people in need more easily identify their location so that rescue crews would not need to rumble up and down the golf course's mile-long stretch of coast.

• • •

On July 3, 2006, the sparkling new Fraser Smart–designed St. Andrews Links Golf Academy finally opened. Meanwhile, the Course No. 7 maintenance facility poked along six weeks behind schedule. Allan Patterson was, however, able to get mowers out to the fourteenth green in advance of Kidd's return in July.

Four months earlier, on the morning after the dustup with McShane at Nahm-Jim, Kidd had bit his tongue while walking about the fourteenth green. It was destined to draw reviews, not all of them rave. What gnawed at Kidd was not the fact that the green was wild. He had told the crew to crank up the volume and they had, though a scooch too much thought Kidd, so he'd asked them to dial it back. Kimber and McShane said they had, but Kidd was not convinced. Back when he was taking orders instead of giving them, Kidd would do what he thought best, then tell the designers what they wanted to hear. That might slide with a boss who popped up on-site four times during the entire build, but it was a dicier play with a boss who spent forty-seven days on-site in the first half of the build. Still, Kidd decided he was better off waiting until conditions allowed Patterson to mow the green down to playing length, so that they could all hit shots into it and roll putts across it. (Typically greens are not cut short until late in the grow-in, so as to allow the grass to deepen its roots.) If the green did not hold approach shots, or if the contours made sections all but unpinable, Kimber and McShane would get the point without Kidd having to say a word.

Seeding the fourteenth hole early in the process worked to Kidd's advantage, as by the middle of the summer there was sufficient grass for Allan Patterson to get the green cut down to five millimeters and have it running about seven on the Stimpmeter (which measures the speed of a putting green). Under normal conditions the green might roll around nine, but seven was plenty enough to allow Kidd, Kimber, Patterson, McShane, and Walsh to take a handful of golf balls and a few wedges and putters out to the fourteenth hole. Firing shots high and low and from left, right, and center, the green performed like the waxed tabletop in the midway at a county fair where people toss coins and try to get them to stick. A few balls did, a few more didn't, and for the most part holding the green required only slightly more skill than luck. Rolling putts proved a similar test of ability and karma. Getting balls close to the foreseeable pin placements required a deft touch, courageous imagination, and blind faith, but it was not altogether impossible. Kimber and McShane were satisfied, and Kidd was mollified—for the time being. It would be an unmitigated disaster if all eighteenth greens were schizoid, but Kidd had no problem with having one putting green late in the game that is wickedly unpredictable.

21

Love/Hate

When Kidd first climbed on the merry-go-round, it looked like so much fun. There was lots of cool stuff to see and do and time to enjoy it. The pace was comfortable yet exciting. Then it started to speed up. There was no sudden shift of gears, no jarring leap to hyperspace. The ride intensified incrementally, just enough to go unnoticed until Kidd suddenly found himself having to hang on. He looked back, but the horizon had become a blur. He looked to his left and to his right; however, the scenery whizzed by so fast he could not fix his gaze. So he stared straight ahead. The pace was invigorating yet unsettling.

For Kidd, August felt like forever. He spent the first three days of the month in Taghazout, Morocco, then flew to San Francisco to peek in on Stonebrae, before returning to Oregon for a weekend with the family and two days in Bend, at Tetherow. Then it was back to St. Andrews for three days via San Francisco, London, and Edinburgh, before returning to London for two merciful weeks in the office and the eighth birthday of his son, Campbell. Following a one-day site visit to Portugal, Kidd flew back to Oregon on August 30, Kimber's thirty-fifth birthday.

For Kimber, McShane, Walsh, and the rest of the crew in St. Andrews, August felt like that stretch during the senior year of high school between spring break and graduation. They'd had their fun, but now the end was near. Kimber's August 1st progress chart showed ten holes completed (numbers one, seven, eight, ten, twelve, thirteen, fourteen, sixteen, seventeen, and eighteen). McShane and Walsh had the sixth all but shaped, and holes two, four, five, and fifteen were over three-quarters of the way there. The practice area still needed to be built, and there would be ongoing tasks like shaping along the edges of the roads and the maintenance yard that would bring one if not both of them back to St. Andrews in 2007, but all things being equal, McShane and Walsh's jobs at No. 7 would be done by the middle of September.

Kimber hoped to buy them a wee stay when he conceived the idea for a nineteenth hole. Not a pub, but a bonus par-3. DMK had done something similar a few years earlier while building the West Course at Powerscourt Golf Club in Ireland. Powerscourt's first course, the East, is a parkland layout opened in 1996 and designed by two-time British Amateur champion Peter McEvoy. His sixteenth hole is a pretty little par-3 fronted by a pond that pays homage to the twelfth hole at Augusta National. Unfortunately, the greenkeepers had a devil of a time caring for the green because of its positioning in the shade, so when DMK was building the West Course, they created an alternate par-3 that was put into play for the East Course while work was done to fix their sixteenth green. Afterward, DMK's nineteenth hole on the West became a practice hole that could be rotated in to maintain an eighteenth-hole loop should work be required on any of the other holes.

In the expanse between No. 7's twelfth and fifteenth holes, Kimber laid out a par-3 that would play some 150 yards slightly uphill from a tee box near the forward tees at the fifteenth hole to a small green near the middle of the twelfth fairway. A teeing ground between the alternate green and the twelfth green would set up a drive with a stunning view of the sea back to the fifteenth fairway and, ideally, a landing area before the burn that would front the fifteenth green. In addition to offering flexibility and a full eighteen when working on another hole, the bonus hole would serve as a perfect turf nursery when not in play.

The proposed nineteenth hole was on the agenda for a meeting of the Working Party scheduled for Friday, August 11, at 11:30 A.M. Kidd thought about catching an early flight from London that morning, but instead he decided to shuttle up the day before, so that he could have a good look at the latest work on-site and review with Kimber the PowerPoint presentation to the Working Party. On a morning that started out like so many others, Kidd drove the half hour from his house in Essex to the long-term lot at Stansted Airport. He parked, grabbed his briefcase and carry-on bag, locked his car, and strolled leisurely into the terminal. He was early, as usual, so he bought a cup of coffee before taking his place in the easyJet queue.

Kidd liked Stansted. It was convenient, and it wasn't Heathrow. There was one terminal, on a single level, that was brilliantly conceived to be all but idiot-proof. More than that, though, it appealed to Kidd's artistic aesthetic. The terminal, opened in 1991, was designed by Sir Norman Foster, a lion in the world of architecture, whose works include Beijing's international airport, the largest construction project on Earth, and a gleaming seventy-eight-story office tower to be built in New York City as part of the World Trade Center redevelopment. Foster's work at Stansted took the modern airport and literally turned it upside-down. All of the infrastructure that normally goes on the roof (heating, ventilation, air-conditioning, etc.) went in the ground. The distribution network for all services comes from the subterranean level up into the terminal through stanchions that rise from the floor like tree trunks and support a roof that functions simply as a canopy. The weather stays out, but natural light floods in, filling the building with mood instead of fluorescence. Kidd had only just noticed the mood inside begin to change when his mobile phone rang. The queue had slowed to a stop. It was Kimber calling. Everyone around him seemed to be talking on his or her cell phone. Kimber sounded anxious. No one seemed to be smiling.

Kimber said something about a plot, but it was hard to hear. Kidd squinted, as if that might improve his hearing. A terrorist plot, he caught. The surrounding clatter intensified. As the news spread, conflicting information came in waves from all sides. All planes were grounded. Planes were flying, but carry-on luggage was not allowed. The airport was being evacuated. The threat level was raised to critical. Security was checking for liquids and gels. Kidd was not sure what to think, so he followed his gut instinct, picked up his briefcase and carry-on bag, walked calmly but briskly back out of the terminal to the long-term parking lot, unlocked his car, climbed behind the wheel, left the airport, and headed north.

Or so he thought. Kidd accidentally turned south toward Essex, his internal autopilot leading him the way he always went. He was knackered from the nonstop travel, still trying to figure out which way was up after having flown from Oregon to San Francisco to London the day before and slept like shite that night. What Kidd wanted was a nap, but what he needed was an off-ramp.

The next exit, he knew, was just a few minutes down the road. There, he could right his wrong turn and get going north. Or so he thought. Red brake lights suddenly popped up on the motorway like an acute case of measles. Traffic stopped. The wail of sirens grew louder, slowly though, as the emergency vehicles struggled to push through the clogged artery. The airport was behind Kidd, but the problem was up ahead. It was not related to the terror plot, Kidd thought. It had to be an accident.

It was a bad accident, as five minutes passed without Kidd's tires rotating an inch. Ten minutes passed. Kidd was going nowhere fast, so he turned off the engine, locked the doors, reclined his seat, unbuckled his safety belt, and took that nap.

The plot was chilling, its potential horrifying. Upward of fifty conspirators were allegedly involved in a long-conceived, well-orchestrated plan to simultaneously suicide bomb a dozen or so transatlantic flights originating in the United Kingdom and bound for the United States. The suspects intended to smuggle liquid and gel explosives onboard in common carry-on items like bottles of shampoo and tubes of toothpaste, then detonate the bombs using everyday electrical devices such as laptops or iPods.

British officials, working off a tip following the London subway bombings in July 2005, decided to act when they did rather than wait for the plot to unfold any further, due to concerns over an imminent dress rehearsal to make certain that the bombers could indeed get their explosives onboard undetected. Had the foiled dry run succeeded, officials believed that the actual attack would have been just days away and the carnage could have rivaled 9/11.

Blaring horns behind him roused Kidd from a deep sleep. He wiped the drool from his chin and checked his watch. Nearly an hour-and-a-half he'd snoozed. The catnap helped make the ten-hour drive to Scotland only slightly more bearable.

• • •

Kidd meant no disrespect by his yawning during the meeting of the Working Party. He had driven straight through, though not to St. Andrews, where Kidd knew he would wind up in a pub. Instead, he drove to the family home in Auchterarder, where Kidd knew he would find peace and quiet with his parents still at Sandy Lane in Barbados. Twelve hours of uninterrupted slumber helped clear the cobwebs from his brain if not the spiderwebs from his bloodshot eyes.

After Peter Mason reported that the Links Trust appeared to have cleared its final hurdle with Sandy Fyfe by agreeing to the fence line along the braes, Kimber delivered the PowerPoint progress report:

Clearance	*100%*
Topsoil strip	*100%*
Bulk earthworks	*99%*
Shaping	*95%*
Drainage	*90%*
Irrigation	*85%*
Topsoil respread	*80%*
Greens and tees	*80%*

The greens, tees, and approaches had done quite well, said Kimber. Those pieces were maturing nicely, with a good blend of desirable grass species. Even if not all members of the Working Party knew exactly what that meant, they could feel confident, given the conviction with which Kimber spoke. The fairways and semi-roughs were slower to grow in spots due to the warm, dry weather, though overseeding the thin areas would help. The lack of rain over the summer had hindered the grow-in of areas of deep rough that were not otherwise irrigated. All in all, no news was good news. Asked what risks could prevent construction from concluding by the end of the season, Kimber answered only the weather. Niggling issues with the irrigation installation and rootzone supply had caused the schedule to slip one week, but they were on target to finish seeding all golf areas by the first week in October.

Kimber's proposed nineteenth hole won easy approval. The Working Party grasped the concept and needed little convincing that the benefits outweighed the incremental budget increase. Also receiving a thumbs-up was the plan to utilize the warm-up area and designated areas on the third and sixth holes for any future air ambulance helicopter landings. Kidd piped up when asked if Course No. 7 was being promoted in the US. "For a course that is still two years from being opened to the public," Kidd said, "this project is creating the most interest and buzz I have ever encountered."

When Kidd returned to St. Andrews ten days later, he walked Course No. 7 from the first tee through to the eighteenth green. It was the first time that he, or anyone, had done so. All the dots were connected. Where once sat a flat, boring, brown potato field now rose a rollicking, engaging, mostly green golf course. Beneath the emerald carpet and the woolly landforms and the quirky tees and the vexing greens lie buried all of Kidd's doubts. Experiencing the course in sequence, totally shaped, mostly grassed, and so close to completion, reaffirmed Kidd's conviction that this golf course could never have been created on paper or on computer or by a designer who merely fulfilled his contractual obligation and turned up for six site visits.

Exactly as intended, the anticipation grew as Kidd made his way around the back nine and down to the water at the sixteenth green.

Standing on the seventeenth tees he was overcome by a sense that the crew at No. 7 had not designed this course so much as discovered it. It had always been there, like a sculpture inside a block of marble, longing to be revealed. All it took was a team of artists with the vision and the caring and the commitment and the patience to unlock it.

Striding up the eighteenth fairway, Kidd's pace slowed. He wanted to savor the moment, the rush, the triumphant march that champions enjoy when victory is at hand. Upon reaching Kinkell Point, Kidd lingered on the green, burning every detail of the instant into his memory and bursting with pride over his team's having achieved everything they had envisioned—and then some. "Love it or hate it," he told the lads at the pub that night, "people who play it are never going to forget it."

Kidd took Kimber, McShane, and Walsh for dinner at the Dunvegan that evening. There would be no replay of their memorably forgettable night at Nahm-Jim. The mood was sedate; McShane was quiet. Kidd had seen this before. It was the same on every job: the party was all but over, and the partygoers grew increasingly nervous about what was—or wasn't—next.

Kimber had at least another year of loose ends to tie up at No. 7, though he could oversee that, as well as pick up other projects, working out of the office in Essex. Given his druthers, Kimber would happily be based out of St. Andrews. He had grown attached to the Auld Toon. He'd joined the New Club and had an eye on joining the St. Andrews Club, too. He bought an apartment in town that he planned to fix up. Kimber lobbied Kidd to move the operation to Scotland. It would also be more convenient for Jimmy, Kimber reasoned, but Kidd's pat answer was that the office would stay in Essex as long as his son, Campbell, was in Essex.

DMK Golf Design's docket had projects under way and in the works, but come the autumn of 2006 there were no golf courses starting construction. There were plenty of jobs that shoulda, woulda, coulda come through but nothing onto which Kidd could easily move McShane and Walsh. Walsh was safe. He was like the rookie phenom who had a breakout season but could not yet command the big bucks.

Kidd could carry his salary over the winter. McShane, on the other hand, was like the veteran All-Star whose talent was unquestioned but whose beaucoup price tag fairly forced Kidd to let McShane test the free agent market.

Kidd wanted McShane to stay, but you can't always get what you want.

22

Beautiful Music

Kidd dearly wanted to attend the "topping off" party that the Links Trust had planned for the cast and crew at Course No. 7 on Saturday, September 9, 2006—even though Kidd's impacted work diary dictated he would essentially have to fly over just long enough to say *Cheers!* and chug a pint or two before having to turn right around and fly back home again. His recent encounter with the terror plot coupled with the prospect of flying from Heathrow to America on the fifth anniversary of 9/11 made it an altogether unpleasant proposition.

Besides, the celebration might have been a bit premature, like the big, bold headline in the September edition of the Links Trust's monthly newsletter, which declared, "Seeding Completed at Course No. 7." The lead heralded, "A significant landmark in the development of Course No. 7 has been reached with the seeding of all fairways, tees, and greens having been completed." Tees and greens, yes. The fairways were another story. All golfing areas needed to be seeded by the end of the first week in October at the latest. A four-day stretch in mid-August that dumped two inches of rainfall had resulted in a disconcerting setback. It meant that from the start of September to early October just one rained-off day per week would jeopardize the seeding target. Potentially more calamitous was the very real possibility of a few ill-timed ill-weather days, because rain was bad but wet was worse.

Lingering damp conditions kept crews from prepping the grounds for seeding and, worse still, might require time-consuming repair work. By mid-September Kimber's best guesstimate had the crews completing the seeding at the fourth and fifth fairways, leaving only the fifteenth hole with a big, bold question mark.

• • •

Finding flights from Oregon to Edinburgh that were available, much less reasonable, was next to impossible. The hitch was getting to St. Andrews in time, as two months prior Kidd had committed to play a round of golf at Bandon Dunes with the trio of high bidders in a charity auction. Kidd donated his time as a favor to a friend named Paul Milton, the CEO of Hart Howerton in San Francisco, an architectural and design firm that often referred DMK Golf Design for the golf component of Hart Howerton master-planned communities. Three fat cats plunked down $15,000 for the experience, which included transport between San Francisco and Bandon in Hart Howerton's King Air 350.

As it worked out, Kidd was to tee it up with the big spenders at Bandon Dunes on Friday morning, September 8, after which he planned to hop a ride on the King Air out of Bandon down to San Francisco in time to catch Virgin Atlantic's 4:30 P.M. overnight flight to London. If the flights were on time, he could connect out of Heathrow and feasibly arrive in Edinburgh by 12:30 P.M. Saturday, which would have him on-site at No. 7 right around the time the party started at 2:00 P.M. However, the winning bidders pressed to play another round that Friday afternoon. Kidd need not have been present for that; however, if the trio stayed so, too, did the King Air, and Kidd could not make the Virgin flight if, after playing in the morning as committed, he then tried to catch a commercial flight from North Bend through Portland to San Francisco.

Luckily for Kidd, all three Bandon courses were booked that afternoon. The hurdle Kidd was ultimately unable to clear was not much time for a whole lot of money, as the airfare priced out at $4,491.25. Just one hitch in the giddyap and that promised to be a shockingly expensive ticket to a party Kidd might well miss altogether.

It seemed that the honchos from the Links Trust might miss out as well. Peter Mason was on holiday, Gordon Moir intimated that he preferred to keep his tee time on the Old Course, and Alan McGregor called Kimber and Patterson earlier in the week to regret due to a conflict with his grandson Jamie's third birthday party. With or without the brass, dozens of others who'd had a hand in the creation of No. 7 fully intended to have their fill of fun—and Guinness, and Tennent's, and Corona. Kimber brought a case of Taittinger champagne and handed out bottles as a token of thanks to the subcontractors and other key contributors. Those bottles did not stay corked for long.

The party was in full swing when Kidd awoke in Oregon. He wanted to be there, but he needed to be here. He needed to be home with Jill and Ailsa after spending essentially the entire month of August away. While the girls slept, Kidd tiptoed downstairs, made a pot of coffee, and fired up his computer. Nothing like a month's worth of receipts to sort and expenses to file, Kidd thought, to keep his mind from wandering across the pond to the party he was missing.

In addition to the DMK and Links Trust guys, the fifty-odd people who made the scene included the earthworks guys from Geddes Group, the drainage guys from Meiklem, the sprinkler guys from Turf Irrigation Services, irrigation designer Phil Langdon, and site surveyor Jack Jarvis. Kimber invited Skippy up, but he could not slink away from the New Inn. Chef Richard Brackenbury from the Links Clubhouse gave up a Saturday off to barbecue burgers, sausage, chicken, and chops for the lads. There were lassies, too. A local caddie named Davey Lindsey, invited along by McShane, brought his mum, and it wouldn't have been a party without a group of Estonian girls who had been placed at No. 7 by a local employment agency specializing in affordable Eastern European labor, to work on-site as stone pickers (thus their nickname, "The De-Stonians"). Mother Nature even graced the proceedings with a temperate, mostly windless, stunning sunny day.

Through the morning fog hovering outside his glass patio door Kidd spied the old salmon eagle perched on the snag atop the Douglas fir tree. It was just the excuse to procrastinate he'd been looking for. Kidd refueled his coffee cup on the way through the kitchen to the garage, where he grabbed a driver and a handful of range balls. Teeing it up on his front lawn, Kidd reared back and fired a shot right at the old bird.

Mason was away on holiday, but Moir and McGregor made it to the party after all. Moir arrived early to help set up, then said his thank-yous before bolting back down to the links in time to make his match on the Old Course. McGregor, God willing, would attend many, many more birthday parties for his grandson, but this—this gathering, this golf course, this group—would never come round again. He did not want to derail the revelry, but McGregor asked those assembled for a moment of their time so that he might offer a few words.

"Today is a true watershed," he began. "Earlier today you finished seeding the fourth green, meaning that all eighteen greens are now complete." McGregor applauded the effort, and the guests responded in kind.

"Congratulations on what has been a monumental effort," said McGregor. "Everyone here has been involved in creating a truly special golf course. I think back three or four years to when I first walked these fields with the farmers. I remember thinking to myself, 'Right, this looks pretty boring! It's flat but has nice views. I suppose some architect might produce a half-decent golf course.'" The gathering laughed in unison. "Well, I look around today and I simply cannot believe what you all have achieved. I do not see one weak hole on the golf course.

"On reflection," he continued, "one of the best decisions we made was to bring in the trades ourselves to the exclusion of a main contractor. I believe this has led to a better product, as it has given us more flexibility and control. Further, I have found this to be a motivational place to come to over the last eighteen months. This is in thanks to the great teamwork. Our thanks go to Stuart Meiklem and his crew, to Donald McKerracher and the Geddes crew, to Calum

Oliphant and the irrigation crew, and to Mick McShane and Conor Walsh, shapers supreme. Many have been involved from the Links Trust, whether that has been full-time up here under the expert guidance of Allan Patterson or imported from our other links courses, and of course you've all done great.

"Then there's DMK," said McGregor, pausing for dramatic effect. "I see in today's *Daily Telegraph* that the former home secretary is calling the chancellor of the exchequer, 'a deluded control freak.'" McGregor cast his eyes directly on Kimber, whose reputation as a control freak was not lost on anyone. As laughter erupted, Kimber jokingly took cover behind a van. "Well, the controls have paid off," said McGregor, his tone heartfelt, "and I speak for the Links Management Committee, the Trustees, and management and staff when I again say thank you and well done!"

McGregor implored everyone to eat, drink, and be merry, then Kimber stepped up to speak.

"I'd like to thank Alan and the Links Trust for hosting this barbecue today," he began, "and for leaving us alone these past two years to do what we do best!" That drew a raucous cheer from the crowd and a mock glare from McGregor.

Back in Oregon, Kidd's tee shot buzzed the bird, but it did not flinch. It did, however, appear to raise its head, as if to say, "Well played." Kidd ducked inside, to find Ailsa toddling about and Jill shuffling a step behind. The coffee was all gone, so she made another pot. Kidd turned on the TV, which was still tuned to channel 913, the Classic Rock digital music channel that Kidd and Jill had been listening to the night before. Ailsa pulled her daddy down to the family room floor to stack blocks.

Flying high above St. Andrews Bay, the Royal Air Force's aerial acrobatic squad, the Red Arrows, highlighted the annual Leuchars Airshow. On the ground the entertainment at No. 7 included an unintentional impression of a Keystone Kops routine when one of the partygoers, attempting to shuttle what appeared to be at least a dozen people from the clubhouse site up to the car park, pitched a golf cart into a ditch. By 7:30 P.M. the temperature had dipped, the food was all eaten, and, more importantly, the beer was all gone, so the circus packed up and headed into town.

The New Inn was chockablock that Saturday night, looking less like the neighborhood pub it is than the Lizard Lounge or Ma Bell's or one of the other lemming-packed university hot spots in town. Skippy's cash register rang like a slot machine stuck on perpetual jackpot. Everyone kept buying rounds until everyone had a pint in one hand, another in the other, and a third waiting on the bar. Huddled at the corner of the bar, Kimber, Walsh, and McShane were feeling no pain, only pride. McShane made his way to the jukebox, pumped in 25 pence, pressed 69-13, then raised his glass and led anyone who cared to sing along in a rousing rendition of Neil Diamond's "I Am . . . I Said."

Ailsa squealed and giggled as she toppled the tower of blocks her daddy had built before her. Kidd lay sprawled on the carpet nursing the dregs at the bottom of his coffee cup when a song came on that he knew by heart. As he restacked her blocks, Kidd smiled at his daughter and sang along.

You can't always get what you want
You can't always get what you want
You can't always get what you want

But if you try sometimes
Well, you just might find
You get what you need

Kidd hoped to keep the band together—for the foreseeable future anyway, if not the forty-three years that the Rolling Stones have made beautiful music together. That would put McShane on the eve of his ninetieth birthday, and while it was not hard to picture the crotchety old coot still waiting to meet the man who would knock him off his Ivory Tower, the reality was that the individual wants and needs of Kidd, Kimber, McShane, and Walsh would sooner contribute to a parting of their ways.

Making a golf course is like making an album. Each hole is like a song. Each has a beginning, a middle, and an end. Each has twists and turns and highs and lows intended to provoke thoughts and stir emotions. Each is an adventure unto itself, but strung together they compose a greater journey.

These creations are the expressions of artists who devote themselves wholly to their craft and shape something from nothing, only to let go and offer their art to others for their enjoyment. People will form their own opinions. They will interpret the work differently than the artists ever imagined. Some critics will rave while others will snipe; such is the subjective nature of art. Some people will love it, others will hate it. Just as long as they do not forget it.

Enjoyment can be had if it is played only once, but deeper exploration invites discovery. Play it again, and again, and again, and each time the artists' work will reveal something new, some layer, some nuance, some enlightenment, some answer.

Therein lies the ultimate satisfaction: the experience will never be the same, forever.

• • •

Postscript

 •   •   •

"No. 7" was never anything more than a working title, and when the time came to bestow a proper name upon the course the Links Trust turned for help to its largest constituency: the worldwide golfing public.

In November 2006 the Trust staged a month-long competition via its Web site, inviting anyone from anywhere to suggest any name he, she, or they saw fit for the new course. The grand prize was an invitation to the VIP course-opening ceremony, as well as one of the very first tee times when the course opens for public play in the spring of 2008. The lucky winner, drawn at random from a pool of those who submitted the chosen name, turned out to be an American, Edwin Burtnett, a thirty-nine-year-old industrial engineer from Tampa, Florida.

Entries flooded in from all corners of the globe—4,000 in all with over 300 unique submissions. Many invoked the location, offering The Kinkell, The Brownhills, The Cliffs, The Braes, The Town View, The Seaview. Some cited famous golfers, recommending The Old Tom, The Morris, The Bobby Jones, The Woods, The Nicklaus, even The Payne Stewart Memorial.

The Pilgrimage and The Holy Grail seemed fitting. At least one person suggested The Wallace, though no one thought to name the course after the movie in which Scottish hero Sir William Wallace was immortalized: The Braveheart.

Royalty was represented: The King Bruce, The King David, The King James IV, The Queen Mother, The Victoria, The Elizabeth, and The Prince William. So, too, were the commoners, with a number of ballots cast for The People's Course.

The Trustees sought a name that was relevant to both the course and also to St. Andrews, that fit with the family of names of the other six Links courses, and that was easy to understand for golfers the world over; thus were nixed such Gaelic favorites as The Ailnich, The Dunnbraes, The Failte, The Kinrimmund, and The Nadurra.

Ultimately, one name rose above the rest. At a meeting of the Trustees on January 12, 2007, it was decided and decreed that thereafter the seventh at St. Andrews should be called: The Castle Course.

•   •   •

Acknowledgments

• • •

For putting me first all these many years I foremost wish to thank my dear wife, Lisa. There are no words that do you justice, though *selfless*, *classy*, *remarkable*, and *stunning* begin to paint the picture. Your grace touches everyone you encounter, and I am honored and blessed to have shared a life with you these past twenty-five years. You are, therefore I am. Forever.

My deepest thanks to my children, Ella, Swen, Calvin, and Lars. You possess understanding beyond your years, as well as a gift for seeing past the person that, at times, I don't intend to be and drawing out the daddy I know I can be. I love you all the way to everywhere.

Thank you to my family, who, sappy as it sounds, provides me the strength to pursue my passion for writing when any sane person would have bailed ages ago. You are my enablers. My profound thanks and respect to my parents, Allen and Dale, who continue to amaze, awe, and inspire.

I have yet to divine suitable thanks for David Kidd. I hope this book is a start, and I trust the words will come to me one day soon, likely over pints after golf. In the meantime, thank you for giving without a thought of taking, and for sharing the art of getting to *Yes*. Thanks, too, for handing me the paint can and allowing me to design my bunker on the twelfth hole.

I cannot say enough about Paul Kimber, Mick McShane, and Conor Walsh. You are exceptionally gifted artists, consummate professionals, and you deserve more recognition than you get for your behind-the-scenes brilliance. I truly appreciate your time, trust, and friendship, and I am a better person (my liver notwithstanding) for having "earned the right."

Heartfelt thanks to the entire DMK family, with a special nod to Elaine Alabaster, Jimmy and June Kidd, and Jill Kidd.

Thank you to the St. Andrews Links Trust. I am most grateful for the help and confidence of the good people at Pilmour House, notably Alan McGregor, Peter Mason, Gordon Moir, Allan Patterson, Mike Woodcock, John Stewart, Barbara Ardley, and Shelia Buntin. You cannot please all of the golfers all of the time, and yet you continue to try.

Sincere thanks to my agent Scott Waxman and to Farley Chase, and to my publisher, Bill Shinker, and editor, Brett Valley, and also to Patrick Mulligan at Gotham Books. You made the experience not only painless but also enjoyable, so much so that I have half a mind to try it again.

Posthumous thanks to Mickey and Edna Leuenberger, Swen and Hulda Gummer, Willis L. Winter, Joshua Simon, and Sir William Wallace.

Thank you to Brad Russell and to Ramatu. Thank you to Stewart Smith, Ian Hamilton, Neil Cunningham Dobson, Rosemary Dewar at *The Citizen*, Fife Council, and the helpful staff at the St. Andrews University Library.

Stateside thanks to Armen Keteyian, a tremendous mentor and even better friend; to Kris Van Giesen, with whom I first discovered St. Andrews; to Dan Okrent, David Friend, Kevin Cook, Steve Smith, and Dick Michaux; and to the many friends who have provided encouragement and support, as well as rides for my children to and from school and practices while I was holed up writing.

Thank you to the Hertz guy at Glasgow Airport for not charging me for the dented rims and the hubcap I lost somewhere in Scotland after repeatedly clipping curbs while driving on the wrong side of the road. Thanks also to Skippy, Jack and Sheena, and the many kind publicans of St. Andrews, and to Hamish the taxi driver for delivering us home safely.

Apologies
My apologies to the pedestrians in the Royal Burgh of St. Andrews, whom I inadvertently terrorized while driving on the aforementioned wrong side of the road.

Sincere apologies, too, to my daughter, Ella, for my regrettable decision to call you from the New Inn at 2:30 in the morning with Mick McShane. My bad.

Cast

• • •

Will Adams	Colin Dear	Mike Horkan
Margaret Allardice	Eric Drentlaw	Colin Hutchison
Quentin Allardice	William Duncan	Sergei Izjumov
Mike Allcock	Richard Duthie	Lyle Jameson
Jan Andreas	Greig Easton	Jack Jarvis
Kenny Andrews	Ozbignies Felkner	Todd Jerome
Stuart Bisgrove	Malcolm Fenton	Callum Johnstone
Davie Brown	Euan Ferguson	John Kemp
Douglas Brown	Melanie Findlay	David McLay Kidd
James Brown	Neil Finlay	Paul Kimber
Jim Bruce	Robert Finnegan	Paul Kirkwood
Blair Cameron	Agustin Fontanes	Kuzma Kovevnikov
Gary Cameron	Ian Forrest	Uldis Krancins
Ross Campbell	Eric Forsyth	Charles Laing
Josh Chabon	Graham Foster	Phil Langdon
Ganesh Chand	Mario Gagliardi	David Lawlor
Willie Clark	Graham Geddes	Mike Love
James Clement	Daniel Gilman	Gary MacDougall
Dave Cochrane	Ross Gilniany	Euan MacGregor
Keiron Coll	Drew Glover	Bob Manneran
Simon Connah	Vassili Gontsarov	Lorna Marroney
Stuart Cowan	Ken Gray	Jim Marshall
Liz Crowley	Ian Hamilton	Igor Martsenko
Danny Cunningham	Drue Hannah	Peter Mason
James Dalton	Trevor Harris	Martin Maver
Artjom Danilov	Gregor Harrow	Kenny McCallum
Fraser Daun	Terry Hastings	Raymond McCauley
Zane Davis	Andrew Hodge	Grant McCoutires

Tommy McFadden
Alan McGregor
Ben McKee
Donald McKerracher
Harry McNab
John McNaughton
Colin McRitchie
Jim McRitchie
Clint McShane
Jock McShane
Mick McShane
John Meiklem
Stuart Meiklem
Brycen Meng
Chick Menzies
Viktoria Merkulova
William Miller
Gordon Moir
Chris Moore
Andrew Murray
Bob Murray
James Murray
Thomas Neame
Gavin Neill
Jared Nemitz
Jim Nicol
Jim Ogilvie
John Ogilvie

Calum Oliphant
Simon Page
Allan Patterson
Stephen Paul
Nolan Pauly
David Peebles
Ben Percy
Doug Petrie
Neil Porteous
Jamie Raeside
Dave Ramsay
Ian Ramsay
William Ramsay
Willie Redpath
Derek Reid
Natalja Repinskaja
Tom Richardson
Spencer Roberts
Mike Rogerson
Veronica Ross
Brad Russell
Peteris Sadovskis
Dougie Sankowski
Cameron Semple
Gary Semple
Dougie Shearer
Tim Sibicky
Julia Sidorkina

Ian Sinclair
Fraser Smart
Scott Smeaton
Mark Smith
Jonathan Spraul
Sveinn Steindorsson
Charlie Stewart
Richard Stirling
Duncan Strathearn
Danny Sweeney
Lani Togi
John Torrie
Paul Tulleth
Martin Tuma
Andrea Ulitin
Oksana Ulitina
Hugh Waddel
Rodger Waldron
Alex Walker
George Wallace
Conor Walsh
Giles Wardel
Dave Watson
Colin White
Craig Wilson
Richard Windows
Sonja Wohlwend

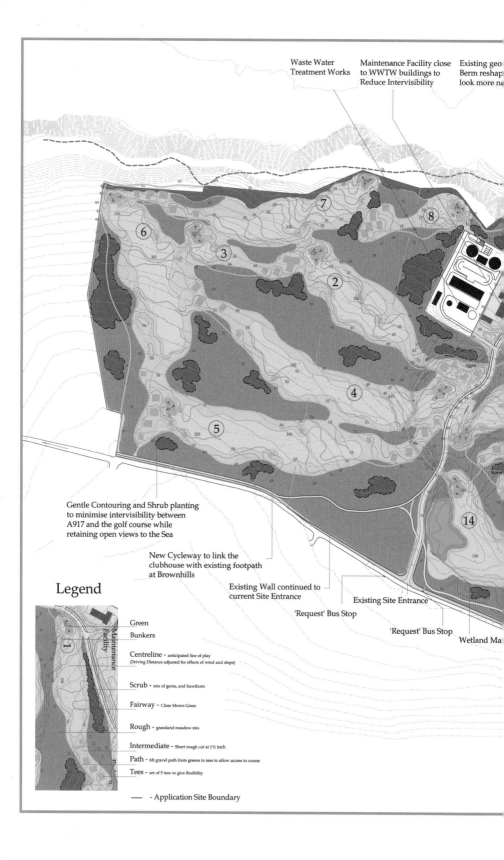

Waste Water
Treatment Works

Maintenance Facility close
to WWTW buildings to
Reduce Intervisibility

Existing geo
Berm reshap
look more na

⑦

⑧

⑥

③

②

④

⑤

⑭

Gentle Contouring and Shrub planting
to minimise intervisibility between
A917 and the golf course while
retaining open views to the Sea

New Cycleway to link the
clubhouse with existing footpath
at Brownhills

Existing Wall continued to
current Site Entrance

Existing Site Entrance

'Request' Bus Stop

'Request' Bus Stop

Wetland Ma

Legend

Green

Bunkers

Centreline - anticipated line of play
(Driving Distance adjusted for effects of wind and slope)

Scrub - mix of gorse, and hawthorn

Fairway - Close Mown Grass

Rough - grassland meadow mix

Intermediate - Short rough cut at 1½ inch

Path - 6ft gravel path from greens to tees to allow access to course

Tees - set of 5 tees to give flexibility

— - Application Site Boundary